REVIEWS

"I take great pleasure in reading inspiring biographies of faith. As I read them, I often find myself jealous, wishing somehow, I could be personal friends with the protagonist, could somehow share in their journey, and find their secret in tapping the power of omnipotence. These giants of faith and experience cause me to "covet" (1 Corinthians 12:31) their experience with the divine.

"In this case, however, there has been no jealousy, no wishing to know the author of this biography that you hold in your hand because for four years I've had the distinct pleasure of personally engaging with Elena and Emil as their pastor. I've watched in real time a person who has gone through the pain of Communism, infidelity & divorce, PTSD causing events, injustice, and devastating health issues, continue to hold fast to her faith, and that with a sense of joy that is contagious.

"Elena is someone you want to be around. Though living in a world with real pain, loss, and tears her cheerful and sustained selfless service to others in concert with her faithful Emil, is at once a rebuke, a challenge, and an effervescent reminder that it is good in this world, brought to birth by simple faith in a loving heavenly Father.

"As you read these stories, I trust you too will be challenged to pray to a living God, embrace a living faith, and experience His real transformative heart-changing repentance."

— *Pastor Charles Byrd*
President of QuestLine Productions

"It's been quite some time since I've taken the time to read a book about someone's life story. God's providential working in the life of Elena and her husband, Emil, will move you, as it did me, to tears of joy and gratitude for God's amazing love and tender care for His children. Your faith and love for God will grow if you will invest the time to read this amazing story of Elena and Emil's sojourn on this planet that is embroiled in a great controversy that is soon to end."

— *Pastor John Witcombe*

"*Under the Shadow of the Almighty* by Elena Bujor is a most captivating and gripping autobiography. The author's story begins on the southern plains of communist Romania, continues through several urban centers of her native land, and then relocates in the bustle and economic activity of the western United States. From beginning to end, the author's commitment to prayer and love for the God she adores shines through its pages. This is all the more remarkable since much of the story unfolds during the dark days of Marxist rule in Romania. The struggle to make ends meet, the need for a caution under the watchful eye of a controlling regime, and the need to find satisfaction and fulfillment under very difficult circumstances, are skillfully interwoven throughout the overall story. The numerous details of everyday life, the challenges of changing workplaces on two different continents, and the struggle with ravaging disease and health problems, come alive in the grip of the author's able pen. The climax of the journey occurs as the saga shifts from the Old World to the New. Obviously, the thrill of freedom and relative prosperity help to bring the story to a happy end. Above all, the author is thankful for God's goodness and guidance, and the warmth of family and friends."

— *Robert G. Pierson*
Retired Professor
Andrews University Theological Seminary

"From the opening lines in a sleepy little village in post-war Romania, through the trials of a severely ill son, to her life now in America, Elena's story is truly captivating. I was encouraged to read about her incredibly rich life from a young girl to what she now describes as their twilight years. Seeing the many times God stepped up and came through for her and her family is just remarkable. The truth and the heart that Elena writes with are also tender and honest. Her love for her Creator God and her family is unmistakable. This is a book you will want to read more than once and pass on to your friends and family. This book is filled with hope and story after story of modern-day miracles. It should cause you to honestly believe in something bigger than yourself."

— *Jeanette Stark*
Editor, Director, and Producer at Better Life Broadcasting Network

"In this heartwarming story of tenacious faith and fortitude, Elena recounts memories of God's miraculous care during her years growing up in Communist Romania as well as God's continued guidance throughout her life. This book is filled with promises that God has faithfully fulfilled in her life, promises which everyone may claim against all odds."

— *Stephanie Martin*
High School Teacher

UNDER THE SHADOW OF THE ALMIGHTY

From Communist Romania to Freedom

Elena Bujor

TEACH Services, Inc.
PUBLISHING
www.TEACHServices.com • (800) 367-1844

World rights reserved. This book or any portion thereof may not be copied or reproduced in any form or manner whatever, except as provided by law, without the written permission of the publisher, except by a reviewer who may quote brief passages in a review.

The author assumes full responsibility for the accuracy of all facts and quotations as cited in this book. The opinions expressed in this book are the author's personal views and interpretations, and do not necessarily reflect those of the publisher.

This book is provided with the understanding that the publisher is not engaged in giving spiritual, legal, medical, or other professional advice. If authoritative advice is needed, the reader should seek the counsel of a competent professional.

Copyright © 2022 Elena Bujor
Copyright © 2022 TEACH Services, Inc.
ISBN-13: 978-1-4796-1500-1 (Paperback)
ISBN-13: 978-1-4796-1501-8 (ePub)
Library of Congress Control Number: 2022912857

All scripture quotations, unless otherwise indicated, are taken from the New King James Version®. Copyright © 1982 by Thomas Nelson. Used by permission. All rights reserved.

Some of the names in this book have been changed to protect the identity and privacy of the individuals.

Published by

www.TEACHServices.com • (800) 367-1844

DEDICATION

To my precious son Silviu, his wife Alina and my granddaughter Emma.

CONTENTS

Foreword 7
Acknowledgments 9
Introduction 11
Prelude 13

Chapter 1   First Steps to School 15
    The Flight from the Natal Nest 18
    An Unforgettable Winter Break 21

Chapter 2   Fear of the Unknown 27
    Again, in the Cradle of Childhood 32
    The Angel of the Lord, My Angel 36

Chapter 3   The Wonder Child 41
    Deep Pains Are Mute 49

Chapter 4   In the Fiery Furnace 55
    Through Death's Valley 59
    Stop Crying! 63
    Nothing to Wonder 67
    Face to Face with Reality 71
    A Passing Shadow 78

Chapter 5   On Eagles' Wings 91
    The God of Open Doors 97

The Mirage of Freedom 101
Happy Birthday, Free Romania! 106

Chapter 6   The Rope Braided in Three 109
In the Shadow of His Wings 114
The First Visit to Free Romania 118
At the Crossroads 121

Chapter 7   Gold Beach—Oregon's Paradise 125
Empty Nest Syndrome 134
At the Border of Time 136

Chapter 8   The Year of Great Pains 139
It Is Good to Wait 145
Blessings in Disguise 148
2004—A Stormy Year 151
The Year of Difficult Decisions 156

Chapter 9 The Mysteries of Providence 163
A New Perspective 168
Where Does Your Heart Draw You? 170
July 2006 174
Great Performances—Dramatic Changes 184
A Pleasant Surprise in Romania 187
Talking with Dr. Leonard Bailey 188
A New Hope 190
November 13, 2014 191

Chapter 10   Goodbye to the Ocean! 197

    Grants Pass—A New Beginning 201

    Great is the Lord! 203

    May 24, 2016 205

    2017—A Year of Mysteries 208

    December 30, 2017 216

    New Year 2019 220

Chapter 11   In the Twilight 223

FOREWORD

Protected by guardian angels, this story of a lifetime begins in the gentle lands of the Vedea, Romania and descends in the dim light of day, somewhere in an American town near the Pacific coast. But dusk is not the end, rather the recapitulation of the journey.

The unnatural deprivations of childhood, the early confrontations with a regime hostile to the faith, the almost mysterious opening of an escape route, the severe impact on immigration, and the rewards of later years, all gather around an epicenter of the book, which the author called "the miracle child." The child of God's miracles. The irreversible diagnosis is recorded with professional precision, and the names of the doctors who fought against their own medical expertise to save this child are noted, thus signing with their own hand an indisputable document that proves that beyond the laws of nature, Someone greater than us hears our prayers.

This book could be useful not only to the believers but even to those who find it hard to trust. Those who, beyond the boundaries of rationalism and demonstrability, seek from the depths of their being the simple and clear touch of a Savior.

Maybe not all the requests mentioned here respected the valued order of things, yet the Spirit of the Lord is near to us, teaching us to pray and wait, not for our small answers, but for the exceedingly high ones that God has prepared for us. When it comes to prayer, no one should feel underprivileged. For even if we are not all answered in the same way, we are all answered in the best way.

These pages are a beneficent respite in which, like the ancient writer, we can ask, "How will I reward the Lord for all His goodness toward me?" Maybe by simply telling others about His goodness and mercy. Looking back, all that remains of the vortex of the clouds is the quiet mirror of heaven in which one thing is reflected: the goodness of God.

—Dan Burtescu

ACKNOWLEDGMENTS

To God be the glory, for He wrote in His book each chapter of my life, long before He knot me in my mother's womb. He is the true author of all the amazing stories that unfold in this book. For His unfathomable love for me, for giving me the courage and inspiration to scribe my life story in this book, I will be eternally grateful.

To Emil, my beloved husband, and my best friend - for your endless love and untiring emotional, spiritual, and technical support. Without your tenacious encouragement, this book would never come to life.

To my sister, Mari, my brother Peter from Romania, and Viorica, Cornel, and Mihai, my siblings from America - your love in action helped me tremendously in my trials.

To Jo Engelhorn – for your inspiration and help in shaping the manuscript.

To my editor, Jeanette Stark - for your love for my story, your dedication, and your skillful assistance in polishing my manuscript.

To Stephanie Martin - with gratitude for your marvelous guidance and your graceful, passionate, and professional finishing touches to my book.

To Timothy Hullquist – Author Advisor for TEACH Services, Inc. – for generously sharing your time and wisdom in the decision-making process I struggled with.

To Rebecca Silver – Editing Director at TEACH Services, Inc. – for your kindness and your major contribution to the final editing process.

To Alyssa Newman – Production manager at TEACH Services, Inc. – for your courtesy, professional assistance, and creative designing of my book.

INTRODUCTION

I promised to write a book ...

> *"My heart is overflowing with a good theme; I recite my composition concerning the King; My tongue is the pen of a ready writer." (Ps. 45:1, NKJV ... A Contemplation of the sons of Korah ... A song of love.)*

I would like my pen to be that of a "ready writer." Oh, to have the inspiration of Korah's sons!

By trade, I am not a writer nor a poet. I was a dental laboratory technician in Romania.

At the age of thirty-eight, I left for the United States, where I became a dental assistant and eventually was privileged to practice my previous skill as a dental laboratory technician.

My greatest professional satisfaction was to be able to give back to the patients the smile they had lost due to missing teeth. The smile that blossomed on their faces, the tears of joy, the hugs, and the words of gratitude gave me the satisfaction of a duty fulfilled.

Most of the patients, especially those whom I saw for the first time, asked me where I was from because of my accent. It was obvious from the start that I was not American. And when they found out where I came from, the question followed invariably: What brought you to America? Why did you leave Romania? When and how?

This was the starting point of my story of coming to America. And depending on the time I had available, I briefly expounded on the reason for my departure from my homeland, as well as the string of miracles by which Providence facilitated my coming to this country.

Almost every one of those listening to my story said to me, "Elena, you have to write a book! I want you to promise me that you will do this!" I promised many of them that I would. It is the book you hold in your hands.

I chose to be vulnerable and honestly express my feelings, my frustrations, and my failures. At times I got carried away by the tide of reliving very intense memories, usually painful, and it felt more like my struggle than His work but I know that the Lord has always been by my side, holding my hand and not letting me go, even though, at times, I was not able to perceive it.

As you may see, I live intensely both the pains and the joys. Reliving my memories as I laid them on paper, I understood more, not only about myself but about my Lord. I realized that He always spoke to me through His Word, which I cherish so much. That is why the book is sprinkled with many biblical texts.

Now, as a retiree, I fondly remember the beautiful experiences God carried me through in order to know Him on a personal level and acknowledge Him as my personal Savior. I made mistakes in my life, even though, at times, I did not perceive them as such; but the victories were all His. From this perspective, I would like you to understand everything I am sharing with you on the following pages.

The book you hold in your hands, dear reader, is not the product of a mind educated in the art of the word, nor is my pen of a ready writer. It is rather a song of praise to my Lord, the King of kings. It is a song of love for my beloved Savior, sung in human language. My prayer is that, through divine touch, it may resonate with your soul as well.

Above all, since the Lord is the author, this book is intended to be an altar of gratitude on which I offer my sacrifice of thanksgiving, consumed by the fire of His boundless love. May the sweet fragrance of this sacrifice permeate your heart and give you a new revelation about God and His unfathomable love for you.

May the reading of this book remind you of your own experiences, and out of love for Him, join me in a song of praise, telling others how wonderful is our God, the only One who works miracles.

—The Author

PRELUDE

"For You formed my inward parts; You covered me in my mother's womb. I will praise You, for I am fearfully and wonderfully made; Marvelous are Your works, and that my soul knows very well." (Ps. 139:13–14)

January 6, 1949

It is not daybreak yet. The village sleeps peacefully under the burden of the newly-laid snow, above which the starry vault reflects its silver rays.

Among the snow heaps, polished by the frost, is a silhouette of a man hurrying to the other side of the village.

Arriving at the door of Ms. Geta, he knocks and shouts as loud as he can. Although awakened suddenly and dazed by sleep, the mistress of the house understands the reason for this early morning visit.

Florica, Grigore Iorga's wife, was ready to give birth. Knowing that Florica does not take long, nor does she have the patience to wait, midwife Geta had to hurry. Thus, shortly after Geta arrived, the eighth child of the Iorga family sees the light of day.

"It's a girl!" exclaimed the midwife excitedly.

Tears of joy ran down the mother's face while the father, sobbing, repeated, "She is a girl! She's a girl!"

They both had longed to have another little girl after the family tragedy four years prior. They had lost their little Elena. She was the family's sweet singer and was only five years old when death claimed her life. In those days, transportation (especially in winter), the doctor, and the medicines, were not easily accessible in case of an emergency. Little Elena died of pneumonia shortly after the arrival of the doctor from a nearby town.

The indescribable pain that plagued the Iorga family for many years, especially when two years later, they lost Valeriu at a mere two weeks old, would be alleviated by the birth of another little girl, which, without thinking, they named Elena.

Elena, now the youngest in the family, would soon become the adoration of her older siblings, as well as the comfort and delight of her parents.

The post-war times were hard for poor Romania, especially for the peasants. After Communism came to power, Romanians were deprived of their most basic means of livelihood. A few years after the end of the war, the Iorga family, like many other well-to-do families, was left in poverty.

By the time Elena was a toddler, the food was more and more scarce. As a young child, she did not understand why Mama did not put enough food on the table. One day she looked at her mother's tear-stained face in bewilderment as their food supplies were being confiscated. Mama insisted on them leaving something to feed her hungry children.

The news that the Iorga family had their barns emptied reached the ears of the nearby villagers. Soon, thanks to the generosity of their Adventist friends, the flour multiplied, and the smell of warm bread returned to the house, however, only for a while.

Despite severe poverty, there was love and faith, peace and joy, harmony and understanding in the Iorga family. Both parents were God-fearing people and patiently and lovingly instilled in their children the knowledge of God. Elena grew up in a fertile field under her parents' training, learning from an early age obedience and respect for her parents and, implicitly, for God.

CHAPTER 1
FIRST STEPS TO SCHOOL

"Fear not, for I am with you." (Isa. 43:5)

On the first day of school, I felt shy and reserved, surrounded by unknown faces. I noticed that some children were better dressed; they even had uniforms, notebooks, pencils, and satchels, but more importantly, they had a corner of bread hidden in their pockets, concealed for fear of it being stolen by a friend who was hungrier than they.

The fact that I had old, half-used notebooks and pencils, a strapless cardboard backpack, all left by older siblings, did not bother me much. The thing that I truly coveted was a piece of bread held by my classmates. I looked at it with longing when they consumed it during recess. I knew from home that bread was a luxury item that only the wealthy had; however, I did not envy children from such families. When we joined in playing, who could tell who was hungry and who was full? We were all children, and we shared the exuberance and innocence of childhood equally.

I had looked forward to the first day of school without giving much thought to the fact that I did not know anyone but my cousin Gabi. Gabi and I would be classmates.

I had grown up in what felt like a little piece of paradise. Although the nest was poor and small, I had felt the love and closeness of my parents and older siblings, and, like any baby of the family, I had a decent dose of spoiling. It was for this reason, I thought it would be the same in the new world I was about to explore, away from the warm and fluffy nest of the family. And after all, why should I be afraid? I knew how to count to one hundred, I could read very well—even the newspaper—and I knew how to write in cursive. I had learned all this from my older siblings, just "playing school." However, I did not have a uniform or school supplies.

The classroom seemed inhospitable to me. The wooden floor, freshly treated with diesel, spread an unbearable odor into the air. I resigned myself quickly, thinking that this was how school was supposed to smell. The benches were made of carved wood, cold and unwelcoming. We were seated by the teacher, each at a desk with a chosen desk partner; the strategy was unknown to me. However, I felt privileged to be placed on the first bench. Tudora was my desk partner, and that did not feel like a privilege. You see, she came from the poorest family in the village, and I was afraid to be close to her, knowing that she had lice. I had already started scratching my head, thinking that soon I would become a second Tudora in the class.

The roll was called. Each student was to stand when their name was heard. When it was my turn, I stood up with the dignity of a well-bred child, hoping to make the most beautiful impression. To my great surprise, the teacher introduced me to my classmates as an "idiot child" who believed in God, went to church on Saturday, and thought she would go to heaven. And, to make the children laugh at me, he said sarcastically, "When the Lord comes to take you to heaven, I will cling to your foot, and I will get there, too."

> *I stood up with the dignity of a well-bred child, hoping to make the most beautiful impression.*

The whole class burst out laughing; I wanted to hide under the bench in shame.

I felt a little better when I was asked if I could count to a hundred. I was amazed to see that I was the only "idiot" child in the class who knew how to count to one hundred!

To my great joy, the next day, Mrs. Stefania Marinescu appeared in the classroom. She would be my teacher for the first four years of school. I breathed a sigh of relief at the thought that I was rid of Mr. Marinescu ... and he was rid of me.

Mrs. Stefania Marinescu was a wonderful teacher who knew how to instill in me the love of learning. I loved her a lot, although I did not understand why she did not care. I received the best grades; I was a model student of whom she liked to brag; but the fact that she would express her outrage and hostility toward my religion made me reluctant, confused, and even afraid of her.

A few times, she sent me home, telling me not to come back until I agreed to attend school on Saturday. At the end-of-year celebration, when the awards were given, my name was called first with the mention that I deserved first place, but because I missed school on Saturday, the first prize was to be awarded to another student.

This is how I learned from the first years of school to accept injustice with dignity and to trust in the God of my parents, the only One who will grant me justice. Through experiences like these, He became for me a personal God whose love conquered my heart for life.

I read this definition of victory given by American author Dennis L. Wilcox, who is also a professor of public relations and strategic communication:

"When you are entitled to receive honors and appreciation, and another passes in front of you and receives what you deserve, and this does not make you change your feelings nor your attitude toward them, that's victory."

The Lord had given me the first victory of this kind as a young child, which encouraged me to accept injustice, knowing that God sees everything, and He never remains indebted but rewards those who trust in Him.

By the time I started fifth grade, I had another set of teachers. I must admit my affinity for Miss Simona Stefan. She was a Romanian language teacher, a young woman who had just graduated from high school, and she came to class dressed in a high school uniform. I was fascinated by her talent and passion for the Romanian language. She had the gift of instilling in her little disciples a love of letters. Romanian language class was a delight for me. I loved Miss Simona, although I always had the impression that she did not understand this.

I spent my vacations helping my parents at home, in the garden, or with the cow grazing in the pasture. The time spent alone in the heart of nature, on the green hills, in the groves animated by the chirping of birds, along the waters with their gentle whisper, constituted the paradise of my youth.

Childhood, with its innocence and charm, passed like a pleasant, nighttime dream. I look nostalgically at the past, trying to relive the most beautiful moments of my former years.

***

THE FLIGHT FROM THE NATAL NEST

"Like a bird that wanders from its nest is a man who wanders from his place." (Prov. 27:8)

After finishing elementary school, my teacher, Mr. M. Dumitru, advised my parents to send me to high school, knowing my potential and eagerness for learning. To my surprise, I was the only one in the class who was admitted to the high school in Rosiori. The entrance exam was very difficult at that time, and there were few who entered without some type of bribe.

I did not understand at the time how much my poor parents sacrificed to support me during my four years in high school. Forced entry into the CAP (Agricultural Production Cooperative) meant, for the poor peasant, the dispossession of the most basic personal goods that ensured his existence: land, agricultural machinery, poultry, and animal farm as well as private craft workshops. My father was even forbidden to have beehives, the only source of income for our family at the time.

My father would have to go to work as an unskilled worker on the construction site for only 500 lei, or approximately 120 American dollars, per month in order to keep me in school. The average salary at that time was about 1,000 lei per month. In high school the requirements were much stricter. The uniform was mandatory. Supplies, the rental in the city, food, and other extra expenses required hard work in construction for my father as well as strict savings at home.

In spring and autumn, I would commute on foot every day in order to save money to pay the rent in winter. That meant almost twelve miles a day, back and forth. I left at ten o'clock in the morning to get to class in the afternoon. I was learning on the road as I walked through the woods and sunny fields. I rarely met people on the road. I was not afraid of them or wild animals since I was studying my books and did not have time to think about anything else. In the evening, on my return, my mother, knowing I was afraid of the dark, would meet me at the entrance to the forest. Although the trek was tiring for both of us, my mother's love for me, my love for learning, as well as my father's dedication to hard work away from home on the construction site in Bucharest, motivated us to move forward.

In the winter, I could not commute due to bad weather, so my mother started looking for a rental in town. My first place was in the elegant home of two widowed sisters with whom my mother had become acquainted years prior.

They were very rich ladies with big hearts; they wanted to help my mother and host me in their home. My mother gladly accepted the offer and took me there, fully confident that everything would be fine. I was received with warmth and love by these two women; even so, from the moment my mother left, I felt alone and empty, and no one could fill the void in my soul. It was the first time I was away from home and family and I was lonely.

That beautifully decorated house with Persian rugs, massive furniture, and luxury items looked like a palace in stark contrast to my country hut, but I longed for my mother to come and take me home.

A few days later, my mother came to see how I was getting along, and without saying too much, she understood that I had to go home. And that is what I did.

Soon after, I moved in with "Mother Zoe," a nice Adventist widow whom my parents had known for a long time. The small room in which she was living, an addition to the big house, resembled my native nest more. The only furniture in that confined space was a small stove heated with sawdust, a small bed—just big enough for one person—and a small kitchen table. Next to it was the kitchen and the pantry. It was warm there, and I loved it. We both slept in the small bed with separate covers. I slept at the wall side—so as not to fall out of bed—but at the opposite end. I felt safe. Mother Zoe shared breakfast with me, which was invariably a cup of warm milk with a slice of bread with homemade jam. It was a delight!

The next year, I had to move from Mother Zoe's. My host felt the space was too small for two people in that little room. At the new place, I had a roommate who stole my food from the fridge when I was at school. I understood that she was hungry but I was hungry too. Poor Mother had to move me yet again.

This time I was alone in the room; however, the old woman who was hosting me stole my wood in the winter when I went home on the weekend. I will never forget that Sunday night when I returned and had to sleep in an ice-cold room. All the wood had disappeared in my absence, and the host refused to talk to me. I literally thought I would freeze until daybreak. I snuggled in my bed, dressed up with all the clothing available and covered with the heavy blanket my mom had made for me. I prayed to the Lord to keep me alive, and I could not wait for the morning in order to go to school to warm up. That was a long night for me, shivering and praying not to freeze till morning.

At dawn, after a night of nightmares, I set off for school, determined not to return to this host. Smaranda, a classmate, took me to her host, Mrs. Mozolea, a decent woman, who kindly received me in her house and prepared a small bed for me in Smaranda's room. It was warm and safe there. I told my mother to come to the new residence, and by agreement with the mistress of the house, I stayed there until the end of the year.

Although I wanted to come home on the weekends, I did not always succeed due to bad weather. I missed home, and sometimes I risked trying to go home without thinking. So it was on that unforgettable Sunday morning, in the middle of winter, that I took off on the snowy road, driven by the need for food, supplies, and clean clothes for the following week.

It was snowing quietly, and the city was buried in snow. Everything looked enchanting as I peered through the window steamed by the mist of heat left in the room overnight. No trace of man existed on the street.

There was no point in being alone in the house all day. How good it would be at my house! My mother, coming out to greet me, the warmth and smell of fresh food, the warm bed in which I would sleep at night, all these thoughts gave me wings. Whatever would be, I must go! I had a backpack on my shoulders and hoped it would keep me warm. I was not very well dressed, but I knew I would warm up as I made my way through the snow.

The road was completely buried under the snow. I struggled forward, making my way through the freshly laid snow, wondering why no one was on the road. It was so beautiful outside! I arrived safely at the edge of town, where I expected to see the man in the booth guarding the railway crossing. But the man was not there. There was no sign of any passers-by either. The sky had darkened with the growing blizzard. I was completely disoriented. I could not see ahead. Where was the road? The barrier was my last landmark, and I did not have the courage to walk away from it.

Suddenly, I remembered the wolf story my father used to tell us when we were little. He told us how one winter day, when he dared to go to town, the blizzard had caught him on the way, and the wolf came out ahead. With our faces tense with horror, we waited anxiously for the outcome of the story. After a short pause, my father asked us, "And what do you think I did?" He answered, "I cried out as loudly as I could to the

Lord to deliver me, and immediately, the wolf turned around and got lost in the fog." The story of the wolf was so vivid in my memory as if I had seen it through the nebulous curtain blocking my path. I thought it was best to pray before I met the wolf and I decided to turn around. I returned to my host residence and prayed that the weather would change so that my mother would be able to come and bring food and the change of clothes I needed for the following week.

I do the same now; every time I am confused because of the foggy horizon or the clogged road, I pray. *"Whenever I am afraid, I will trust in You" (Ps. 56:3).*

***

AN UNFORGETTABLE WINTER BREAK

"Unless the Lord had been my help, my soul would soon have settled in silence." (Ps. 94:17)

The longing for home could not be tempered by the bad weather. I only had a few days until the winter break. I packed my bags on time and, with great joy, set off after the last day of school. The weather was beautiful, and I had nothing to fear.

My mother was waiting for me with the necessary preparations. The house was well heated, and there was warm bread and good food, just like the holidays. I was now in the tenth grade. After a plentiful meal, I lay in bed with no intention of sleeping. Just to relax. I was on vacation at my house. The sun was smiling seductively through the window. I do not know if I fell asleep, but after a while, I felt that my eyes were blurred, and I could not see well. I climbed out of bed and went to the mirror to see if I had anything in my eyes. I was very dizzy and I was afraid I would collapse. The only thing I remember is the noise made by the vibration of the mirror that I think I hit in an attempt to balance myself so that I would not fall. I do not remember anything else.

Suddenly, I began to see again. In fact, I could see very clearly. I was lying on the snow in front of the house, leaning on the arms of a neighbor who was rubbing my cheeks vigorously. All around, familiar faces looked at me in dismay. They were our neighbors. I saw my mother. Her face was as yellow as wax. A smile quickly sprang from her frozen lips as I opened my eyes. I began to tremble and I was quickly ushered inside the house.

The neighbors all disappeared as if somebody commanded them to leave the place. I did not insist on finding the answers to my questions. I understood that my mother was going through a crisis, so I left her alone. I felt tired, exhausted even. Poor Mother was watching me, anxiously watching my heartbeat and my breathing. It was Friday night. When I felt that the atmosphere was more relaxed, I asked my mother for an explanation of what had happened the day before.

She explained that everything was fine in our home. My mother let me relax in bed and went for a short visit to see the next-door neighbor. Suddenly, she heard a voice telling her in a commanding tone, "Go home immediately, or you will find her dead!"

> *"Go home immediately, or you will find her dead!"*

She hurried home and scurried to my window to first look inside and see what I was doing. The window was open, and I was leaning my head against the window frame. She asked me what I was doing, but without waiting for an answer, she quickly ran into the house, knowing that something was wrong. She found me unconscious, lying down on the floor.

With the strength of despair, she dragged me out into the fresh air. At the desperate cry for help, all the neighbors gathered. They rubbed my face with snow, slapped me, and screamed to wake me up. They did everything they knew best. And this old-fashioned treatment, they believed, revived me back to life.

My mother had lost track of time. Only the Lord knows how long I had been unconscious, trapped in the clutches of death. The final conclusion, after the drama was over, was that I had suffered from carbon dioxide poisoning. My mother had put too much wood on the fire, and the room was not well ventilated.

The lack of oxygen induced a state of unconsciousness from which I would not have awakened if God, in His mercy, had not intervened. My guardian angel took me out of bed, then, after I fell in front of the mirror, lifted me up and led me to the window he had also opened to keep me alive. In the meantime, I believe another angel was commissioned to alert my mother that my life was in danger. And, to be sure that my mother would immediately carry out the order above, the angel spoke to her resolutely—in a commanding tone—"Go now! Otherwise, you will find her dead!"

With boundless joy and gratitude, we thanked our God for His miraculous intervention. This extraordinary experience marked both my mother and me for life. I will be eternally grateful to God for the many miracles with which He has enriched my Christian experience. I also wonder, like the psalmist David: *"What shall I render to the Lord For all His benefits toward me?" (Ps. 116:12).*

"For You have delivered my soul from death." (Ps. 56:13)

This is one of the first wonders through which I have personally felt God's involvement in our lives; how He mobilizes heavenly messengers to intervene in our salvation when we are in danger.

I cannot imagine what would have happened to me if the angel of the Lord had not turned me away that blizzardy Sunday when I had tried to go home on my own without realizing the danger to which I would be exposed. And when my guardian angel intervened again to save me from death, I realized how grateful we should be to God for the work of angels in our lives.

"For He shall give His angels charge over you, To keep you in all your ways. In their hands they shall bear you up, Lest you dash your foot against a stone." (Ps. 91:11–12)

My last year of high school, 1967, was a good one. It was the best. A classmate, Nina, took pity on me and invited me to her house. Her mother, a very kind, poor widow, agreed to let me sleep in the large bed with her and her daughter, having no better place for me.

I was charged a low rent, which helped me save a little bit of money. How well we all three warmed up at night, even if the fire did not burn all night in the stove. In the morning, I would get up early to buy my bread on the ticket before going to school. (Ceausescu provided tickets for the students to secure their daily portion of bread, which was not available for everybody—only for students and employees).

Staying at school was a pleasure. Good classmates, good teachers. Missing home, however, consumed me. I knew my mother was home alone, thinking of me and of my father working hard on the construction site to keep his daughter at school.

Toward the end of the year, a bus connecting the city of Rosiori with my home village became available. Although I had to depart at five o'clock in the morning, the bus being packed with people commuting to work, I was happy that I did not have to walk anymore and that I had more time to study.

That year was the shortest one; that is how it seemed to me anyway. I had reached the threshold of the baccalaureate. My dream of going into medicine was a path that I had been chasing since I was a child. I understood that it was not possible, since I could not afford to be in school for six years and would have to choose a technical school. I found out about the Medical College in Bucharest, and I enrolled there in the dental profile where the highest competition was. I thought it had to be a good choice.

What scared me was, after the baccalaureate exam, I only had three weeks to prepare for the admission exam to the Medical College. I studied intensely and I prayed that the Lord would help me to pass the exams if it was His will for me to attend this school.

The written exams went pretty well. The oral chemistry exam came first after written tests were taken.

In alphabetical order, hundreds of candidates presented daily to the exam room. I also went on the first day, out of curiosity, to find out about the topics written on the "tickets" the candidates would draw randomly at the oral examination.

It was like a lottery.

One of the candidates boasted that he drew ticket number one, which was very easy. He also told us what topics he had. One of organic chemistry and one of inorganic chemistry. I said to myself, "Ah, if only I were to snatch up this subject too!" How could I draw this one ticket out of hundreds of tickets? Tickets were folded in such a way that you could not see anything, just a white, wrapped paper. I remembered that **"The Lord is near to all who call on Him, To who call upon Him in truth"** *(Ps. 145:18).*

I called on Him with all my heart. I also went to the exam and prayed before it began. "Lord, if it is Your will for me to enter this school, show me ticket number one because I want that one. I promise that if You will help me to pass these exams, I will never go to school on the Sabbath, even if I am expelled because of my absences."

There I was in the exam room, in front of the table with hundreds of tickets. I was very happy when I picked up the ticket, and on its back, I saw number one. I already knew the subject. The rest is history.

On the day the results were displayed on a huge billboard on a building wall at the school, I was thrilled when I saw my name on the list of those who passed the exam. I thanked God with all my heart and renewed my promise to honor Him by obedience, no matter the consequences. One more time, I experienced God's promise:

"Cast your burden on the Lord, And He shall sustain you." (Ps. 55:22)

CHAPTER 2

FEAR OF THE UNKNOWN

"For I, the Lord your God, will hold your right hand, Saying to you, 'Fear not, I will help you.'" (Isa. 41:13)

It had started to smell like autumn. The ripe crops were waiting to be gathered into barns. The vine press groaned under the weight of grapes ready to be crushed in the press. Housewives hurried to finish canning before the frost fell.

This is how things were in the Iorga family, with one exception. Elena thought she had to make her *own* nest for the winter and a little further than the native one. She would leave behind the most precious treasure, childhood. Her parents consoled themselves with the thought that the last little chick had found her wings and must fly but that she would return, like a swallow to the nest in which she was hatched.

School would start in a few weeks. Luggage must be packed, although to be honest, I did not have much to pack. My heart skipped a beat at the thought of being away from home and dealing with the unknown. The arrangements had been made, and my new residence for the next two years would be in the capital city of Bucharest, in the home of my sister, Viorica.

Val, her baby of just a few months old, was the biggest attraction for me. I was as proud of him as if he were my own, and when I went for a walk with him in the park, I received compliments. People mistook me for his mother and marveled at such a young parent and such a lovely child. I was eighteen at the time.

The first day of school was fascinating. Although I knew absolutely no one, I felt at ease. I knew the Lord had brought me to this place, and I was sure of His protection. The biggest dilemma was, what to do with Sabbath? How will I tell the teachers that I will not come to school on Saturday? What will be their reaction?

I had heard from students in post-secondary schools or students at universities that, after a number of unexcused absences, they were expelled. Could I be an exception?

Students were crowded around the billboard where the schedule for the first trimester was displayed for all five profiles, including dental. There were so many posters that I did not know where to find myself. I quickly learned the dental profile had three classes of forty students each. I found my name in class B. Before I found the list of classrooms and the schedule specific to class B, I heard voices of protest around me. "Such a thing is not possible! It's not fair." "There must be a mistake. Why does class B have no classes on Saturday when all the others have?"

The dilemma was soon resolved. At the bottom of the panel was written in bold letters—"*Not having enough classrooms, school management has decided that Class B Dental will have no classes on Saturday.*" But why class B and not A or C, the students of those classes wondered. I was the only one who had the answer. It was a secret that I could not reveal to anyone at that critical moment. I myself looked at the billboard in amazement and became speechless. God had providentially orchestrated the events, honoring my confidence as a child and further strengthening my belief that He was in control. In that tumultuous atmosphere, I rejoiced. I would be free to practice my faith without fear of consequences for an entire quarter! Then and there, on the first day of school, in front of that huge billboard, I sealed my decision to be loyal to Him and keep the promise I made before I was admitted to this school. I renewed my vow not to desecrate the seventh-day Sabbath, even at the risk of being expelled. The fact that I obtained this undeserved favor ex officio for the first trimester opened new horizons for me. From that moment on, I was convinced that this was just the beginning of a journey to a glorious end. And so it was.

In the first term, I had the opportunity to meet my colleagues, to befriend them, to get to know my teachers, and they to know me. High grades accumulated next to my name, and I was more and more fond of the profile I had chosen. My conduct, so different from that of my colleagues, garnered respect and admiration. I was loved by both classmates and teachers. I was so different from those around me and yet so compatible with everyone.

My mother had taught me how to knit when I was little. Mohair was fashionable at the time, so during breaks in between classes, I knitted for myself a white mohair sweater. Many girlfriends signed up for me to make them a sweater as well. They supplied the mohair, I knitted the sweaters, and that is how I earned money for the train so I could go home on vacation.

Staying with my sister Viorica and her husband Eugen was one of the greatest blessings to me. Here I saw the hand of the Lord at work, and I was always grateful to Him. At church I made friends quite easily. Carmen was my best friend. She also struggled with keeping Sabbath during her six years of schooling as a student at Mathematics University. She was a brilliant student and graduated with the highest degree, in spite of missing classes on Saturdays. We remained friends for life, although we were geographically challenged after my departure to America.

At church I acquired new spiritual values that marked my youth. After a year of study in the baptismal class, I made a covenant with the Lord and dedicated myself to Him for the rest of my life. I was baptized in secret one evening, without an audience so as not to have problems at school. You see, the baptism of students was banned under Communist regime. Carmen was also baptized in secret, somewhere in a mountain creek. There were other young people like us who did not go to classes on the Sabbath, although they had difficulties. We prayed together, shared experiences, and encouraged each other. We always had stories to share when we met on Sabbath at church.

My first term went well and, after a short vacation, I was back at school. With great apprehension I found myself once again in front of the panel where the new schedule for all profiles was displayed. New subjects, new teachers, new classrooms. And this time, the schedule was full. I noticed that I would have classes on Saturday that were not repeated at any other time: maxillofacial surgery and fixed prosthesis. I wondered how I would make up these courses as we did not have textbooks, so we had to take notes.

Class attendance was scrupulously recorded. I knew from the previous term that, after a number of absences, many students had been suspended and some even expelled from school. My absences began to accumulate. I was up-to-date with the study material, as I took notes from one of my best classmates, and everything was fine from an academic point of view. Some of my classmates were absent from class and were suspended. They noted that my name did not appear on the blacklist at the end of the month, but they knew the reason. One student, Andi, once jokingly asked me if he could also become an Adventist to have his absences overlooked.

One day I was called to the principal's office. He first complimented me on my academic excellence, impeccable conduct, etc., and then, without asking for the reason for my absences, asked me to give a written statement that, for personal reasons, I could not attend certain classes and to ask to have my absences excused. He took my written statement and assured me that everything would be alright.

I felt unworthy of this great favor, and I wondered: *"What shall I render to the Lord For all His benefits toward me?" (Ps. 116:12)*.

I now understood that, at least for a while, the problem of Saturday's absences was solved. Without being asked for any explanation, without negotiation, without my contribution in solving this sensitive problem that all Adventist pupils and students were facing at that time in Communist Romania, my issue was resolved.

There was still a problem. As winter approached, the day shortened, and the Sabbath began earlier on Friday night. I had understood from a young age the importance of keeping the Sabbath edges from sunset on Friday until sunset on Saturday. With the new schedule, I had laboratory hours until late on Friday, well after sunset. I had a new instructor who noticed my good grades and watched me closely, eventually entrusting me as a manager of the lab. She handed over the keys to the storage and asked me to distribute the necessary tools and materials to the students before starting the program each day and, at the end of each class, to put everything back. The key was to remain with me permanently.

Everything went smoothly until Friday. From my previous experience, I did not have to give explanations but simply announced that I had to leave at that time. The instructor agreed to let me go, assuming it was an exceptional situation. Next Friday night, I asked again to leave early. It did not suit her very well, as she had to put everything back together at the end of the program; however, she let me go. Seeing this repeated every Friday night, I suspect that she found out about the Sabbath issue but, without asking questions, gave me the freedom to leave without asking for permission.

However, the solution had to be found to be able to take the tests on other days, on the subjects assigned to Saturday only. I negotiated with the teachers, and they agreed that I could take the tests on any day except Saturday. I took the notes from my classmates and studied on my own.

I passed with the best grades that term, as well as all the others, until the end of my second year of school. I still had a big obstacle to pass: the final exams. We had been informed that no absences were allowed for the diploma exam. Whoever did not show up for the finals would have to repeat the entire second year of school. A special examination committee was coming just for this session.

This was my final test. I had finished the two years of school with excellent results, and I was not afraid of exams. I prayed to the Lord that no exams would be held on Saturday. I had assurance knowing that He was in control. I had enough evidence of His divine intervention during the two years of school. I relied on the Lord's promise: ***"Trust in the Lord with all your heart, And lean not on your own understanding"*** *(Prov. 3:5).*

However, to my great bewilderment and grief, one of the written exams had been scheduled for Saturday. Again, I reminded the Lord of the covenant made with Him, and I moved forward with unwavering confidence, without doubting His tender love and care for me. I remembered another verse from the Bible: ***"Rest in the Lord, and wait patiently for Him"*** *(Ps. 37:7).*

Saturday's exam was the last. I was called to the principal's office, and he warned me that nothing could be done for me this time and reminded me that if I did not take the exam on Saturday, I would have to repeat the second year. I thanked him again for his understanding and told him unequivocally: "I am very sorry, but I cannot violate my conscience and, as such, I will not take the exam."

I had chosen to have a special Sabbath of fasting and prayer, knowing that my parents, family, and friends were praying for me as well. On Sunday morning, when I went to school to see if there was a poster on the bulletin board, I read something amazing. "The Dental Technology Commission will meet again on Monday to test the students who did not appear for Saturday's exam." I soon learned that I was not the only one missing the exam, and I found my name on the list of students who would be given the test. My heart cried out for joy:

> ***"I sought the Lord, and He heard me, And delivered me from all my fears ... Oh, taste and see that the Lord is good; Blessed is the man who trusts in Him!"*** *(Ps. 34:4, 8)*

The next day I took the exam with a heart full of gratitude. The Lord had opened the way for me to take the Saturday exam on another day. Now I understood a little more of the mysteries of Providence. Sometimes He allows us to be tested for the strengthening of our faith and for the glory of His Name. He knew that I would have many more exams to take in life, and He gradually strengthened my faith and dependence on Him. My love for God motivated me to remain faithful to Him in some of the most unfavorable trials I would go through over the years.

> **My love for God motivated me to remain faithful to Him in some of the most unfavorable trials I would go through over the years.**

My last day at the medical school was when we were called to receive our diploma. The distribution of work was done depending on the demands. It was announced that the students who graduated with the highest grades would have the privilege of choosing their workplace. I was very surprised when I heard my name called; I did not have to think long. I chose Rosiori, the town where I attended high school, the closest place to my parents' house. Nothing more beautiful. Nothing more wonderful. I would like to shout out loud, let everyone hear what a wonderful God we have:

"Oh, how great is Your goodness, Which You have laid up for those who fear You, Which You have prepared for those who trust in You." (Ps. 31:19)

***

AGAIN, IN THE CRADLE OF CHILDHOOD

The hut in your land is more than a palace abroad. (Dimitrie Cantemir)

I was overwhelmed with nostalgia as I took leave of Bucharest, moving far from my family there and my friends from church. I said goodbye to all, exhilarated with the desire to step into my new life with my head up, serene, and confident. I took Jesus with me *"Because He is at my right hand I shall not be moved"* (Ps. 16:8).

The joy of returning home was great for me and for my parents as well. I had graduated from college at the age of twenty, one year earlier than my colleagues. To my benefit, the medical school had reduced the term from three years to two years. I had also graduated from high school one year early, allowing me to finish my education two years earlier, and this was another great blessing to me.

I do not remember taking my well-deserved vacation before starting my new career. I presented myself at the dental clinic in Rosiori with a neatly packaged diploma and asked to speak with the head of the clinic. I was taken to Dr. Mihai Balan's office. I was nervous. It was my first experience of this kind. I was determined to tell him who I was, what I believed, and what I wanted. I was intimidated by his posture and especially his prestige as a man of power. He was a tall, well-built man. He looked like a boss, but at the time, he was not my boss, and as such, I had no reason to be shy. I gathered my strength and told him who I was and why I had come to him. He did not ask me too many questions. Probably the candor of my innocent face weighed more than my words. After a brief interview, he asked me when I could start working. Now I realized I needed to tell my future boss about the Sabbath.

The moment I told him that I was an Adventist and that I would not be able to work on Saturday, he gave me a friendly smile and said, "No problem. My aunt is an Adventist, and I know what it's about. I'll do everything I can to help you. As long as I'm here, I will not let anyone harass you." He kept his word. I signed the employment contract at the hospital to which the dental clinic belonged, and, in a short time, I started work.

I had very good colleagues, and I adjusted quickly. There were a total of twelve dentists and twelve dental lab technicians plus auxiliary staff. Everything went smoothly for the first two years. I worked on Sundays to make up for Saturday hours, and I praised the Lord for the wonderful way He orchestrated all things for me.

Although Dr. Balan was a man with a big soul, he sometimes had a bizarre behavior that no one could understand. When we heard his hurried footsteps on the stairs leading upstairs, we all knew that the "boss" was coming. He was not always in a good mood. Sometimes he would quickly open the door to the lab where I worked and call me to his office. Once, he sent one of the nurses to call me. He always treated me with respect, and I had no reason to be afraid of him, although when he was angry, no one stood in his way.

He invited me to take a seat in the office chair while he, together with his assistant, worked on the patient positioned in the dental chair. He did not say a word, nor did he ask me to do anything for him. After a while, he sent me back to the lab without any explanation. I was puzzled, but I did not dare to ask questions, although I wanted to understand why I was called to his office. Soon enough, I would find out.

One day shortly after that, Steven, the head of the laboratory, revealed the mystery to me, who said he had heard it firsthand from Dr. Balan's mouth. "When I have moments of anger and nervousness, I call Elena into my office and ask her to take a seat at my desk. Her presence reassures me at once. Elena is a revelation for me!" When I heard these words, a similar Bible story came to mind regarding King Saul. When the king was troubled by an evil spirit, he would give orders for David, a young shepherd by trade, to come and play the harp for him. His presence, as well as his songs played on the harp strings, had a soothing effect on the capricious emperor, and the evil spirit left him at once. Little did I understand at that time why I, at only twenty years old and nicknamed "that little one," had a special impact at work, not only on my boss but also on my colleagues in the laboratory. In my presence no one swore or made bad jokes.

Although I felt loved and respected by all the staff, something completely strange and unexpected happened during a time when Dr. Balan went to Turkey on vacation. An inspector from headquarters came to the workplace to investigate, following an anonymous notification. I was called to the director's office and informed that after three "systematic" absences, I would be fired. The only option: to work on Saturday.

I replied that I could not violate my conscience, no matter the consequences. After several failed attempts to convince me, the local leadership convened a meeting with all the medical professionals in the city of Rosiori, hoping to intimidate me and make me give in to pressure from the local power.

In the meantime, my boss, Dr. Balan, had come back from his vacation. He was very indignant at what happened in his absence and made it clear to me that he would do everything he could to support me at that meeting.

I heard my name shouted. I got to my feet. The director of the hospital, after criticizing me for my "narrow mind and retrograde ideas," asked me in plenary why I was so stubborn and refused to come to work on Saturday. One of my co-workers, a good friend of mine, firmly held my hand and whispered to me to be strong and not give up. I declared in a loud and clear voice: "I am a Seventh-day Adventist and, according to the fourth commandment, I cannot violate my conscience to work on the Sabbath, even at the risk of losing my job."

Dr. Balan, trying to defend me, took the floor and described me as one of the ideal communists: honest, hardworking, conscientious, fair at work, etc. Of course, his arguments were not strong enough. I did not have a

Communist mentality, an essential quality, and that nullified all the other good things.

After a predetermined deadline, during which time the director of the hospital tried to negotiate with me, proposing that I only make an appearance on Saturday without working, I was fired. I had refused the option, stating that I could not compromise, acting against my conscience. I was given about a month to make up my mind and return to work, comply with the schedule of the office and work on Saturdays. What followed was the unlawful termination of my employment contract. I started searching for a job elsewhere.

Shortly after, an article appeared in the local newspaper about Elena Iorga, "a narrow-minded and stubborn Adventist" who was fired from work because she refused to work on Saturday.

After a period of fasting and prayer, the Lord offered me a job at a hospital near Bucharest. I would have my Sabbath free.

I was satisfied even though I was commuting by train for twenty minutes to Vidra, where there was a small laboratory with only eight dental technicians.

There, I worked in a disgraceful environment without the most basic equipment. Once I became head of the laboratory, I struggled to improve the working conditions.

At a staff meeting, I tried to bring plausible arguments by describing the conditions in which we worked, comparing ourselves—the technicians—with "mechanics in white gowns." The director liked this metaphor and, impressed by my plea, ordered the allocation of funds for the purchase of equipment and materials needed by the laboratory. In a short time, working conditions changed radically and gradually continued to improve.

I worked there for almost nineteen years until I left for America. I was very attached to Dr. Maria Ivan, a wonderful woman with whom I collaborated beautifully and made a lasting friendship.

On Thursday afternoons, I would work at the nearby clinic to compensate for Saturday. There I worked with Dr. Fotinia Botez. This was the most fruitful time for me, not only professionally but also spiritually.

The struggle to keep my faith pure had become second nature to me. I could see how wonderfully the Lord was leading me, and I felt safe under His protective wing. Although I understood little about the workings of Providence, I had learned to listen to Him without questioning. And I was never disappointed.

At Dr. Botez's office, I acquired clinical knowledge of dentistry outside the technical spectrum taught at the medical school. There, I gained proficiency that would be of great use to me later in my new career as a dental assistant in the United States.

***

THE ANGEL OF THE LORD, MY ANGEL

"The angel of the Lord encamps all around those who fear Him, And deliver them." (Ps. 34:7)

How grateful should we be to the guardian angel who was appointed at the birth of each of us! Only in eternity will we know how many times we have been delivered from great dangers and even from death through the supernatural intervention of the angels commissioned by our heavenly Father to watch over us, step by step, in our wanderings on this earth.

It was a cool autumn morning. I was getting used to commuting, although I had to change the means of transportation three times from home to the railway station. The thing I did not like was that I had to be at the station at a fixed time. If there was heavy traffic on the route and I was only one minute late, the train would leave without me. The late passengers were at the mercy of the movement clerk who ordered the train to leave. If you would happen to be seen running after the train, and the clerk was merciful, he would whistle for a long time, and the train would stop. The late man clung to the ladder of the last car and then breathed a sigh of relief that he had not lost his day's work. The next train was at noon, so catching the train was priority number one for all commuters.

One particular morning, the trolley arrived at the station only a few minutes before the train was scheduled to leave. I saw from the trolley that the train was still there. I was on the front steps of the trolley, ready to jump and run a few hundred yards to the station, hoping to catch it before its departure. As soon as the trolley stopped, I jumped through the front door and began running toward the train station. I did so without making sure the road was clear on my left side. It was the end of the line, and another trolley that I had not seen was just departing on the line parallel to the trolley that I had just gotten off.

The only thing I remember is the squeaking of the trolley brakes and a strong current that pushed me to the other side of the line. I looked around in dismay and did not realize what had happened. The trolley was gone ... only my guardian angel and I were left at the spot. By the time I arrived at the station, the train had already left; its long, loud whistle still lingered in my ears. There was nobody around to scold me for my recklessness or to congratulate me on escaping from my certain demise.

I had no reason to hurry now, but I had reason to thank God for the saving angel who pulled me off the trolley rail before being caught under its wheels. This was the second time in my life, after the carbon dioxide poisoning incident, that my guardian angel snatched me from the clutches of death. My heart was full of gratitude.

> **The trolley was gone ... only my guardian angel and I were left at the spot.**

I want to praise the Lord unceasingly and tell everyone about this wonderful God, my God in whom I trust. *"Unless the Lord had been my help, My soul would soon have settled in silence" (Ps. 94:17).*

The year was 1973. May 1. Labor Day in Romania. A day of joy for Romanians, especially when we were not obliged to "celebrate it through work." The weather was nice enough to go outside in the forest, in the green grass, in the fresh and cool air in the mountains, and for the most adventurous, even at sea, although the water was cold as ice.

It was the month of flowers, the month of rebirth, both for nature and for the oppressed man bent under the harsh yoke of Communism. In Bucharest, spring had come earlier than usual. An unanticipated heat wave, brought by the south wind, beckoned the entire community to come out. Out of the house, out of town, on the beach to the Black Sea, out of the crowds and the daily tumult.

With anticipated joy I scheduled a trip home to visit my parents. There I could breathe a sigh of relief in the peace and comfort of childhood to which I was still attached with body and soul. My mother was waiting for me with lilac flowers from our garden and freshly blooming peonies placed in an earthen pot.

The joy of coming home was even greater when I saw that I was expected not only by my parents but also by my nephews and niece from Bucharest. They were the five children of Mihai, my older brother, brought to their grandmother by their dad.

They were all dear to me and very close to my heart. During my student years, when I had a little time off from school, I loved going to their home to play with them, to teach them songs, to tell them one more story. The four boys, Val, Mihai, Cornel, and Claudiu, were very naughty. Lumi, the "princess" of the family, was attached to me in a special way.

We all decided to travel to the valley, to the forest, to the coolness and the green grass. Grandma made sure to take a blanket with her to spread on the grass in the woods. There, on the bank of the River Vedea, the little ones often came to swim. Here, children could run freely without restrictions. They came, like me, from the heart of Bucharest. Upon arriving at the forest only fifteen minutes from home, the children zigzagged through the forest, giggling and squealing with joy.

My mother had just sat on the blanket in the shade, and I was watching the children, when suddenly, I heard Val, the ten-year-old boy, shouting loudly, "The oxen!! Look at the oxen!! They are coming toward us!!"

I hurried in the direction I had heard his voice. From the other side of the river, three giant bulls were running to the place where they had seen Val and Mihai, the younger brother. They quickly crossed the river and started climbing the high bank of the river. We immediately realized that we were the target of these angry beasts, and we were in grave danger. There was no time to waste. I quickly gathered the children, and, along with my mother, we all started running out of the woods. The roars of the angry bulls resounded terribly in the silence of the forest. I looked back to see how close they were to us and was surprised to see them stampeding on a forest road in the opposite direction. I assumed they had lost sight of us, and we continued running down the valley toward our house.

Suddenly, we heard angry roars and loud hooves pounding behind us. I was in despair. Where were we to go? I was far from any place of refuge. Humanly, there was no escape. My greatest concern was for the children. They did not understand the danger we were in. On the contrary, they laughed and had fun looking back at the "big oxen" running after us. I felt totally helpless.

Next, without knowing why, I turned right, and we all started the hard, steep climb up the hillside where there was a farm, a possible place of escape if someone were there to rescue us. It was awfully hard to scamper up the hill. I hurried the children to pass in front of me and kept alerting them: "Run, kids! Run!"

I was carrying the youngest of them on my back, a boy only three years old, who could not keep up with the rest of us. Claudiu was holding me so tightly by the neck that he almost suffocated me. I pushed the other kids from behind, urging them to run as fast as possible. We were all climbing. I turned my head to look for my mother and saw her far behind us, very close to the bulls. I heard their angry snorts and bellows as they continued climbing the hillside, chasing their prey.

I could hear the rattling of the chains around their necks, and, with the force of desperation, I pushed the children to the top of the hill and over the other side, where they could not be seen by the angry bulls. They were safe there. I hurriedly returned to help my mother. The climb was much harder for her, and she was far behind us. The bulls were so close to her! My poor mother!!! She was exhausted. I could read the horror of impending death on her face. With the last drop of energy, I pulled her after me without looking back. When we reached the top of the hill, we both collapsed to the ground. We were exhausted. In the middle of the hill, the bulls had stopped to rest. My mother later confessed to me that my face was as white as snow. I was shaking like a leaf. I had reached the maximum level of adrenaline. From the top of the hill, I could no longer see the bulls, nor did they see us. I could finally breathe a sigh of relief. We gathered the children around us and lifted our eyes toward heaven with words of praise and thanksgiving to our great Savior.

We later learned the bulls that terrorized us had escaped from a reservation across the river and that the caretakers were desperately looking for them. They were extremely dangerous, so they had been kept in chains.

Looking back, we marveled at how the Lord urged us to change direction, not knowing that bulls cannot climb hills with the speed with which they charge down the plain. He also gave us the energy to flee to a safe place, saving us from the danger.

One of His promises was ringing in my ears after coming out from the state of shock: *"For He shall give His angels charge over you, To keep you in all your ways. In their hands they shall bear you up, Lest you dash your foot against a stone"* (Ps. 91:11–12).

***

The beautiful years of my youth, with the age-specific exuberance and love of life, were blurred by the health problems I faced beginning at the age of twenty-eight. Like any girl in her prime, I dreamed of getting married, having a family, and then becoming a mother.

The devastating earthquake of March 4, 1977, measuring 7.2 on the Richter scale, shook the Romanian community from its foundations and caught me off guard. I was not feeling well, not only emotionally due to the psychological trauma caused by the earthquake but also physically. In the chaos after the earthquake, the hospitals in Bucharest were packed with victims. My friend, Dr. Botez, realizing the seriousness of my situation, intervened for me to be seen immediately at the Emergency Hospital.

I was diagnosed with acute appendicitis and was immediately hospitalized and prepared for surgery. I was told that I was on the verge of peritonitis, that is, on the verge of death. After the surgery, I was placed in a hospital hallway on a folding bed, alongside the victims of the earthquake. I was soon discharged due to lack of space in the overcrowded hospital.

Once again, I thanked God that He saved me from death and that I remained under His loving care.

Among the many people scared by the earthquake who left Bucharest was my sister, Viorica, together with Eugen, her husband, and their son, Val. They left behind a beautiful apartment located at the outskirts of Bucharest, which I decided to buy myself. That is how I moved to a new house that summer, even though it would take me an additional hour to commute to work. I was young, and I did not mind.

A year later, in 1978, life had another surprise for me. I was diagnosed with a uterine fibroid of an unusually large size. I needed surgery. Through relationships, I managed to be admitted at one of the best hospitals in Bucharest and operated on by the famous obstetrics surgeon, Dr. L. Ratiu. After the surgery, I received good news and bad news. The good news was that, although the size of the tumor required a total hysterectomy, through an extremely laborious surgical maneuver, the surgeon and his team managed to keep the uterus intact. The unwanted news was that I would not be able to have children because of the uterus scarring due to the operation.

This news saddened me deeply. However, the tumor was benign, and I had plenty of reasons to thank God that I was anatomically and functionally intact and, especially, that I did not have cancer. A year later, in 1979, I married, but not before notifying Cornel, my future husband, that I would not be able to become a mother, according to the doctor who operated on me.

CHAPTER 3

THE WONDER CHILD

"Is anything too hard for the Lord?" (Gen. 18:14)

Neither my husband nor I could come to terms with the idea that we would not become parents, although, theoretically, I had accepted this reality when I found out from Dr. Ratiu that I would not be able to have children.

I knew that our Lord is a God of the impossible. We were just going to test Him. We prayed that His will be done in this regard, knowing from experience that this is the wisest choice.

Only three months after marriage, typical pregnancy symptoms appeared. My first thought was to see Dr. L. Ratiu and tell him the good news. When he met me at his office and heard my unrealistic story, he smiled at me candidly and said: "You're a naive child. How can you believe such a thing?" He then elaborated, reminding me how traumatic the surgery was, how I would never be able to conceive and carry the pregnancy because of my scarred uterus; in other words it would be impossible for me to become a mom. Period.

After he found out that I was right, he exclaimed, "You're a great success for me. A unique case, which I cannot explain. This must be a miracle! However, the risk of losing the pregnancy is high, due to the fact that your damaged uterus will not be able to expand as the fetus develops. You must be under strict supervision because your life is in danger."

At that time in Romania, as a patient, you had to be recorded at the medical clinic or hospital according to your residence. In order to schedule an operation by Dr. Ratiu, who was outside the network, I needed to obtain special approval from the Minister of Health. I had no right to register with him permanently, even though I wanted to. He was one of the best OBGYN specialists. Not coincidentally, Dr. L Ratiu's brother was an obstetrician-gynecologist at that medical clinic in my county. The surgeon wrote a note to his brother and asked me to present it to him on the first visit, entrusting me in his care.

From the start, Dr. Eugen Ratiu proposed to discontinue my pregnancy as the safest alternative to avoid a miscarriage with the implied risks. As parents, both my husband and I adamantly said, "NO!" The doctor respected our decision and advised close medical supervision.

To protect myself and the fetus, I was forbidden to go to work. Under Ceausescu's dictatorship, the unjustified loss of a pregnancy was punishable as a criminal act both for the mother and for the providing physician. Abortion was allowed only if the mother already had five children or for well-justified medical reasons, such as the mother's life being jeopardized. Otherwise, both the mother and the obstetrician were liable to imprisonment up to ten years for causing an illegal abortion. And because contraceptives were smuggled, many young girls and mothers with fewer than five children resorted to empirical methods to provoke a miscarriage. Many of them lost their lives because they refused to disclose the truth for fear of going to prison. In such cases, it was an illegal act for the doctor to intervene in rescuing the victim from certain death.

Surgical instrument kits designated for legal abortion were sealed and inventoried. They could only be opened and used with special approval from the Ministry of Health and in the presence of a police body.

I stayed at home during the entire pregnancy to prevent miscarriage and attended regular check-ups each month. The baby developed normally, and I did not experience any discomfort or pain.

When I had about two weeks left until full term, I thought it would be good to see Dr. Ratiu for arrangements of a C-section, which was mandatory. Contractions at birth could cause my scarred uterus to rupture from lack of plasticity.

At the visit, everything looked normal. The doctor had no clue that my baby had another plan, however. Overnight, he "cracked the shell," although he was not ready to see the light of day. I lost the amniotic fluid without pain or contractions. I awoke at 4:00 a.m. to a wet bed but without symptoms. Cornel called the ambulance, and I was taken to the Municipal Hospital, where I was registered. I was planning to go to the Minister of Health the next day to get my approval for delivery at the hospital where Dr. Ratiu was permitted to perform the surgery. The OB doctor in charge at Municipal Hospital did not pay attention when I told him that a C-section must be performed due to my cicatricial uterus. No labor, no pain.

He gave me medication to induce labor. Nothing happened. He presented the case to the professor, and he immediately ordered the

C-section. I was taken to the surgery room, and soon after, our baby saw the light of day. It was May 6, 1980.

Lusa, a friend of mine from church, happened to be the nurse who accompanied me to the operating room and attended the cesarean section. "It's a boy! And he is hairy, like Esau!" Lusa exclaimed with a loud voice. Those were the first words I heard after I awakened from the general anesthesia.

At that time in Romania, the baby's gender could not be identified during pregnancy. A deep emotion flooded my soul when I heard that I had delivered a baby boy.

> "*It's a boy! And he is hairy, like Esau!*"

The baby was taken from me before I could see him, and I was transferred to a special unit for C-section mothers. Unfortunately, I had to stay in the hospital under close supervision with antibiotics for two weeks. I had lost amniotic fluid more than twelve hours earlier, and surgery should be performed quickly in order to prevent infection for both mother and baby.

The next morning I woke up, and with the effect of the anesthesia over, I remembered my friend's words from the operating room: "It's a boy."

"I need to see my baby!" I told myself. I got out of bed, although the nurse on duty had told me that I was not allowed to get out of bed before I was seen by the doctor during the morning visit.

The desire to see my child knew no bounds. I left the room and, holding onto the wall, I managed to walk down a long corridor, looking for my baby, who had been taken from me the day before. I found out that he had been taken to another wing of the hospital for special care. I was looking forward not only to seeing my baby but to holding him, to feel him, to hug him, and to nestle him in my heart forever. It was a legitimate desire in me as a mother to experience "live" the unprecedented feeling: bonding body and soul with my offspring.

I was very anxious to see my baby. I had already outlined the portrait of my son in the most vivid shades; small and plump, with beautiful hair, a nose like a little button between his chubby cheeks, and a smile on his face at the first eye contact with his mother!

Leaning against the wall, I could hardly walk down the long corridor, my whole body racked in pain.

Arriving at the place where the babies were stationed, I was not allowed to enter. Through a glass screen, I could see inside an incubator full of naked babies, blindfolded, exposed to a light-lamp. I thought that was the way it should be, and I did not ask any questions. Through a small open window, I was given my wrapped baby to hold only for a short time. My baby was so small! And so fragile! He weighed only 5.95 pounds, and, as was common in that day and age, I was not allowed to breastfeed him due to having a cesarean section. I also learned that he would have to stay under the ultraviolet lamp because he developed physiological jaundice. He had weighed over 6 pounds at birth, and I could not leave the hospital until he regained his birth weight.

At first glance, although my eyes were full of tears, I saw the most beautiful baby in the world. He was mine and could not be otherwise. Before he could feel the warmth emanating from my body, after I whispered in his ear how much I loved him, he was taken from my arms and placed back under that source of ultraviolet heat.

When I was told I was not allowed to breastfeed my baby, I was stunned. After much insistence, I was given permission to visit the nursing room according to the established schedule to see my baby. Nothing else.

I could not wait for that golden time when I could touch him, hold him tight to my breast, and admire him sleeping peacefully in my arms. At lunchtime, he was already full and asleep because he was bottle-fed before breastfeeding. I would have loved to see him awake, to smile at him, to talk to him! And especially to feed him the best milk in the world, breast milk.

One day, to my great surprise, the baby was awake when he was handed to me at breastfeeding time.

My first reflex as a mother was to breastfeed him, even though I had been told I was not allowed to. With boundless joy and total dedication, I offered the most abundant meal to that little baby. It seemed too good to be true. After he fell asleep, I started "inventorying" him to see if he really was my baby.

He had a distinct sign by which I could identify him: a small chip at the pavilion of his right ear. A strange feeling troubled my soul. I felt something was wrong, and I was right. The sign was not there. Not even my baby's name on the bracelet! I quickly went to complain about the confusion. At the nursing station, a mother was alarmed that her baby could not be found. The dilemma was solved when that mother recognized her baby in my arms and thanked me for the free meal generously offered to her son.

By and by, I got my own baby and, with tears in my eyes, I hugged him and told him how much I loved him. This was a short visit due to the fact that breastfeeding time was already over. With every "mealtime," I left with a broken heart. My baby was not allowed to be breastfed for the first two weeks when we had to stay in the hospital.

Finally, we were home at last. Everything was beautifully decorated for the great celebration of the arrival of the youngest offspring of the family, our child. In the meantime, his father had taken care to declare our son at the Civil Registry Office. The name we had chosen was SILVIU. Wonder baby!!! The greatest gift from the Lord, for which I will be eternally grateful.

The news of our arrival at home brought great joy to the whole family; however, less to little Silviu. The transition from the baby bottle to the mother's breast was impossible.

From now on, the baby had to make a sustained effort to get the milk directly from the source, and it did not suit him. It was much easier for him in the hospital to receive the milk straight from the bottle with less effort than sucking it from Mother's breast. He decided to go on a "hunger strike." The doctor came to our home to assess the problem. She convinced herself that breastfeeding was not feasible and advised me to continue bottle feeding. I really wanted to give my child the best food, and I decided to fill the bottle with breast milk for all meals. I managed to do this for four months without a milking pump. I don't even know if, at that time, there was such a thing on the Romanian market.

After four months, the trauma of manual milking became unbearable, and we had to switch to Similac, the best milk powder at the time. Although he was gaining weight quite well, intestinal colic not only tormented the baby but also us, the parents. We were exasperated and exhausted physically as well as emotionally. Every hour he would wake up screaming and wake up the whole family. This nightmare lasted almost a year.

During this time, the baby had been diagnosed with an inguinal hernia. The surgeon told us he was too small to have surgery.

I had to start working. I slept standing in the crowded trolley on the way to the railway station from where I took the train to work. Baby's hernia started causing pain periodically. Such episodes would occur randomly, day or night.

The first thing I did when the train arrived at the station, on my way back from work, was to call home and find out how the baby was doing. If he was in a crisis, we had to take him to the hospital immediately, where the surgeon reduced his hernia with an extremely painful maneuver. I learned from the doctor that in times of crisis, the pain is incredible, but we were told the baby should not cry because the pain would increase.

At the age of ten months, Dr. Zamfir decided to operate on him. After the surgery, in order to prevent the incision's rupture, Silviu was not supposed to cry! The whole family, parents and grandparents, were all watching the little "terrorist."

We took turns as we stood over his crib like sentinels during the night to calm him down when his crying episodes occurred. After a year, the ordeal ended.

We hired a very good nanny, Geta, who stayed with us to care for our little boy so that I could go back to a full-time work schedule.

***

The phone was ringing! It was bedtime, an unusual time for calling unless it was an emergency. With justified apprehension, I answered the phone. From the other end of the line, I recognized my mother's voice. In a trembling tone, she asked us to urgently come home because my father was in the hospital in a serious condition.

Cornel and I went to Rosiori, my hometown, as soon as we could. We were shocked by this unexpected news. I knew my father as a healthy and strong man despite his age of eighty years old.

We found out he had cancer in the fourth stage with bone metastasis, which caused incredible pain. The whole family was alerted. We did our best for our father. With drugs from abroad, his life was extended for almost two years, and his suffering was also prolonged to the maximum. Together with my brother, Peter, I witnessed the passing away of our father, whom we loved and who loved us so much.

Mother, left alone, suffered the most after the loss of her life partner, who had been an integral part of her being for more than fifty years. At that time, she was seventy years old.

After almost a year, she decided to have a relatively simple operation for a perineal rupture, which she had postponed for a long time. I brought her to Bucharest and took her to the same hospital where my baby was delivered three years prior.

We made the necessary arrangements, and the surgeon who performed the C-section on me would operate on my mom. She came out of the surgery anemic, and a blood transfusion was performed. Shortly after that, she went into shock. The doctor in charge was very puzzled, not knowing what was happening.

It seems that the blood type was wrong because her body refused to accept it and expelled it immediately. After that, she had kidney failure. Her kidneys would not eliminate even a drop of urine. Every effort was made to force the diuresis. She was not responding to any medication. I was desperate to hold on to my mother.

A dialysis doctor was brought in and explained to me that her heart was not strong enough and that we should not cause her death by trying this procedure. I was shocked at what had happened in such a short time. I remembered how, a few hours earlier, my mother went to the operating room singing and encouraging me to be strong and trust in the Lord that all would be well. I could not accept the cruel reality that my mother was going to die soon.

I cried out to the Lord with a heart torn with grief: "Lord, I know that You can save my mother! You are our only hope! You are a merciful God! The doctors looked at me in dismay, not understanding my refusal to accept that my mother had no chance. I watched her on her deathbed for days and nights, urging the doctors to keep trying the impossible, while I believed that *"**All** things are possible to him who believes"* (Mark 9:23).

The days were getting more and more exhausting. My mother's condition was getting worse and worse. She was like a balloon ready to pop. The fluid pumped by the IV accumulated in her body without being able to be eliminated. She had a cadaverous color, and the state of delirium completed the clinical scenario of a dying person. Laboratory data confirmed imminent death. She had gone into a kidney coma.

The whole family was gathered around the bed, frozen in pain. Every breath, every beating of my mother's heart, gave me hope and motivated me to not stop praying for her. Doctors, professors, and urologists looked helpless and shrugged in bewilderment. They did not understand how my mother could survive despite her extremely critical condition.

After several days of tense waiting for the imminent outcome, something completely inexplicable happened. The "balloon" burst! By defecation, all the fluid accumulated in my mother's body through the IV was eliminated. The toxins not eliminated by the blocked kidneys were expelled in this way, and my mother began to recover.

She opened her eyes and smiled at us all, not knowing that she had been on the verge of death. She wondered why the whole family came to visit her, including Cornel, her son from America. Her kidneys began to work at normal parameters. Everyone was stunned, especially the doctors! They had never seen anything like this.

On a urography, her kidneys looked completely normal. Having no explanation for what happened, they had to admit that, indeed, this was a miracle. The professor doctor who struggled the most to rescue my mother from the clutches of death, said that I was the one who motivated him to not give up. My trust in God and the tenacity with which I persisted day and night in prayer was rewarded. Mother recovered completely, with no kidney sequelae.

After thirty days and nights of hospitalization, a time of nightmare for the whole family, my mother was discharged. The urologist told me that she had been completely healed, and that she would never have kidney problems again. And so, it was. What more can I say? A real miracle!

This is my God who I have trusted and will continue to trust all my life. I owe Him all the praise and gratitude for this miracle, and for many more He would do for my family and me.

> *"I love the Lord, because He has heard My voice and my supplications.... Because He has inclined His ear to me, Therefore I will call upon Him as long as I live ... For You have delivered my soul from death, My eyes from tears, And my feet from falling." (Ps. 116:1–2, 8)*

***

DEEP PAINS ARE MUTE

It was summer. The heat wave, which was hard to bear, especially in the city, forced people to the mountains or to the sea, looking for some small respite.

In the distance you could clearly see the horizon, bathed in the light of a beautiful sunrise. The blue, cloudless sky announced a gorgeous day. On the "Sea of Life," the mast of a small boat emerged, floating confidently.

Suddenly, heavy clouds gathered in the peaceful, serene sky. A fast-moving storm aroused the sea, and its gigantic waves crashed angrily into the small boat as if to swallow it. The young helmsman, taken by surprise, did not know what to do. Forgetting the precious cargo in the ship, he jumped off the deck and, without looking back, let himself be carried away by the waves, and then—suddenly—he was gone!!

The mother did not know how to swim, and the baby was totally helpless. In those moments of bitter confusion and despair, thinking of her husband, who disappeared in the tumultuous waves of the sea and her little one, only three years old, the poor mother cried out in despair: "Lord, save us!" Her cry reached heaven.

Although the boat-of-life was shattered under the attack of the raging waves, its precious cargo was brought ashore safely by an unseen hand. Many tears were shed by the poor wife for her husband stolen by the waves of the world.

In such a time of distress, she claimed the Bible promise: ***"Call to Me, and I will answer you, and show you great and mighty things, which you do not know"*** *(Jer. 33:3).*

After three days of fasting and praying, a mysterious voice spoke to the young woman in a gentle and clear voice: "Stop crying!" Then the voice unraveled the secret of her husband's mysterious disappearance: "He had gone to the beach with a woman who lived just five blocks away." She was devastated.

Nothing that could have been done to save the wrecked home was left undone. The wounds of her soul, though caressed with the balm of heaven, were still bleeding a year after the shipwreck.

In that period of maximum uncertainty and emotional turmoil, her little boy, who was now four years old, was her only relief. He often caught his mom crying, even though she tried to hide her pain, and with his little hand, he would wipe her teary cheeks. His innocent gaze, his delicate touch, were the only cure for her broken soul, the only antidote to the inner pain that consumed her. He was the joy and comfort of her soul.

The emotional trauma caused by this catastrophe and its ravaging effect cannot be described in words. After many years of torment and agony, healing came, but the scars remained, deeply embedded in the heart of the mother and the heart of the child. And yet, *"**He heals the brokenhearted and binds up their wounds**" (Ps. 147:3)*.

***

> *After three days of fasting and praying, a mysterious voice spoke to the young woman in a gentle and clear voice: "Stop crying!"*

The fall of 1983 lost its usual charm. Through my teary eyes, I could not discern the beauty of this wonderful season. Everything was sad, and felt cold all around me.

Autumn, with its nostalgia, took flight to other worlds, making room for a harsh winter with a leaden sky, like my soul. The flu season dragged on longer than usual, especially in crowded areas such as Bucharest.

Silviu, my son, began to complain of a sore throat. I took him to the doctor, and he was prescribed antibiotics. A common cold. Nothing more.

When the treatment was finished, instead of getting well, his condition worsened. I went to the specialist, the necessary tests were done, and I found out that he had chronic tonsillitis with golden staphylococcus. We had to change the treatment with injectable penicillin. I was very sad, knowing from my own experience how painful such injections were. I understood that this infection was dangerous, and I had no choice. I had to inject him four times a day. I was alone. It broke my heart to see him screaming in pain. I had to ask a neighbor to come and hold him every time I gave him the injection.

After completion of the treatment, the infection persisted. Due to the inflammation in the throat, my boy could barely breathe. I rushed him to the hospital, and he was immediately admitted at the request of the ENT specialist with the diagnosis: Chronic adenotonsillitis, outbreak of Staphylococcus aureus infection. The next day, Silviu underwent surgery.

That very day, I was scheduled for my first court appearance. My state of mind cannot be described in words. My heart was torn with grief, both for my child and for his father.

After the operation, the doctor explained to me how serious the infection was. He said that my baby's tonsils were rotten and that it was possible to have postoperative complications with massive hemorrhaging. He told me that I had to keep an eye on my son and that complications may occur after surgery. My boy was breathing hard and had a high fever.

I watched him constantly and prayed for him. After midnight he woke up, vomiting large amounts of blood. I immediately alerted the doctor, who ordered a blood transfusion to prevent the hemorrhagic shock. Silviu was transferred to ICU, and a vial of blood was attached to the catheter on his vein. The doctor who operated on him soon appeared. He expected such a complication, given the serious infection to which my boy had been exposed.

Another complication occurred after the transfusion—staphylococcal pneumonia. We had to stay in the hospital for two weeks for intensive treatment and medical supervision. It was a nightmare for both of us. I cried out in despair to God for another miracle, and my prayers were answered. My son's condition improved.

At discharge, I was outside at the hospital gate with my boy hunched over in my arms, trembling with cold and emotion. I prayed that the Lord would send me help. Suddenly, a taxi appeared and took us home. At that time, it was difficult to find a taxi. When a free one appeared, it was grabbed by whoever was faster.

It was mid-December 1983. It was cold outside and cold in the house. At the apartment building, the heat was allocated according to the Communist Party's order. My soul was cold—colder than the house. I was so alone.

Winter had settled in earlier than usual. I was physically overworked after many sleepless nights in the hospital. Mental and emotional exhaustion far surpassed physical exhaustion.

I clung to the Lord with my weak faith, and slowly but surely, my boy began to gain strength. After much prayer and special care, he saw a complete recovery. His sprightly voice filled our home and my soul again. Life seemed to return to the new "normal" for a short period of time.

***

Dramatic changes occurred in the family after the "pillar of the house" collapsed. Geta, my child's nanny, decided to retire and soon left us.

Not long after, I decided to move out of my house, trying to fade away the sad memories of a dismantled home. I managed to sell the apartment and buy another one in an area closer to the train station, thus shortening the commute to work.

I also found a good nanny for my son, a beautiful and pure-hearted girl. Her name was Angela, and she loved Silviu very much. I continued my commute in the province and worked hard to support my family.

After a cold and gloomy winter full of adventures, we waited for spring with auspicious hopes.

> **Life was beautiful in our home, for love and innocence reigned here, and Jesus was our daily guest.**

The visits of my mother, as well as of Silviu's grandparents and Uncle Mihai, filled our house and our souls with joy. The wound of my heart had begun to heal, thanks to the Great Healer.

The summer, with its long and hot days, was desirable only for holidays at the beach and in the mountains. I often took my child to the country, either to my mother's house or to my in-laws, who loved me as their daughter. There, far from the hectic and crowded life of the urban environment, I found an oasis of peace and comfort.

From time to time, I would take Silviu to stay with my mother, especially when a heatwave was announced in Bucharest. I always went home on the weekends to spend time with him. Although I missed him a lot during the week, I preferred to keep him in the country, in the cool, fresh air, green grass, and well cared for by his loving grandmother.

On the eve of autumn, when the weather began to cool, I intended to bring my boy home. My legitimate desire to have him permanently home had become imperative. Life had somehow entered a normal path. The support of family, church, and friends had made a huge contribution to the healing process. My child was the apple of my eye, my only treasure, the object of my boundless love. He was a beautiful and intelligent little boy, full of life, of inexhaustible energy. He overwhelmed me with his love, which he expressed so convincingly through chosen manners and words.

Life was beautiful in our home, for love and innocence reigned here, and Jesus was our daily guest.

CHAPTER 4
IN THE FIERY FURNACE

"I thought it good to declare the signs and wonders that the Most High God has worked for me. How great are His signs, and how mighty His wonders!" (Dan. 4:2–3)

October 1985

Autumn settled into its legitimate borders after an unusually hot summer. A pleasant breeze vibrated in the air, loaded with scents that caressed the soul. The outdoor market plaza groaned under the burden of beautifully decorated fruit and vegetable pyramids for Harvest Day. Nature, in golden robes, arrayed for the holiday, invited us to take a walk outside, away from the tumult of the busy streets, at the edge of the lake or in the forest, for relaxation and meditation. The trees proudly displayed their multicolored ornaments, inviting the weary traveler of the day to a stop under the cool shade.

I was exhausted after a day of work. My house was not welcoming. My child, who was usually jumping into my arms when I appeared in the doorway, was still at my mother's, where I had taken him for the hot days.

Arriving at the apartment door, I realized I did not have the key with me. I had forgotten it at home. I hurried to a public telephone to call my brother Peter to ask him to bring me the spare key that I had given him some time ago. It was already dark, I was tired, and I did not feel like going for the key.

He answered the phone and, before I could tell him why I called him, he promptly interrupted me, giving me astonishing news. Our mother had called. She said I must come to her home immediately; Silviu was seriously ill. He had a high fever, as well as an inflamed and very painful leg.

This unexpected news was like a dagger in my heart. I was crushed. I did not know how to get to the country sooner to help my child. I needed a car so that I could quickly transport him to the hospital in Bucharest.

I cried out in despair, "Lord, help me!" I was immediately urged to call Uncle Cornel, a brother of faith who had a car and could help me in my emergency. Every time I turned to him, he was kind enough to help me. I must mention that at that time in Romania, a car was a luxury item that not everyone could afford. In the divorce, Silviu's father had taken our car, and we depended on public transportation. Realizing the state of emergency, Uncle Cornel left immediately, and we were soon on Alexandria Road leading to my mother's house. It was October 25, 1985.

We arrived at our destination late at night. I burst into tears when I saw my child, burning with fever and in incredible pain. His left leg was red and very much inflamed.

I carefully placed him in the back seat, his head on my lap and his left leg propped up between the pillows. We asked Uncle Cornel to take us to the Children's Hospital in Bucharest.

Silviu was immediately admitted into the hospital, connected to an oxygen mask, and hooked up to an IV. The necessary investigations were soon made to determine the cause of the foot infection. X-rays and laboratory tests helped establish the diagnosis: acute osteomyelitis, left tibia. The surgeon on duty that night warned me that this type of bone marrow infection was extremely dangerous and involved many risks.

How he contracted such an infection was a mystery. The staphylococcal entrance gate could not be identified. "Staphylococci trot all around us without affecting us," the doctor told me.

Silviu was a perfectly healthy child, not showing any signs of illness until then. How and why did he get so seriously ill? Why was his immune system not on guard to protect him from an enemy invasion? Why had he not shown signs of the disease until the infection reached the bone? I had many questions that went unanswered.

My little five-year-old was immediately taken to the operating room.

The waiting moments until he was brought back to the ward were long and excruciating. I prayed fervently for the Lord to intervene.

After the operation, the surgeon told me that he had removed "a bowl of pus" from the infected leg. My boy was now calm under anesthesia. But I was not at all calm. I watched him through the night, watching every breath, every heartbeat.

Everything was so nebulous as I awaited the post-operative prognosis. Even the doctors could not guess what was to come. I was told to keep an eye on him and to call the nurse if there were any problems. I stayed up all night and prayed. My soul was melting with pity for my child. If it had been possible, I would have taken all his suffering upon myself. My pain was unimaginable!

By daybreak, I noticed that his condition was getting worse. He was breathing very hard, and his heart was pounding. I alerted the nurse in charge, and she called the doctor on duty, the same doctor who had operated on him the night before. The surgeon immediately came to the room, and seeing the critical condition of my son, ordered him transferred urgently to the ICU. In a few moments, a team of doctors and medical staff gathered around the bed, collecting new laboratory samples.

The new diagnosis pronounced the death sentence for the little patient: Septicemia with staphylococcus. Pleuro-pulmonary staphylococcus. Septic myocarditis.

The doctors told me that the vital organs—heart and lungs—were drowning in pus, and my son had no chance of survival. I was shown a lung x-ray. Only 10 percent of his lungs were still functioning. The rest was flooded with infection.

He was taken to the operating room, and a pulmonologist placed a drainage tube to remove the pus from the lungs. The cardiologist declared herself powerless, telling me that my child's heart was severely damaged, resembling the result of a massive heart attack. Her little patient's body was vibrating, due to tachycardia, at 210 beats per minute.

> **The new diagnosis pronounced the death sentence for the little patient.**

Later, Silviu was taken back to the operating room to have a catheter placed into his vein for antibiotics, as well as blood transfusions. A special medication was injected into his spine to prevent the infection from spreading to his brain.

A blood transfusion was performed, and three types of antibiotics were administered intravenously. His fever was close to 104º F. The scene was horrifying.

An infectious diseases specialist was called to evaluate my son. As he stepped into the room and saw Silviu's little body vibrating due to tachycardia, he was astonished and looked dismayed and utterly helpless.

Eventually, the ER doctor on duty advised me to call my family, stating that I should not be alone, as my child would not make it through the night. I was shaken to the core. My heart torn with grief, I burst into tears. I asked for explanations for the death sentence pronounced on my child.

The doctors explained that staphylococcal sepsis is relentless, and that the patient was too young to survive, and that he was not responding to any medication. His immune system was totally compromised, and his body "refused to cooperate." He had contracted all the possible complications, and in conclusion, we needed to be prepared for the final verdict—imminent death.

I called my family. I also called the pastor, asking him to convene the church for an urgent prayer for little Silviu. I was totally devastated. Fear of death tore my heart. Oh, if I could have taken his place, I would not have hesitated for a moment to give myself completely for him.

Suddenly, an inspired thought flashed through my mind: **"With *God, all things are possible"* (Matt. 19:26).** I clung desperately to this promise and continued to pray as I watched my precious baby struggling between life and death.

Peter, my brother, stayed by my side all night, stunned by this incredible scene. No words, only tears. The silence was terribly oppressive. Nobody had anything to say. Only God could understand what I suffered through that night. I was constantly praying. I tried to hide my tear-stained face, turning my head and wiping away my tears whenever Silviu opened his eyes.

Many of the promises of the Lord Jesus reverberated in my memory. The miracles He performed in my life, especially when He saved me from death, more than once; when He saved my mother from death, all these memories came back to my mind and gave me hope of life for my dear son who was stuck in the clutches of death.

Bible promises resonated in my mind, giving me hope and confidence:

"Yea, though I walk through the valley of the shadow of death, I will fear no evil; for You are with me." (Ps. 23:4)

I watched intently for every breath, every beat of my son's heart. Even though, due to tachycardia, his breathing was very laborious, as long as there was a breath in his chest, life could not be extinguished.

I spoke to the Lord in my mind and said to Him, *"I know that You can do everything, And that no purpose of Yours can be withheld from You" (Job 42:2).*

As I was pleading with God in prayer, I was more and more confident that the Lord would perform a miracle for my child, although his condition was profoundly altered. I was wondering what the doctors would say at the morning visit when they would find their little patient still alive.

***

THROUGH DEATH'S VALLEY

"Call upon Me in the day of trouble; I will deliver you, and you shall glorify Me." (Ps. 50:15)

A faint ray of light crept through the partially camouflaged window of the intensive care unit. For me and my brother Peter, it was a nightmare. The eyelids, although tired, refused to close. I was physically and mentally exhausted after an extremely tense day and two sleepless nights.

From the previous night, when Silviu was admitted to the hospital, I sat next to his bed, watching his breathing and his heartbeat, listening to what the doctors had to say, and asking questions.

His condition had not improved, as far as I could see. However, my faith and trust in God helped me not to lose my courage. I knew from experience that I could trust my God, the God of the impossible.

The time for the morning visit arrived. The professor doctor came with the whole team: specialists, residents, students. They surrounded Silviu's bed, all with their eyes fixed on him.

Dr. Davidescu, who had been on duty at the time when Silviu was admitted into the hospital, later confessed to me that she cried when she returned home and told her husband about Silviu, a hopeless case. The next day, when she was in the elevator going up to the ward, she asked a staff member if Silviu was still alive. She could not believe that he had survived overnight.

New laboratory results, radiographs, and other tests were studied and discussed. I retreated into a corner to make room for the medical team, but I attentively listened to their words.

I heard the professor, who was holding the patient's chart in his hands, whispering to the team, "If you look at the clinical and laboratory data in the chart, you would think that the patient was already dead. Look at the child, though! He is still breathing. I'm amazed! I don't know what to think. And look at his mother's bright face!"

I was constantly connected to Heaven through prayer. Only in this way could I resist the furious attacks of discouragement and despair. I was later told that my faith had motivated everyone not to capitulate in the face of death.

The fight was fierce. Everything was attempted to save my little Silviu. Dr. Oraseanu, the lung specialist, told me to call him at any time at night if the drainage from the lungs was blocked. I even called him once after midnight, and he immediately came to fix the problem.

The infected leg was so swollen that the stitches popped open, and pus came out through the open incision. He was taken back to the operating room to remove the collected pus and suture the incision. His extremely high fever could not be controlled. I was told to apply cold water compresses only to his healthy leg and left arm, where there was no IV attached.

Mari, my sister, arrived on a night train from Constantza and stayed with me all the time, helping me change compresses and watching Silviu when I went home to take a shower and to change.

The members of my family could hardly get into the intensive care unit. They came in turn, wept at the bedside, and left. I asked not to be visited by anyone but my family. My soul was crying in pain. I did not want to be comforted.

My brothers and my sister from America called me several times a day. I only asked one thing of everyone: "Pray for Silviu!"

The doctors became more and more pessimistic. At one point, Dr. Zamfir, the chief surgeon in the hospital's surgery ward, raised his hands in the air and exclaimed helplessly, "I am not God to save your child!"

Although pessimistic, his testimony affirmed a truth on which I had anchored all my hope: "God has power to save!"

A ray of hope lit up my face at the thought that the Lord heard the cry of my despairing soul. Like the prophet Jeremiah, I consoled myself with confidence in the goodness of the Lord: ***"This I recall to my mind, therefore I have hope. Through the Lord's mercies we are not consumed, because His compassions fail not. They are new every morning; Great is Your faithfulness"*** *(Lam. 3:21–23).*

In the morning, I thanked God that another night had passed and that Silviu was still alive.

The chief physician in the intensive care unit often visited us and left without saying anything. The cardiologist came to see him several times a day. Her deep sigh said it all. I wanted to ask her about my child's condition, but she totally ignored me. She simply refused to talk to me. She later confessed to me that she avoided me because she did not want to tell me the truth and amplify my pain.

X-rays, lab tests, EKGs, and blood transfusions were the order of the day. The three antibiotics given intravenously had to be replaced every ten days with new ones. The staph virus mutated and became resistant, and meds were inefficient.

After a while, a new element appeared in the laboratory results: an extremely high level of enzymes, which, together with the pigmentation of the skin of an intense yellow, indicated an acute liver disease.

Dr. Tudor, a specialist in infectious diseases, was brought in, and he confirmed that my child's liver was affected by an acute, out-of-control hepatitis. "Of course, high doses of nonstop medications intoxicated his liver," the doctor thought. The liver should also be kept under observation, in addition to the other vital organs affected by the infection.

The days were extremely tense, and the nights were long and torturous. The fever increased to 104º F., and the general condition worsened from one hour to the next. I had often been told that nothing could be done to save my child.

From time to time he was taken to the operating room to have the pus that accumulated at the surgical site removed. After a while, the catheter stopped working and had to be replaced. A surgeon specialized in this procedure, Dr. Basca, placed a new one on the other hand.

Silviu was perfectly lucid, but extremely weak. He spoke in a whisper and could barely be heard.

After the new catheter was placed, Dr. Basca came to me and explained to me how difficult the procedure was. The veins had collapsed due to the acute infection. Then he confessed with tears in his eyes that, while he was trying to push the catheter into his vein, Silviu had whispered in a pathetic tone, "I see you are struggling in vain. Either you can't ... or you don't know how to do it ... if you don't know, call someone else."

Due to the many drugs administered nonstop through an IV, a rash broke out all over his body. My baby was tormented by terrible itching and was not able to scratch himself since both hands were immobilized.

Mari and I both scratched him gently to distract him from the itching.

One morning, the pulmonologist came to see him. When seeing the doctor, Silviu begged him in a pleading tone: "Doctor, could you scratch my back, please?"

"Of course, I can!" the doctor answered candidly and immediately started scratching his little patient's back.

In the brief moments of silence, after the morning rush, when a lot of doctors came to see Silviu, Mari and I were trying to alleviate his pain, talking to him, singing, and telling him stories, trying to distract him from his pain and suffering.

Once, while I was singing something to him, he said to me, "Mom, sing me that song: He healed many sick, as He was going from place to place."

It was a song he had learned in the Sabbath School class at church. I was deeply moved by the fact that he was thinking about this song now when he needed healing. Of course, I sang it to him many times and assured him that the Lord Jesus would heal him, too.

I was praying and waiting for something special to happen to us. I wanted Silviu to be able to eat, to gain strength, to get out of this lethargic state. We were trying to tempt him with all sorts of culinary "baits." He refused to open his mouth. The doctors told me I had to persuade him to eat. Easier said than done.

One day, Dr. Davidescu offered to try to feed him. She asked me to leave the room, to leave her alone with my son, thinking that the boy was fussing to eat in the presence of his mother.

After a while, she called me inside, and with tears in her eyes, she said, "I'm convinced he cannot eat." I forced him, and he threw up. She apologized and, deeply saddened, left the room.

Every day, especially at night, when the condition worsened, all the medical staff panicked. The fear of death had become obsessive. The results of all the tests were getting worse. From time to time, a blood transfusion was needed.

His lungs and heart were flooded with pus, making breathing more and more difficult. Leg amputation would have been an extremely drastic alternative, but the patient's general condition was so compromised that he would not have endured such a traumatic intervention, not to mention the mental trauma of both the child and the mother, which would have marked both for the rest of their lives.

The pus at the incision site accumulated quickly, and the patient had to be taken again to the surgery room. Eventually, after several consecutive interventions, the anesthesiologist was afraid that Silviu would not be able to come out from the general anesthesia due to his extremely debilitated condition. A decision had to be made as soon as possible—maybe with fatal consequences.

I had to give my consent for a new surgery. I was told that the risk was just as great, whether he was operated on or not.

I was terrified. "Lord, what should I do?"

More than three weeks of atrocious suffering for my child, physical exhaustion, and mental anguish for me as a mother had already passed, watching him day and night and shedding tears for him.

It was heartbreakingly painful to see him suffer without being able to help him. I would have liked to take his pain, to sacrifice myself to death for him, if it were possible.

All this time, I prayed to the Lord not to take my child, for he was everything to me. He was all that was left for me, and I could not imagine life without him. I was at the end of my rope.

Like Jacob, in the face of imminent death, I was persuaded to entrust my child into God's care, aware that He had kept him alive until that moment, and He could save him from loss of life.

***

STOP CRYING!

"Thus says the Lord: Refrain your voice from weeping,
And your eyes from tears; For your work shall be rewarded,
says the Lord." (Jer. 31:16)

Confident that the Lord was in control, I gave my consent for Silviu to be operated on again. He had already become "the miracle boy." Later, I found out that every day, upon arrival at the hospital, before arriving at the ward, everyone wanted to know if Silviu was still alive.

The anesthetist on duty told me that he did not have the courage to put him to sleep, not being sure that he would wake up from the anesthesia. The little patient was so weak, and he could barely breathe. The chief anesthetist was called in, and my son was taken to the operating room.

I accompanied him up to the door, knowing I had to stay there. But Silviu asked his mother to be with him in the surgery room, and his request was honored, given the very special situation he was in.

As soon as the anesthesia was injected into the catheter, Silviu fell asleep, and I had to leave the room.

On the way to the door, with tears in my eyes, I turned my head to see my child once more. My heart, torn by pain, could not detach itself from him.

I was alone in that empty hallway of the surgery ward. I pressed my ear to the padded operating room door, trying to hear what was going on inside. I could only hear sounds of surgical instruments being handled. Nothing else. Nobody was talking. Only I, beyond the door, was talking to God. I did not know if I would ever hear my dear baby's voice calling me again. The thought that he might not wake up shook me.

In those excruciating moments, not knowing what else to ask, I cried out in despair, "Lord, Thy will be done! Not as I want, but as You want!"

> **In those excruciating moments, not knowing what else to ask, I cried out in despair, "Lord, Thy will be done! Not as I want, but as You want!"**

This was the hardest thing I ever asked of the Lord. And from that moment on, an inexplicable peace flooded my soul. I entrusted my baby, my only earthly treasure, into the hands of my heavenly Father. And I waited.

I do not know how long I waited or how long the operation lasted. I lost track of time. My ear was still glued to the operating room door. I knew it would have to open eventually, but I did not want to think about what would happen next. I had entrusted my child to the Lord, and that was enough for me.

I was stunned when eventually, I heard my child's voice calling me, "Mom!" From that moment on, realizing that my son was alive, that he had survived the general anesthesia, I believed, more than ever before, that he would not die but get well.

He was soon taken out of the surgery room, and when our eyes met again, I experienced the joy of my son's "resurrection from the dead." My heart cried out with joy, and, with my eyes looking up, I uttered the most fervent prayer of thanksgiving:

> *"I love the Lord, because He has heard My voice and my supplications. Because He has inclined His ear to me, Therefore I will call upon Him as long as I live. For You have delivered my soul from death, My eyes from tears, And my feet from falling." (Ps. 116:1–2, 8)*

***

One afternoon I received a totally unexpected visit. Doctor R. Beloiu, the president of the hospital to which the dental clinic where I worked belonged, knowing what we were going through, wanted to see us.

Being himself a pediatrician and finding out that my child was on the verge of death, he was very moved by our condition and showed his compassion and empathy toward us in a very special way. He handed me an envelope with cash. My entire salary for the month of November was inside that envelope. I told him I had never worked a day during this month, as I was in the hospital with my son.

"I know that," he said. "And I know how much you need money here in the hospital for your child's care." He knew that patients in the hospital do not get the best necessary care unless they bribe the medical personnel for the service provided. Deeply moved by his noble gesture, I thanked him respectfully as tears of gratitude rolled down my face.

The struggle for survival continued with the same intensity after the miraculous awakening from the general anesthesia. This was my child's struggle.

As a mother, the struggle with discouragement was fierce. My faith was hard tested after the Lord gave me the assurance that my son would live and get well.

Doctors were increasingly skeptical about the healing of the little patient because he did not respond to any of the intravenous antibiotics. No sign of hope, from a medical point of view.

His heart was just about to fail; his lungs, too. Blood transfusions were an almost everyday event. His badly infected blood needed to be replenished with clean blood to keep him alive. The fever was rising alarmingly, especially at night. Mari, my sister, and I could barely replace the hot compresses with water-cooled ones from the sink. There were no ice packs available to lower the fever.

Although my son was often on the verge of death, I chose to trust in the Lord with all my heart. However, the enemy was trying to bring me down with discouragement. I did not understand the mysteries of Providence. I put my hand to my mouth, and I was silent. And I wondered, as did all the doctors, how my child could survive this out-of-control infection.

The whole range of antibiotics existing at that time on the Romanian market had been exhausted, and again, the doctors declared themselves totally powerless.

Dr. Zamfir, the surgeon who handled this extremely difficult case, learned that I had relatives in America. He advised me to call them and ask for them to send a new generation of antibiotics from there, which had not yet reached our country.

As my overseas brothers called me every day to find out about my child's condition, I told them we needed medicine from America; my brother Cornel did not stop to think.

Without waiting for a visa, he flew to Bucharest with a large dose of antibiotics (samples offered by a doctor friend of my sister), knowing that he would not be allowed to enter the country. Upon arrival, he called me from the airport, and, according to the instructions given to him, I brought proof from the hospital that I needed the medicines as soon as possible because my child was dying. I obtained the paper from the hospital management, and as quickly as I could, I headed to the airport. My brother was not allowed to cross the border, although we could see each other from a distance. A border guard brought me the medicine, and I soon returned to the hospital.

New hope was rekindled in my heart at the thought that these "miracle drugs" would have a powerful effect and bring the long-awaited healing.

The next day, my brother, Cornel, appeared at the ward door, looking for us. I thought I was dreaming. He had managed, after much effort, to negotiate with the airport authorities and, after paying a large sum of money, he obtained the visa to enter the country.

He stayed with us for two weeks and was a great comfort and encouragement for me. He had brought Silviu toys from America, including a small piano toy that played in his ear and often put him to sleep.

When he left, Cornel took our mother with him to America. She already had the plane ticket to visit there, but, due to the trouble with Silviu, she had given up leaving. I wanted my mom to go to America to protect her from witnessing my distress and pain.

Since we had plenty of antibiotics, at the doctor's suggestion, we agreed to share them with another patient in Silviu's room, a baby who had meningitis and was struggling in terrible pain. The doctors were very happy that this little baby had another chance. However, after the first week of treatment, the results were not as expected. There was no change for the better in either my son or the other patient. The doctors were increasingly discouraged.

However, my optimism and tenacity did not weaken. Although the battle seemed lost, after more than a week, the other baby cried less, was calmer, and the tests were better. The doctors began to take courage.

Slowly, ever so slowly, Silviu started to feel better. Laboratory results and many other tests were promising.

From one day to the next, everything went from good to better with both patients. The other mother and I were at the height of our happiness. The doctors began to take courage and continue the fight. A smile of joy and hope flashed across everyone's faces.

Songs of praise and gratitude to God made the strings of my weary soul vibrate and rejoice in the Lord.

"I will bless the Lord at all times; His praise shall continually be in my mouth." (Ps. 34:1)

"In my distress I called upon the Lord, And cried out to my God; He heard my voice from His temple, And my cry came before Him, even to His ears." (Ps. 18:6)

***

NOTHING TO WONDER

"Behold, I am the Lord, the God of all flesh. Is there anything too hard for Me?" (Jer. 32:27)

"Silviu, I want to listen to your heart again!" said the cardiologist before leaving the room.

Her face shone with joy. For the first time, she looked me in the eye and said in astonishment, "I can't believe such a thing was possible! I can't understand what happened to his sick, 'drowned in pus' heart. It cannot be scientifically explained how healing was possible. This child has a new heart. A perfect heart. That must be a miracle!"

I agreed with the doctor and confessed that I also believed in miracles and in the God of miracles.

Pulmonary radiography showed perfectly healthy lungs with no signs of disease. My boy was breathing normally as if he had never been ill.

Dr. Oraseanu, who took care of his lungs, confessed to me in a trembling voice how much he was affected by my child's suffering, as he, too, had a little boy of the same age and the same name, Silviu.

The drainage tube was removed from his lungs, and the oxygen tube was also removed. From now on, Silviu was breathing normally, and I could breathe a sigh of relief. All the doctors who took care of him admitted with amazement that "Silviu was a miracle child."

ICU doctors had spent many nights in the clinic and had deep emotions when they saw themselves helpless, thinking they could not save the little patient from death.

One of them, Dr. Petrescu, came to the hospital one morning with a friend of his who wanted to see the miracle boy and to meet me, "the hero mother," whose son survived the deadliest infection. But more than that, he was told something completely out of the ordinary about me.

In one of the most difficult moments, when the doctor found himself powerless to get my child out of the crisis, he glanced at me and was stunned; my face was glowing. He wanted to know the secret of my peace and serenity in the middle of my ordeal, and mostly, the miraculous healing of my son. I pointed up to heaven, declaring triumphantly that "God Almighty is the author of this miracle." I trusted in His love and earnestly prayed for divine healing. My constant connection with the Divine Source empowered me to remain calm and unflinching in the most critical moments when my son's life was at stake.

Another visitor, Dr. Davidescu's husband, wanted to see the miracle child, for whom his wife had shed many tears at home.

I felt privileged for the opportunity I was given to testify to unbelievers about God as my personal Savior and friend.

Gradually, the atmosphere was more and more relaxed. I could go outside for a few more hours, without emotions, without haste. My boy was getting better and better from day to day. We hoped we could go home soon.

Now, I could take him out of bed, hold him in my arms, and, carrying the IV bag with us, walk around the room. He once asked me to take him to the window to look outside. Surprised by the enchanting picture outside, decorated with frost, he asked me in amazement, "Mom, where are the leaves of the trees?" He retained the last image in his mind before entering the hospital when the trees were still adorned with multicolored leaves at the end of autumn. We started talking about home and day-dreaming about life in freedom.

We had grown emotionally attached to the medical staff that had been around us for more than a month, sharing with us the full range of emotions in the battle with death. Now we lived the joy of collective victory. Everyone was happy.

Only Silviu had a less pleasant experience in one of the last nights spent in the ICU.

A nurse of a darker complexion we had never seen before cracked the room door from time to time and, through the diffused light in the room, stared at the IV bag, then she would leave. My baby, who was now very receptive, whispered to me, "Mom, why is this gypsy coming and looking at my IV? Does she want to steal it from me?" (In Romania, little kids were warned by their parents to beware of gypsies because they steal little children.)

I barely managed not to burst out laughing and embarrass my child as I reassured him that I would take care of his IV; it would not be stolen.

* * *

It was Sabbath. "Mother Gigi" (my mother-in-law) came to visit us and thought of a surprise for me: to stay with Silviu so that I could go to church in the afternoon. I was so happy to go outside in the open air, outside the walls of the hospital, where I had been imprisoned next to my boy for almost two months.

Although I hurried, I arrived at the end of the program. I had lost track of time. According to tradition, the end-of-year promises for 1986 had been shared: a text from the Bible, printed on a beautiful bookmark.

At the entrance, I met Pastor C. Alexe. I told him I wanted a promise. He told me that the promises had already been distributed. I asked him to find out if there was one left for me.

He returned with a bookmark and told me that this was the only promise left: *"Blessed are those who mourn, For they shall be comforted"* (Matt. 5:4).

Wonderful promise! I thanked the Lord for keeping it for me, knowing I needed it. I quickly returned to the hospital and, my face radiant with happiness, shared my promise with Mother Gigi and my baby.

I now had the assurance that the Lord would wipe away my tears and comfort me after so much sorrow. I looked to the future with confidence, trying not to think about the things I had been through. We thanked God for new proof of His care for us.

"Oh, taste and see that the Lord is good; Blessed is the man who trusts in Him!" (Ps. 34:8)

> *"Oh, taste and see that the LORD is good; Blessed is the man who trusts in Him!"*

A sense of security and peace took over my soul. I knew the day of going home was approaching. From the doctors' comments, I understood that my child's life was no longer in danger. But we still had a rough road ahead to go.

Silviu would have to start eating and drinking once the IV was removed. I could not leave the hospital otherwise. I had tried to trick him into taking food in his mouth but to no avail.

An x-ray was taken, and I was told that, due to the fact that he had not eaten or drunk anything for almost two months, his stomach was constricted and no longer appeared as a cavity.

They were afraid to remove the IV, although he could receive oral antibiotics if I could persuade him to drink and eat.

"How do you expect this child to drink and eat as long as he gets everything through IV?" asked another doctor called to give his opinion. Hearing this logical statement, I took courage and asked the Lord to bring us out of this last impasse. I was convinced that He would not allow Silviu to die of starvation after miraculously saving him from the deadly infection.

I was asked to give my written consent for Silviu to be disconnected from the IV and discharged. I was given a red pen to sign on the patient's chart that I would take full responsibility for anything that might happen after the IV was removed. And I signed.

***

FACE TO FACE WITH REALITY

"He also brought me out into a broad place." (Ps. 18:19)

It was a long night, like many others, next to my child's bedside. And yet, so different from all the others. It was our last night in the hospital. I could not sleep from sheer joy.

During the morning visit, a medical team surrounded Silviu's bed to see him for the last time and say goodbye to their little patient. Tears of joy rolled down my face. I could not find the right words to express my gratitude to all the doctors and staff that trod my thorny road, wept with me, witnessed my agony, and shared with me the triumph of victory, a true miracle.

Overwhelmed with gladness and gratitude, we said goodbye to everyone, and, on eagle's wings, we headed home, accompanied by our dear family.

I thanked the Lord for being with us moment by moment, answering my prayers, and giving me the strength to endure the flames of the furnace. I will be eternally grateful to Him for the miracle of miracles—saving my child from the threshold of the grave.

After spending endless nights with my son in the hospital, with my head resting on the edge of his bed at night, I would stretch in my own bed, with my head on my pillow. And my child would sleep peacefully in his own bed without being awakened by the terrified screams of other children.

The first night in our home was like a dream. Total silence, without agitation or the many noises specific to the hospital environment. Silviu slept like a baby. I had to struggle for a while to break the routine of checking on his vital signs, making sure he was still breathing and his heart still beating.

Silviu's responsibility from now on would be to learn to eat again and to walk on one leg. Unfortunately, we were not given crutches from the hospital, nor did the staff recommend using them.

My poor baby was just skin and bone. He once asked me, puzzled, "Mom, why do my bones rattle when I sit on the potty?"

When Carmen, my friend, came to see us, she burst into tears. I did not understand why. I was at the peak of happiness that we were home again, that Silviu was well, and I did not understand why she was crying.

After a long time, she confessed to me how shocked she was when she saw Silviu, from a plump child, full of life, as she knew him, now just a skeleton.

The mental trauma I had gone through, as well as the physical exhaustion, had left deep marks in my soul. However, Silviu was my joy and comfort and the purpose of my existence in a sin-sick world.

Radical changes on all levels took place in our life after coming home. We were no longer surrounded by doctors and nurses who would watch over Silviu and intervene in critical moments. He had to learn to jump on one leg because the other was immobilized in a cast. It was very uncomfortable because the cast was heavy, and he was not allowed to lean on that leg. The desire to move, after a long period of lying on the hospital bed, had become irresistible. "Mom, I'm so glad I'm not in the hospital anymore!" he told me one day, hopping on one leg in the hallway between the living room and the kitchen.

One night, Silviu woke up with a high fever. It was dark everywhere. Electricity had been shut off for "energy saving." I tried to make compresses with cold water, but the water did not run either.

Mari lit the candle, and we carefully groped down the stairs from the second floor to the ground. We quickly packed a bag of snow from outside and wrapped Silviu's hot body to lower the fever.

But this was not the biggest inconvenience. A much bigger surprise than shutting off the water or electricity would complicate our existence for a while. When we left the hospital, I took on the responsibility of convincing my little one that he should start eating and drinking, even though he was neither hungry nor thirsty. The doctors in the hospital advised me to give the child fruit and greens.

I insisted on him eating, but he could not understand why I had to torment him with something he did not like. He had simply forgotten how to eat. The masticatory reflex had disappeared, the abdominal cavity could no longer be seen on x-ray, and there were no more gastric juices that would make him hungry and stimulate his appetite.

There was no time to waste. Food and water were as vital to him as air. I asked the Lord, "What should I do?"

Somebody from church recommended Dr. Laza. We called him, and shortly after, Dr. Doru Laza came for a visit with his wife, Doina. The meeting with them was providential. They were kind and loving people. From the beginning, Silviu and "Uncle Doru" became good friends.

Although the juice cure that was recommended to us was a long and very laborious process, Silviu accepted it because "That's what Uncle Doru said."

"I don't trust my mother as much as I trust Uncle Doru," he said. "I don't want to ignore his orders. What he says I must do. You don't 'joke' with him!"

Finding out that we started juicing, Gina, a colleague from work, brought me a sack of carrots and other vegetables. At that time, especially in winter, it was almost impossible to find fruits and vegetables on the market. My in-laws helped me a lot with supplies of carrots, celery, beets, and other roots, plus fresh eggs and dairy products from the country.

My sister, Mari, and I had to get up early in the morning to juice the fruits and vegetables. We had to finish the job before ten o'clock when the power would shut off by Ceausescu's order.

When Silviu heard the sound of the juicer, he would come to the kitchen saying, "Mom, I want to know when the juice is ready, so I can start crying."

Before the meal, we prayed that the Lord would help Silviu drink the juice and not vomit. His prayer was unchangeable: "Lord, please help me to swallow the juice fast and get well!"

I started with very small quantities, dripping the juice with a dropper onto his tongue. Little by little, like feeding a baby bird abandoned by his mother, I convinced him to open his mouth. I alternated fruit juice with vegetable juice at fixed hours, according to the program established by "Uncle Doru."

Meanwhile, Viorica, my sister from America, sent us Barley Green, a green barley powder that we mixed with vegetable juice. This supplement was an excellent energy provider and stimulated his appetite.

Slowly but surely, my boy began to gain strength. He was hopping on one leg and holding up his casted leg so as not to touch the ground. He was a happy boy, full of energy and good cheer.

"Mom, I don't know what to do with my energy. I feel like jumping up to the ceiling!"

After a while, we started implementing solid food in his diet. It was an ordeal, both for us and for Silviu. He ate very little, and he cried at every meal.

Mihai, Silviu's uncle, as well as Silviu's grandparents, visited us often. Mihai would take Silviu outside for a walk in a stroller when the weather was a little milder. When the sun came out, we hurried outside because it was warmer than inside the home. The heat provided by the state was insufficient, and the use of additional electric heating sources was forbidden in order to save energy.

It was a hard winter with a lot of snow and frost. Often, temperatures dropped below zero degrees Fahrenheit. Once I caught Silvicu at the window, fascinated by the enchanting picture outside. It was snowing.

"I'm glad it's snowing, and the snow is settling so that I can go sledding when I get well. I can't wait to get well ..."

***

One day I received a phone call from the management of the hospital where I was employed. I was told that the president wanted to see me.

The meeting with the "big boss" was surprisingly pleasant. I had last seen him in early December when he visited us at the hospital and brought my full salary for the previous month.

He first gave me a Christmas present, an envelope with money that exceeded my monthly salary. For the second time, I was overwhelmed by his kindness and heartfelt sympathy. But, more than that, he explained to me that I needed rest: physical and emotional relaxation after the trauma I suffered in the hospital. Then he offered me the solution to this problem.

He had already spoken to his cousin, the director of a psychiatric clinic in Bucharest, and had scheduled a consultation for me. This specialist prescribed me antidepressant drugs (which I did not use) and ordered a home care therapy, restricting me from work.

This is how, for two months, I was able to stay home with my child, take care of him, and, at the same time, recover myself. During this time, I received money on sick leave. I saw again God's hand stretched out upon us for protection and healing, and I was very grateful to Him for this favor as well.

The good news that we were home again spread quickly. Two other doctor friends from the church came to see Silviu. They brought me financial aid from the church in addition to a personal monetary gift, which was very useful to me.

The long, boring, cold, and gloomy days of a capricious winter were finally over. A warm breeze, with the scent of hyacinths, heralded the arrival of spring. We missed the sun and the leisurely walks in nature after our long isolation indoors. Our first outing, apart from the visit to the hospital, was to church.

Silviu was very happy to be among children again in his Sabbath School class. Anita taught them songs and told them stories from the Bible. Preparations for a Mother's Day celebration had already begun, poems had been distributed to all the children, and the musical repertoire had already been developed. Each child was to represent a flower and had received the corresponding poetry. However, Silviu did not get any of these, as his participation was completely unexpected. No problem! We would find a poem for him, too.

I called Benone, an old friend, an eminent Adventist poet and writer, and asked him to write a poem for Silviu, choosing a spring flower that he could represent at the special program.

Benone was very kind, and the next day, I received the poem over the phone. Silviu was to play the role of a snowdrop just out of the snow. This role suited him perfectly.

The following Sabbath, at the celebration, the pulpit was full of "flowers" of all ages and colors. Each child represented the flower he held in his hands and recited the appropriate poetry.

Here is the poem Silviu recited, holding in his little hands a bouquet of snowdrops. (In Romania Mother's Day is in early spring.)

"THE SNOWDROP"

Look at me! I am a snowdrop,
Tender, beautiful, and tiny.
For whoever wants to see me,
God brought me out from the snow.
A cloud had tried to hold me back,
But I am a bright ray of light.
He took me out of the dark,
'Cause I've been His delight.
Look at me! I'm a drop of dew,
And I hold flowers in both hands.
God brought me back to life anew
And crowned me with His garlands.

Tears of thanksgiving and gratitude streaked my face, looking at my little Snowdrop, a living testimony of God's infinite love.

***

"It's so good to be home! I don't even want to go for a checkup. Let the doctor come here at home if he wants to see me!"

> **Tears of thanksgiving and gratitude streaked my face, looking at my little Snowdrop, a living testimony of God's infinite love.**

That's what my child thought aloud as we prepared to go to the hospital for the follow-up. And, after all, why should we go? Silviu was gaining strength from day to day, he had learned to walk just jumping on one leg, and he was eating well, without tears and insistence from his mother. I knew that the visit to the hospital would stir up sad memories for both of us, but we had no choice, and there we were, once again, at the hospital.

After removing the cast for x-rays and surgical examination, Silviu felt free again and was looking forward to getting rid of this burden.

On an optimistic note, I was waiting for a good report from the doctor. Reading the laboratory results, the doctor exclaimed with satisfaction:

"Of course, the mother gave the child all kinds of vitamins from America. Otherwise, I can't explain these fantastic results. Hemoglobin-15. Like a lad in the power of youth."

When I told the doctor that I had not given him any vitamins, only fresh juices, and some solid food, he was amazed.

I was at the height of my happiness. My toil had been rewarded. I was determined to continue juicing along with the vegetarian diet. Although Silviu would not be happy with my decision, he understood that he must, especially after "Uncle Doru, a smart doctor who knows everything," would explain why.

The x-ray results soon arrived. I watched the expression on the surgeon's face intently as he stared at the x-ray films displayed on the bright screen. He was not at all pleased with what he saw. I read his face with bewilderment and sadness.

"Unfortunately, I have to give you some very bad news. The staph infection your son went through bombarded and destroyed the growth cartilage of the tibia at the ankle extremity. Therefore, this bone will no longer grow at this point, and the left leg will remain shorter than the right. Even more, the fibula, the bone parallel to the tibia, not affected by infection, would continue to grow normally and would cause deformity of the foot."

My child would be left with a short and deformed leg for life. The surgeon went on to say, "One thing I can recommend, knowing that you have relatives in America, is do your best to go there for treatment. Here, the child will have no chance of recovery and will remain disabled for life."

I left the hospital with a heavy heart. Of course, Silviu did not understand anything that was discussed with the doctor, and it was not necessary for him to know. His only disappointment was that his leg was placed in a cast again without knowing for how long. We would know more in a month when we went back for another check-up.

Silviu noticed that something was wrong and asked, "Mom, are you upset with me? I would like you to be happy all day long for having me."

> **Unfortunately, I have to give you some very bad news.**

Although I assured him that I was not upset with him, my face still expressed anxiety and concern. At such times, I needed encouragement. And I received it right from my dear son: "Mom, I'm giving you some advice. If anything happens to my foot, don't worry, the Lord is in control! Whatever happens, the Lord wants us to gather more faith."

My face lit up at the sound of these words. Heaven had spoken to me in the language of my five-year-old boy. I lifted up my face toward heaven, and I began to "gather more faith."

Without hesitation, I started to pray earnestly to God to open the door for us to go to America.

With the invitation sent by my brother from America, I went to the Passport Service and applied for a grant to America for my son's treatment.

After many months of waiting, I went to the Passport Service to inquire about the status of my application, and I was told that I had to wait to be called for an interview.

After almost a year of waiting, I received the interview date and time, and I was asked to bring my son with me to the interview.

It was difficult to find a taxi, and we often had long waits in the cold, blizzard, or rain at the curbside, carrying in my arms the treasure of my soul, Silviu.

The leg with the cast hung heavy, as if heavier than the rest of his body, and it was getting harder and harder to carry him in my arms. After a long period of time, my back hurt so much that I could barely lift my precious cargo up and hold him in my arms.

At the interview, Silviu played the main role. He was asked to walk to prove the validity of my request. As Silviu started hopping on one leg across the room, the interviewer nodded and asked him to go back to his seat. I thought this would be strong evidence for those in power to give us a favorable verdict. I was not asked questions. Just one comment: "We also have good doctors here in Romania, and it is not necessary for you to go abroad for treatment."

I was asked by Silviu's doctor not to disclose his advice, and I kept quiet.

We left the office of the interview under the impression that humanly, we had no chance of success. Even so, I claimed one of my favorite promises from the Bible: *"With men this is impossible, but with God all things are possible" (Matt. 19:26).*

Otherwise, things seemed to be going well in our family.

Silviu finally got rid of the cast, but his walking became more and more difficult. As he was growing, the shortness of his left leg became more prominent and more difficult for his body to compensate. He preferred to jump on his right foot because with the left one, he could not touch the ground. He could not run, although he longed for it.

During his recovery, which lasted over a year, Silviu learned to read and write on his own. He claimed to be a big boy, almost seven years old, and he wanted to go to school. In Romania, enrollment in the first grade started at the age of seven. The following fall, Silviu would qualify for admission to the first grade.

Here is my son's first "love letter" to his mom that I treasured over the years. It still melts my heart each time I remember it. Well composed (of course, in Romanian), grammatically correct, in very neat handwriting:

My kind and beautiful mother, I love you. You love me more than my father. You are a very good mother. You love Me. Happy birthday! March, 22 month 3, Year 1987.

***

A PASSING SHADOW

"Man is like a breath; His days are like a passing shadow." (Ps. 144:4)

May 6, 1987, was a beautiful day with deep meaning in our family. Seven years prior, my dear baby Silviu, the most precious gift from the Lord, saw the light of day.

The night before, he had already had a dream about his birthday: "*I dreamed it was my birthday, and I was very impressed by the gifts!*"

Before leaving for work, I snuck into his bedroom, watched him for a few moments as he was peacefully sleeping, gave him a virtual kiss for fear of waking him, and hurried to the door.

I gave Angela special instructions, asking her to make Silviu's birthday as pleasant as possible until I returned home. I promised to return from work early in order to spend special time with my boy. Mari invited us to Constantza, and we planned to go there on the weekend to make nice surprises for Silviu for his birthday.

Shortly after arriving at work, I got a phone call from Angela. I had no idea why she was calling. I froze in fear, sensing that something bad must have happened at home. Before listening to what she had to say, I promptly asked her, "How is Silviu doing? Is he all right?"

"Silviu is fine," Angela replied. "But ..."

"But what happened?" I abruptly interrupted her again. I realized something was wrong.

"I got a call from America (pause) and ..."

"And?"

"Valentin is dead."

"What ...!!!???"

The next moment my world was spinning, and I became speechless.

I thought of my sister, Viorica, and her husband, Eugen, of the agony they were going through as parents because of the loss of their only son, who had not yet turned twenty.

How did he die??!! That was the most torturous question.

I had to get home as soon as possible, but no train was available to take me back to Bucharest until noon. A doctor friend from work took me to the national road and waved to all the cars going to Bucharest.

After a while, a semi-truck stopped, and a kind driver motioned for me to enter the cab. I did not have time to think about myself or the danger I was exposed to when traveling with a stranger. I knew the Lord was with me.

When I got home, I called my sister, Viorica, and found out that Val was found almost dead in an electronics workshop at Loma Linda University, where he worked part-time as a college student. Shortly after he was taken to the hospital by ambulance he passed away. A month later, the autopsy report concluded cause of death: undetermined.

My sister begged me to do my best to get my passport and visa to travel to America for the funeral. She informed me that the hospital had already sent a document, via telex, to the US Embassy in Bucharest, certifying the death of my nephew.

It was Thursday, close to noon. I soon learned the American Embassy was not open on Fridays and Saturdays. I had no time to waste. I hurried there before the public office closed.

I presented myself to the appropriate desk and asked for the document. The lady at the counter informed me that no such telex had arrived and that I had to wait until Monday.

"Impossible!" I stated. "The telex must be here. I will not leave until you find it!" I replied firmly, in a convincing tone.

The lady understood that she could not trick me and invited me to take my seat in the waiting room and wait. After a short time, I was called back to the counter, and I was handed the telex.

The next day, Friday, I went to the passport service to apply for urgent traveling forms to America.

As usual, the front gate was guarded by an armed soldier who would not let me in because it was not a public service day. I was told Wednesday was the only day for public access.

I froze after finding out I had to wait until next Wednesday. I knew I had to act against time because every day mattered, but I had no one to talk to.

I decided to fast and pray that the Lord would open the way for me to obtain approval and my passport in record time. I left this problem in His care and hastily drew up a "strategic plan."

I knew that to get the approval I needed the consent of the board of the hospital of which I was employed, as well as a document from the mayor's office attesting that I had paid my citizenship fees for that year. I was also required to have the amount of fifty dollars deposited in the Foreign Trade Bank as "pocket money" during the trip.

I had this day available to get the necessary documents. I found out that our friend, Ilia, had just arrived in the country from the USA and that my brother, Cornel, had given him the fifty dollars I needed. I asked him to urgently deposit the money in my name in the Foreign Trade Bank.

At that time, in Romania, it was against the law for Romanian citizens to carry foreign currency unless they could prove the origin of the money and could provide a clear reason for it. Otherwise, you would be subject to arrest, interrogation, and imprisonment for having illegal connections with foreign individuals.

The most difficult issue was how to get to the hospital, which was located far away in the country. I had already missed the morning bus, and I did not know how to get there as quickly as I needed. I prayed, and God heard my urgent prayer request.

The phone rang! Cornel, Silviu's father, had learned of the tragedy that struck my family and wanted to see if what he had heard was true.

I asked him to take me to the hospital, and he agreed, especially when he found out about my intention to go to America.

I got to the hospital quickly, but I felt unnerved when I found out the president was not there. I asked to speak to the vice-president. He listened to my request and understood that there was no time to waste. The Lord moved his heart and summoned the board members for an "ad hoc" meeting.

> *At that time, in Romania, it was against the law for Romanian citizens to carry foreign currency unless they could prove the origin of the money and could provide a clear reason for it.*

The approval was not easy to obtain, considering that I already had asked for this favor a year ago when I submitted a request for Silviu's treatment. I prayed to the Lord to intervene, and the answer came at once. I soon obtained approval and returned home with a peaceful heart, praising the Lord for His intervention. On the same day, the passport pictures were taken for Silviu and me.

I waited for the Sabbath as an oasis in which to breathe a sigh of relief after two days of trouble and grief.

Valentin's death was also announced at the church that Viorica and Eugen attended regularly before leaving Romania. Among their friends who wanted to know details about this tragedy was Paul Bujor. He pulled me aside and quickly addressed the subject: "Don't you think it would be a good opportunity for you to try to go to America for your nephew's funeral? This might be your chance to go for your son's treatment also."

I had not told anyone about my intention to go to America for medical purposes, nor that I was trying to leave for my nephew's funeral. Crossing the border was a secret that should not be divulged so as not to get in trouble with the "Securitate." Any suspicion created on this subject could reach the ears of the Securitate through unsuspected agents, and the right-of-departure could be suspended immediately, without the right of appeal.

Paul's question surprised me. It was clear that he did not know my intentions. Finally, I told him I was trying to leave, but I could not act until next Wednesday because of the Passport Service schedule.

Immediately, he offered the solution to my problem. He advised me to go to the Ministry of Internal Affairs and ask for an audience with the minister. I jotted down the address and the name of the minister, and on Monday morning, I was at the entrance of the Ministry of Internal Affairs.

Although I took Paul at his word, I was puzzled. I had no indication that this was the place I was looking for. There was only a massive, imposing door that opened directly into the street. It made me think of a military institution. There was no sign on the door or on the wall of the building. Boldly, I pushed that massive door and entered.

At first sight I had the feeling that I was in a palace. I looked around in amazement, not sure where I was. But more surprised than I was the armed officer in military uniform, guarding an anteroom with transparent walls.

There was a kind of barrier between us, and I realized I was not allowed to cross.

"How did you dare to enter here, ma'am? You are not allowed to enter! Don't you see that it is a military institution?"

"I want to have an audience with the minister." I uttered his name. "It is a situation of maximum urgency!"

Short and to the point! I was ready to meet the minister, to tell him my pain, to find understanding, and to obtain approval immediately. I knew he had power and authority, so I had no reason to doubt.

The guard's reply was like a dagger to me, "I'm sorry, ma'am, but you're totally misinformed. I do not know anyone with that name in this institution. I have never heard of this person."

I interrupted him promptly. "Isn't that the name of the Minister of Internal Affairs?"

"No! If you need to go there, I'll give you the correct address."

Suddenly, I realized he had invented an address to send me away, to get rid of me!

As I tried to convince him that I was right and that I was in the right place, I saw a person in civilian attire coming downstairs on a velvet laid stairway, holding a stack of folders in his arms.

"What's going on here?" asked the gentleman in a puzzled tone. "Who is this lady, and what does she want?"

"This lady is looking for the Minister of Internal Affairs," the officer answered in an arrogant tone. "I told her she has the wrong address, and she will not believe me."

After a brief glance toward me, the gentleman turned away and motioned for me to follow him.

The mourning-black attire, the tear-stained eyes, and the suffering-streaked face somehow justified my presence there. I was invited to take a seat on a velvet upholstered sofa, placed behind the control station in a long corridor lined with Persian rugs.

He asked me why I wanted to talk to the minister. I briefly explained my grief and why I wanted to go to America. I could not control my emotions nor hide the pain that tore my heart.

After answering a series of questions, he told me to come after him. I followed him humbly, confident that I was in good hands.

We went out into the street, heading toward the passport service, which was located only a few yards away. The gentleman was greeted with reverence by the sentinel at the gate; the door opened wide, and, without daring to ask me who I was, he signaled us both to enter.

I could not say a word. I understood that I was in the presence of a very important person.

I followed him through a maze of corridors, and finally, I came to a waiting room with a few chairs by the wall. I already gave him all the needed documents, including the telex from the American Embassy. He asked me to take a seat and wait. The next second, the mysterious person disappeared through a side door.

Without realizing what was going to happen beyond the padded door, I began to pray that the Lord would decide for me, that His will would be done. Although I wanted to go to America to comfort my sister, I knew it was not up to me. And I knew one more thing: I had experienced the power of prayer and the love of God over the years, and all I could do during that time was to pray. I prayed earnestly, knowing that *"All things are possible to him who believes" (Mark 9:23).*

The door opened. I immediately changed my posture, wiped away my tears, and, rising to my feet, recognized the face of the gentleman who had brought me there.

He had some papers in his hand. My face lit up as I said to myself, "I'm on the right track."

But the gentleman's face was no longer the same. In a hardened tone, he said to me: "I found out a number of things in your file that raise questions. First of all, I found out that you belong to a "winter bird" family. You have a sister and two brothers who went abroad and never returned. Then I found out that you already filed last year for leaving with your child for treatment in the United States. Let it be clear: such requests will never be approved!"

I dared to interrupt with a short reply: "Yes, it is true! But at this time, the purpose of my departure is to comfort my sister after the tragic loss she suffered through the death of her only son."

"If that's the case, why did you ask to leave with your son? The funeral is not such a fun-filled event that your child must attend. He can stay home. He must stay home!"

"You're right. But I have no one who can care for my child at home. He is still in treatment, and I must have him with me." Silviu was still taking oral medication.

"He can stay with his father!"

"Unfortunately, his father is no longer with us ... I am a single mom."

"I see! This would be one more reason for you not to come back."

I was speechless.

Again, he asked me to take a seat and wait. The struggle with doubt was terrible. My file was "stained," and I could not clean it, no matter how many tears I shed. Everything seemed to be against me. Even the unknown gentleman, whom I trusted, seemed to have become my opponent.

I sat back in my chair and bowed my head again like a wounded soldier on the battlefield. But I was not ready to capitulate. The struggle with discouragement was fierce. However, I had no time to waste. In the midst of battle, my soul cried out for help to the One who lost no battle. I remembered another promise from the Scripture: ***"You will not need to fight in this battle ... stand still and see the salvation of the Lord who is with you"*** (2 Chron. 20:17).

After a while, the padded door opened again. The same man, with a different face, a relaxed face, with a benevolent look, entered the room. Hope kindled in my soul. I kept quiet. The unknown gentleman motioned for me to follow him again without saying a word.

After exiting the passport service, on the way to the "secret" place, where I had met him earlier, he informed me that the final decision could not be made because a person from the commission was not present at the meeting. I concluded that an ad-hoc meeting had been convened for a quick resolution of my case. However, the final decision was postponed.

"And how will I find out about this decision?" I humbly asked the man.

"You have to come back tomorrow morning."

"Where should I come? You know that I am not allowed to enter the passport service until Wednesday."

"Come to the same place where I found you today. I will meet you tomorrow morning at eight o'clock, right there."

"But you know ... I'm not allowed there either," I cautiously replied.

"Wait for me outside, at the door."

The mysterious man then disappeared behind the massive door of the nameless institution.

I stood still for a while, trying to recollect the thread of the events that took place that morning. The conclusion? So far, the Lord had always helped me. That was all I could say.

I returned home and shared with my sister, Mari, my stunning experience. We prayed together, and we cried together. She begged me to eat, but I could only drink hot tea when I came home, tired and dehydrated.

The following day, Tuesday morning, before eight o'clock, I was present at the appointed place. I must admit that I had doubts about what I had been promised the day before. Would the stranger keep his word? I was wondering ...

I had no idea whom to ask for, in case he did not show up at the eight o'clock meeting. How could I be so naive, to give credence to a stranger who knew too much about me and of whom I knew nothing? Not even his name.

I did not have much time for doubting, for, at eight o'clock, the gentleman showed up at the appointed place and took me to the same place where he had convened the ad-hoc meeting the day before.

With the lesson I had learned on Monday, I took a seat in the same hot chair and shed even more tears than the day before.

My prayers were even more fervent than before: "Lord, let me go to my sister! I'm not praying for myself or my baby. I just want to go comfort my sister. Nothing else."

Tuesday's meeting was much shorter. Unexpectedly short. How could such a big decision be made in such a short time? Maybe because it was the decision of just one person.

The unknown gentleman came out of the meeting room and motioned for me to follow him. He walked hurriedly, without saying a word. He stopped at a window and handed a file to the clerk at the counter.

"I have an urgent case here. You must immediately issue a passport for Mrs. Elena Iorga."

My emotions at that moment cannot be articulated. I just fell silent. When I was asked to pay for the passport fee, I knew for sure that I would get my passport. Then I was asked to come back in a short time to pick up my passport.

I went out immediately, following the unknown gentleman, out of the Passport Service building. I asked him if I had been approved to leave with my child.

He stopped walking as if surprised by my question. "Didn't you ask to go with your son? Both of you have been approved."

At that moment, I felt like I was floating in another world. I held out my hand, touched his shoulder, and asked him, "Are you a real person or an angel?"

"I'm not an angel. I am a human being like all human beings. I was deeply moved by your situation and did everything I could to help you."

"You are such a mysterious being to me! That's why I touched you to convince myself that you are really human. May I have your name?"

"Why do you want to know my name? I can't give it to you."

"I would like to bring you a gift from America as a token of gratitude for the enormous good you have done for me."

"Let's be serious! I know you will not return. And yet … I wish you good luck and success in the new world you are going to!"

At that moment, I wanted to hug him, to tell him how much I appreciated what he had done for me, but I could not. I felt so small, and he was so big in my sight. Certainly, he was a GREAT MAN.

With my eyes bathed in tears, I thanked him from the bottom of my heart for everything he had done. Then our paths parted forever.

I really wanted to look for him when I returned to the country after the revolution. But I had no point of reference. I did not know his rank or position in the Ministry of Internal Affairs.

I asked the Lord to reward him, and I hope to meet him in heaven, where he will have the courage to tell me his name, and I will have the courage to embrace him.

I soon returned to the passport service and obtained my passport on the spot. Then, hurriedly, I went to the American Embassy to get the traveling visa. I was first directed to the cashier to pay the visa fee. I offered a double sum of money for Silviu and for myself, but I was told that I needed to pay only for myself because the consul would not give me a visa for the child. "Why?!!!" I asked the clerk, puzzled.

"Mothers who leave with their children do not return. For this reason, the consul refuses to grant visas for children." I insisted on paying for the child as well, convinced that I would receive a visa for both of us. The cashier gave in, so I paid the fee for two visas.

The interview with the consul was the most pleasant experience of the day. He was an AMERICAN. He listened to me and understood why I wanted to take the child with me. Without any hesitation, he stamped two visas on my passport. One for me, and one for Silviu. I thanked him and left the embassy, hurrying to the Foreign Trade Bank to get my fifty dollars before closing time.

I arrived shortly after the bank closed. I told the doorman how urgent my need was, and he came up with an idea: "The president is still here. Do you want to talk to him?"

"Certainly!" I replied with a firm voice.

He connected me over the phone with the president of the bank, and I told him of my need. He gave me permission to enter and indicated the place he would be waiting for me. I met him where the currency safe was. I gave him the receipt; he gave me the money, and, after thanking him for his kindness, I rushed to the door, thinking, "What's next?"

The only thing I needed to obtain was the plane tickets. I knew that the next day, Wednesday, was the only day when Tarom, a Romanian airline, had a straight flight from Bucharest to New York. I could not afford to miss this flight. I had to get out of the country as soon as possible. I was afraid of having my passport confiscated before departure, as was the case of my relative, on the suspicion that I would not return to the country.

I could not afford this risk. The next morning at seven o'clock, I had to fly to New York.

Travel agencies were already closed at that time, but I learned of an agency downtown that had extended hours. They were open until eight o'clock p.m.

I still had another urgent problem to solve. The money. I had some money, but when I found out about the cost of the plane tickets, I realized that I did not have enough. I called Uncle Cornel, knowing that he could help me. He told me that he had to hurry to get to the bank before closing in order to get the amount I needed. My brother, Peter, could not help me because he had been rushed to the hospital that morning. I always prayed that the Lord would intervene because I could not do it alone.

I had just arrived home, exhausted, after such a stressful day. I came to take the money and to hurry to the agency before closing. Soon, I realized that I would not make it on time. I cried for help: "Lord, I need you!" Just then the phone rang!

Cornel, Silviu's father, wanted to know how we were doing and if we had any chance to leave the country.

I told him that I needed him right now! I asked him to buy a bouquet of flowers, to go to the travel agency quickly, and to intervene for me so that I could come in after closing time to get the plane tickets.

Said and done!

When I arrived at the agency, I saw Silviu's dad at the door on the inside with a bouquet of flowers in his hands. Outside, Uncle Cornel was waiting for me and gave me the money he promised. Although the travel agency door was locked, I was safe, knowing that Silviu's dad had made the necessary arrangements to let me in.

The door was opened, I stepped in, and a lady was waiting for me at one of the counters to draw up my tickets. I was told how much I had to pay. It was a huge amount of money, the equivalent of my income for an entire year. I counted all the money and had an extra 500 lei. I gave the lady all the money I had. She counted it and returned the extra 500 lei to me. I told her I was offering her this money as a token of appreciation for staying overtime to serve me. Suddenly, she burst into tears.

> **That is how the Lord works—miraculously orchestrating events to accomplish His plans with those who trust in Him.**

She explained to me that at the end of the day, counting the money collected during her work shift, she found out that she was missing 500 lei without realizing what had happened. She was afraid to tell her husband at home that she had to put this money back.

We both went home happy. I, that I had managed to buy the tickets, and she, that she recovered the lost money.

The head of the agency was pleased with the bouquet of flowers received in gratitude for opening the door for us after the program. Everyone was happy.

IN THE FIERY FURNACE

That is how the Lord works—miraculously orchestrating events to accomplish His plans with those who trust in Him.

When I got home with my passport and plane tickets, I breathed a sigh of relief. I did not have time to tell my family what I had been through that eventful day. I was exhausted. However, I had to gather my strength and get ready for the trip.

I told my family not to tell Silviu that we would fly to America the next day. He would not have slept due to excitement. He was amazed by the hustle and bustle in our home, but he was happy to have company without asking questions.

I do not remember falling asleep that night. What happened in the previous days, especially on the last day, the pain of parting with my family in Romania, the emotions related to going into the unknown, and especially the reunion with Viorica and Eugen, all these weighed heavily on my mind.

I was trying to hide my inner turmoil, especially from my mother, who was devastated by the tragic news of Val's death, to which was added the pain of parting from Silviu and me with no hope of returning. The only treasure I took with me across the ocean was my child, Silviu, who meant everything to me.

> **The only treasure I took with me across the ocean was my child, Silviu, who meant everything to me.**

An oppressive silence lingered in the living room where we had gathered as a family before my departure for America. Would we ever see each other again??!

CHAPTER 5
ON EAGLES' WINGS

"You have seen ... how I bore you on eagles' wings." (Exod. 19:4)

May 14, 1987

It was four o'clock in the morning, and we were ready to leave for the airport before the scheduled time.

The road to Otopeni International Airport seemed shorter than ever. And then we were there, the critical point, the moment of parting.

Family and very close friends who accompanied us to the airport were all in tears, torn by the pain of separation. I was deeply moved by the fact that two of my friends with whom I had collaborated over the years, Dr. Ivan and Dr. Botez, were present as well.

Mari, my sister, who had always been with us in the most difficult moments of our lives, neglecting her own family to be with us, was deeply saddened by our departure. Poor Peter had managed to get permission from the hospital to come to the airport to see us one more time before our flight to the New World. Under the Communist dictatorship, our return to the home country involved enormous risks. We were all aware of this.

Among those present at the parting, a dejected and thoughtful soul was especially precious to me. It was my mom. Her face betrayed the deep suffering that had ripped her heart to pieces.

I tried to stay as close to her as possible, but I did not have the right words to comfort her in those oppressive moments. She was seventy-four at the time and had suffered many "partings" in life. But none like this one.

The passing away of two of her children at a very young age, then the departure of three other children to America with six of her grandchildren, then the loss of her husband—all this had filled her cup of suffering. But the source of the tears had not dried up. It was the only way she could express the pain of separation with my child and me, the last buds of joy and hope nestled under the branches of this "weeping willow."

Her silence froze me in place. I prayed secretly for the Lord to comfort and strengthen her. I hugged everybody, and, without being able to say a word, I kissed my mother and embraced her for a long time. I had this overwhelming feeling that these would be our last moments together. In fact, I never would see my mother again. She passed away two years later while still hoping and waiting for my return. My brother and sister took good care of her until she drew her last breath.

Holding my baby in my arms, unable to look back, I lost myself in the crowd.

The thought of never returning home broke my heart. I was leaving behind my mother, whose boundless love I would miss for the rest of my life. I was leaving my brother and sister with whom I got along wonderfully, and who sacrificed themselves for me, helping me when needed. I was also leaving many relatives and friends. The precious memories, embroidered with the golden threads of childhood and youth, seemed to be sinking into nothingness.

Fear of the unknown flooded my heart. Exhausted by the pain of parting from those dear to my soul, I was too tired to find the answers to the multitude of questions that were tumbling in my mind.

The fear that I might be turned back from the airport shook my being. Although I had a sense of security when we took our seats in the plane, until the plane lifted off the ground, my heart trembled with emotion.

As the plane ascended to the blue horizon, I felt I was also flying on eagle's wings to the harbor of freedom. Freedom I had long dreamed of.

A thought came to my mind: ***"Fear not, for I am with you; Be not dismayed, for I am your God. I will strengthen you, yes, I will help you ... For I, the Lord your God, will hold your right hand, saying to you, 'Fear not, I will help you'"*** (Isa. 41:10, 13).

Silviu was happy that his airplane flight game had become a reality, and he was very happy to get his seat by the window. He was fascinated looking down to earth when suddenly the plane was swallowed by a blue cloud. Soon the image changed again to an even more enchanting one. We were now floating above the clouds, and Silviu could not take his eyes off the scenery below.

After a short while, the stewardesses arrived with the morning meal, and the atmosphere calmed down.

It did not take long for Silviu to fall asleep, with his head resting on his mother's lap. My eyelids were getting tired, too, but my soul was consumed by all kinds of emotions. I watched my little angel sleep peacefully, and, in a way, that was enough for me.

As in a panoramic film, the events of the last days unfolded so vividly in my mind! I relived them with the same intensity, although I wanted to get rid of them. The future was so hazy that I could not imagine what life in freedom would be like.

After an extremely long and exhausting journey, we found ourselves above New York. We had been in the air for more than seventeen hours, and I longed to touch the "promised land."

The moment the plane landed, I felt incredibly safe, free from the obsession of being chased or returned home by the Securitate. I was in a new world, in the land of freedom. I was in America!!!

After a short time, we boarded a huge aircraft that would take us straight to Los Angeles.

A young man sat next to my son and tried to talk to us. He spoke English, and, with the very little English I knew, we managed to get along just fine.

It was evening already. I was so tired I could hardly keep my eyes open. Soon, dinner was served, after which Silviu fell asleep again. But I could not.

I felt very strange in the new world, and I longed to get to my destination, meeting my family from California.

Silviu woke up due to strong turbulence that tossed the plane in all directions. He vomited. Then he asked to go to the bathroom. I was so dizzy, and my legs could barely hold me up. I took him in my arms, but after a few steps, I collapsed, completely exhausted. We were picked up immediately by someone, and a flight attendant helped us get to the toilet. Such a thing had never happened to me, and I was very embarrassed. I felt completely helpless.

In a short time, we had to return to our seats and not leave them until we landed.

At one point, gazing down through the window, I viewed a sea of lights.

I soon learned that we were flying over Los Angeles. I shuddered at the thought that we would soon be joining such a crowded world, one I had never seen before.

The moment the plane touched the ground, I thanked God for traveling mercies and asked Him to give me the strength to walk without falling. The young man next to us took Silviu in his arms and accompanied us to the terminal where our family was waiting for us. At our parting I thanked the young man, whom I perceived as our "guardian angel."

The meeting with our loved ones in the New World was deeply emotional. There were hugs and tears of sadness mixed with joy.

I was body and soul attached to my sister, Viorica, while Eugen, my brother-in-law, scooped Silviu up and carried him in his arms. Cornel, my brother, found out where we should announce our arrival as emigrants to the United States.

When I had to meet the man in the black uniform, the American policeman, a strange shiver pierced my heart. The fear of policemen had been instilled in me since childhood.

I was not questioned, as I expected. My brother spoke on my behalf. We received some papers with which we had to report the next day to the emigration service in Los Angeles. My brother would take me where I needed to apply for political asylum.

It was close to midnight when we arrived at my sister's house in Grand Terrace, a small town near Loma Linda. I could not sleep because of the change in time zones. My biological clock was telling me it was morning.

It took me a while to adjust to the new schedule. Jet lag has always been a big problem for me. Often, I woke up scared at night, not realizing where I was. I was still afraid of the Romanian Securitate.

When I would realize I was in bed in my sister's house, I always felt relieved. I had such nightmares for a long time until I got used to the reality that I was in America. Silviu had no problems. He adapted quickly, engaged in play with Aaron, the neighbor's little boy, without stumbling over the fact that he spoke a different language. They got along great. My sister had decorated his room with pictures of him, as well as plenty of toys, so it felt more like home. Here, he also had a swimming pool and, In a short time, learned to swim on his own.

I had learned from other Romanian friends who had emigrated before me that they had no problems with getting residence in America. I was confident that my application for political asylum would be granted, especially since I had suffered persecution in Romania.

Our first summer in America seemed very hot to me, but I did not dare to complain about anything, even though the climate here was so different from the one in my home country.

I never knew what tomorrow would bring. I wanted to work, to adapt to the new lifestyle, learn the language, and blend into the American culture. In short, I understood that I had to integrate into this country where I felt so foreign.

I enrolled myself in school in Redlands in a beginner class—ESL (English as a Second Language).

Mrs. Cox was a kind teacher whom all the students loved. It did not take me long to love both her and the language she taught with great talent and passion.

My brother Cornel helped me get my driver's license, and Mihai, my older brother, bought a second-hand car for me as a gift. My sister introduced me to several families of doctors from Loma Linda and Redlands, who hired me as a housekeeper. I made lasting friendships with these wonderful people, who treated me like part of the family.

I was treated in a very special way by the Bailey family. Nancy, Dr. Bailey's wife, was our greatest help, especially in obtaining our legal rights in America. She often told me to bring Silviu to work with me so that he could play with Connor and Bruce, her children, who were close to Silviu's age. Usually, while I was working, she would take the kids to the park or other places of amusement.

Dr. Leonard Bailey was one of the most renowned cardiologist surgeons in medical science. His name as a pioneer in heart transplants for babies had traveled the world.

The very week we arrived in America, Dr. Bailey had managed to transplant a baboon heart into a baby. This unprecedented surgery aroused the admiration of the whole world, except for a minority who protested the sacrificing of a baboon to save a child. His name is one of the most prominent on the list of Adventist innovators around the world.

Here is how the *Adventist World Magazine* presented him in the September 2020 issue:

United States

Claim to fame: heart surgeon who transplanted a baboon's heart into a baby born prematurely.

Leonard Bailey was known for his pioneering cross-species infant heart transplants.

His efforts paved the way for other innovations in the field of heart-transplant surgery.

Bailey worked at Loma Linda University Health for 42 years. (https://1ref.us/1uj, accessed February 10, 2022)

Dr. Bailey never took credit for the extraordinary procedures that earned him international glory and fame.

From his statements we can see how modest this titan of medical science was:

> *"I'm convinced the Almighty has much to do with it (the success of the transplant program). It's almost humanly impossible, given the condition of these babies."*

—*Leonard Bailey, MD, Transplant surgeon*

> *"All of these children (and many more) had received a death sentence at birth. That they are alive today can only be attributed to God's special blessings, an impressive advancement in scientific knowledge, and the quiet determination and vision of a very special surgeon."*

—*Leonard Bailey, MD.*

(*LLU Scope* story July–September 1989)

I felt privileged to be a housekeeper in Dr. Bailey's home, although I rarely saw the doctor in person. He spent most of his time in the hospital, watching over his little patients. But on one occasion, he came home after I finished cleaning the house, and I was still there. He complimented me, saying, "It's delightful! The whole house smells like Elena."

Sometimes, when I arrived at work in the morning, Nancy, his wife, would warn me to avoid going into the bedroom because "Lenny is sleeping." He had been awake all night next to the baby he had operated on the day before, and now, he needed rest.

On my last day working for the Bailey family, before starting school, I had the honor of meeting Dr. Bailey right at the door before I left. Knowing why I was leaving them, he complimented me with words of appreciation and encouragement, which meant a lot to me. He gave me a warm hug, accompanied by the best wishes in my new career.

***

THE GOD OF OPEN DOORS

"It shall come to pass That before they call, I will answer; and while they are still speaking, I will hear." (Isa. 65:24)

With the arrival of autumn, school enrollment began. Silviu had turned seven on May 6, 1987, the same day his cousin, Val, passed away. With mixed feelings we celebrated his first birthday in America, gathering all the children and their parents at Hulda Crooks Park in Loma Linda.

My sister suggested registering my son in the nearby elementary school that her son had attended years ago. He was enrolled in the second grade, as there was no more room in the first grade. School had already begun. He was assigned to Mrs. Kathy Bell's class.

While we were completing the registration forms, Silviu wanted us to inquire when vacation began. Poor child! He had not even started school and was thinking about a break! He was frustrated because he did not know anyone in the new world into which he was plunged. Not even the language. He also wanted to know how he would be able to communicate with the teacher if he needed to go to the bathroom or get a drink of water. Mrs. Bell suggested Silviu would lift a finger if he wanted to go to the bathroom or two fingers if he wanted to get water.

Said and done.

Everything went smoothly from day one. Although it was the first time he had gone to school, especially since he was in a foreign country and did not know the language, Silviu adapted quite easily. He was happy to be among the children.

From the first days, the virtues of the seven years at home were noticed. Several times he brought home "Trophies of Honesty" that the teacher wanted to bring to his mother's attention: 5- and 10-cent coins that Silviu found in the playground during recess were brought to his teacher. The coins were pasted with scotch tape on a piece of paper with the date found and Silviu's name on it. I was proud of my child and encouraged him to be honest, respectful, and kind to everyone.

One evening, we were at Stater Bros., the neighborhood grocery store, with my sister, Viorica. While we were shopping, Silviu noticed a $100 bill on the floor and hurried to the cashier to return it. I congratulated him for the honesty he showed, regardless of the value of the object found.

My son's only difficulty was walking. His left leg could not touch the ground. For this reason, instead of going to the playground with the other kids at recess, he preferred to visit the library. He would pull a book from the shelf and look at the pictures because he could not read yet. This is how he got the attention of Mrs. Alice Fletcher, the school librarian. She was very impressed with the physical condition of this little boy, jumping on one leg, not speaking English, but always smiling.

> **While we were shopping, Silviu noticed a $100 bill on the floor and hurried to the cashier to return it.**

One day, Mrs. Fletcher called my sister and told her that she would like to talk to us about our child's need for treatment. She said she had a relative who could help. Arrangements were made for meeting Mrs. Fletcher and her close relative, Mr. William Price, in my sister's home.

Mr. Price had learned that we were immigrants, and he suspected that we could not afford the costly medical expenses for treating my son's disability. He offered to help us and took the necessary steps for Silviu to be treated at one of the best hospitals for crippled children in Los Angeles. He told us that my son would be the thirty-fifth child he had sponsored and that Silviu would receive free treatment at this hospital up to the age of eighteen until he was fully recovered. He assured us that he would cover all the necessary expenses for this purpose.

We filled out the paperwork. Mr. Price took a picture of Silviu and promised that he would take care of the rest. It was too good to be true! "This will be the miracle of miracles!" I exclaimed ecstatically.

Shortly thereafter, on May 31, 1988, we received a letter of approval from the hospital stating the date for our first visit. Mr. Price offered to go with us, and we agreed. Silviu was evaluated by an orthopedic surgeon and then scheduled for the first operation.

The night before the operation, Mr. Price offered to take us to the hospital. I thanked him and politely declined the offer. He was a frail, elderly man, and we did not want to needlessly bother him.

The next day we were informed that Mr. Price had been found dead in his house. We were deeply saddened by the tragic news. Our benefactor would not experience the joy of seeing Silviu recovered.

September 27, 1988. The long-awaited day of my son's surgery had arrived.

Silviu was very anxious. As we entered the hospital, he began to cry. Certainly sad memories from the Romanian hospital, the long ordeal with his illness and long recovery, vividly flashed through his mind.

On the way to the surgery unit, he was taken to a toy room to choose his favorite toy that he took with him to the operating room. After waking up from anesthesia, he looked for his toy that was lying on his chest.

The necessary measurements were taken for an orthopedic shoe, which would make it easier for him to walk.

The surgery went very well. Two metal rods were screwed into the tibia to immobilize the fibula in the correct position. The drain tube placed in the incised area bothered him the most.

"I'm going to tell the doctor to get this straw out of my leg because it bothers me!" he told me bluntly the day after the surgery.

I was sitting next to him all the time, trying to make him forget about the pain. The first day was the hardest. I did not know how to distract him from the discomforting condition after the surgery. Eventually, he told me what to do: "Mom, if you play with me, I'll forget about the pain. Then, if you would sing a little song, I would feel much better."

I would have done anything to alleviate his pain. Although he was receiving narcotics, the pain was quite severe, especially on the first night after the operation.

Before leaving the hospital, as a token of gratitude, Silviu made me a promise: "Mom, because you stayed with me in the hospital, I'm going to get you a big present!"

Silviu was released from the hospital in a few days; the postoperative evaluation was very good. He was given crutches and was taught how to use them. Later, we received the orthopedic shoe, and my son easily adapted to the new condition, gaining more mobility. He continued to go to school and was glad that during recess, he could go to the playground and play with the children.

Shortly after coming home, we attended Mr. Price's memorial service. There we met the extended family, including Mr. William Price's son, David Price. He gave me a business card and told me to contact him in the future if we needed any financial help in addition to what his father had donated on our behalf. He told us that his father had entrusted him to take over the charity work if necessary.

Fortunately, I never had to turn to him. Mr. Price's donation was sufficient for all the treatments until Silviu reached the age of eighteen.

Two weeks after the operation, we went for a checkup. We had to leave very early in the morning to avoid the congestion on Highway 10 to Los Angeles.

By four o'clock in the morning, I was already on my way. I placed Silviu in the back seat to sleep. After a while, shivering from the cold, he asked me to turn on the heat. Intentionally, I had not turned it on for fear of falling asleep behind the wheel. I had not slept at all the night before.

I gave in to his insistence, hoping to turn the heat off as soon as my boy fell asleep. I do not know how quickly Silviu dozed off, but I think I fell asleep before he did. I suddenly woke up due to the swerving of my car when it moved out of the lane and crossed the white dotted line. I turned quickly to the left because I saw a car on my right side just about to hit me. I thanked the Lord for waking me up in time before it was too late! I turned off the heat and went on my way. I was scared enough to stay alert behind the wheel. We arrived safely at the hospital, and I found my spot in a nearby underground parking garage.

I noticed that the right side of the car was scratched, and the mirror was bent. Only then did I understand that I had, in fact, hit the car. My guardian angel interposed between the two cars, preventing a more serious crash. Indeed, **"The** *angel of the Lord encamps all around those who fear Him, and delivers them" (Ps. 34:7)*. We thanked the Lord that He saved us from an accident that could have been fatal.

Although I was extremely tired and stressed out by what happened on the road, I gathered my strength and, with God's help, made it safely back home. The surgeon gave us a good report, being very satisfied with the postoperative results.

Silviu would have about two surgeries every year. The doctors were always amazed at how quickly my son healed after each surgery. They saw the "Vegetarian" poster at the head of the bed, intended to inform those who served the meals, and concluded that the vegetarian diet played a major role in speeding up the healing process.

As Silviu grew, the left leg became shorter and shorter because the tibia would not grow at the distal extremity. The surgeon explained to me that after the age of eighteen, when the growing process stopped, Silviu would need a bone graft to replace the bone extremity damaged by the infection. But something amazing happened!

The femur of the left leg grew more than that of the right leg, largely compensating for the difference. The surgeon was very surprised and considered this phenomenon a true miracle. In time, the orthopedic shoe was no longer needed. However, we still had five years to wait until the bone graft, which would be the last one.

We will be eternally grateful to God for how He opened the way for Silviu's treatment when, humanly speaking, all the doors were shut. With no money, no medical insurance, and no knowledge of the most prestigious pediatric orthopedic hospitals in the world, the Lord inspired us to enroll Silviu in Grand Terrace Elementary School because He knew that there was a special person, Mrs. Alice Fletcher, who would put us in touch with our benefactor, Mr. William Price. Indeed, our God is the God of open doors.

***

THE MIRAGE OF FREEDOM

Sweet was the sleep in the peace and comfort offered by my sister after I adjusted to the time zone. However, fear of being turned in to the police and forced to go back to Romania was a nightmare that followed me long after our arrival in the land of freedom.

Slowly but surely, I began to adjust to the American lifestyle. Radical changes took place on all levels. I started to assimilate the language; I got my driver's license and became acquainted with my new profession as a housekeeper.

The Sabbath was an oasis of peace and serenity. Attending church services in my native tongue was a special treat on Sabbath morning. I heard life stories, unique experiences related to the immigrant's status. I took courage, learning that residency in America can be obtained without problems, by the simple fact that you are coming from the Communist camp.

In a relatively short time, I received a letter from the Immigration Service. *It must be my green card,* I said to myself!

What a shock it was when I opened the envelope and read "Deportation Warning"! Apparently, I did not present convincing evidence to justify the request for political asylum. I had to send additional evidence within fifteen days to support my case. And so, I did. I was advised to send the documents certified mail to make sure they would not get lost on the way. I was confident that, this time, all would go well, and my son and I would be granted residence in America in the near future.

However, after six months of waiting in vain, I decided to go in person to the immigration service to find out the status of my application.

Somebody told me that without an official appointment, I could not have access to the place where I needed to inquire about my case. The only solution was to stand in line with all those who were applying for political asylum. There was one condition. I had to be among the first ten in line before the immigration service door would open in the morning. Only in this way could I get an order number to go upstairs where the pre-scheduled interviews would be given. I was told that my name would be called after four o'clock in the afternoon. I was determined to show up early in the evening to make sure I got a place in the top ten. My brother Mihai offered to go with me.

It was December with long, cool nights. We took our sleeping bags with us, not to sleep in, but to be sheltered from the cold during the long wait at the entrance to the Immigration Service. We got there around eight p.m. There were only two people before us. We leaned against the wall of the building and expected to spend the whole night on the street to secure our places in line.

Mihai managed to park the car right next to the curb until dawn. Then, he had to park it in a designated place so as not to get in trouble with the police.

We would not have felt safe in that place at night if we had not trusted in God's protection. All sorts of suspicious-looking people were walking up and down the street.

We decided we would take turns being on alert. I chose to take the first turn before midnight, feeling that I was safer while there was still a bit of commotion on the street.

After a while, I began to tremble with fear and cold. I was the only woman waiting in line at that late hour. Mihai sent me to the car, where I was less exposed to dubious eyes. It seemed even warmer because I could wrap myself better in my sleeping bag. However, even in the car, I did not feel safe, although Mihai could see me from where he was posted. As time went on, the line kept getting longer.

At seven o'clock in the morning, the door opened, and I breathed a sigh of relief as we entered the building. The miserable nighttime wait was over.

The clerk at the counter on the ground floor gave me a number and informed me that I had the right to be represented by my brother as an interpreter at the afternoon interview. I felt safe, knowing that I would not be by myself in the audience chamber.

The upstairs waiting room was full. I knew we would have to wait another eight hours for our turn. And we waited again, this time in better conditions than outside on the sidewalk.

After four o'clock, the palpitations began as I waited to be called. I soon heard my name. Mihai and I jumped to our feet and headed for the open door, where an individual greeted us. There, on the doorstep, he asked me my name, where I was from, and who was the gentleman next to me. I introduced Mihai as my interpreter. He was not allowed to accompany me in the room due to the fact that I "know enough English." I felt frustrated and intimidated. But I shut my mouth, as I did not want to get in trouble.

"Why did you come here? What's the matter?" My interrogator asked in an arrogant tone.

I gathered my strength, and in broken English, I started my plea. "I had applied for political asylum six months ago, and after receiving a deportation warning, I submitted additional documents to support my case. After that, I did not get any result from the Immigration Service, and I am afraid my application might be lost ..."

"Your application has not been lost. It's right here!"

"May I see it?" I asked politely.

Immediately, the gentleman pushed a thin folder toward me and gave me permission to look at it.

Bewildered by the content of my file, I asked, "That's all?"

"This is all you submitted to the Immigration Service," was the reply.

The only document I found in my file was the initial application I submitted the day after my arrival in America. Nothing else.

I expected to see the other documents that I had sent certified mail. When I informed my interlocutor about it, he shrugged and said: "That's all we have."

I was very puzzled and disappointed.

I asked permission to add to the original paper the ones that had been lost. The Lord had inspired me to take with me copies of those documents, and I carefully placed them in my file.

The gentleman assured me that in two weeks, I would receive a letter from the immigration service.

I went home with the confidence that soon, my status and that of my son would be permanently established.

Indeed, after two weeks, I received a certified letter. Sender: US Department of Justice. I could not control my emotions. With anticipated joy I opened the envelope. The title of the letter, written in bold letters, took my breath away—**DEPORTATION ORDER.**

I was completely confused. I had done everything I was asked to do. I had presented plausible evidence that I had suffered religious persecution in Romania and had personally submitted the necessary papers to my file. I did not know if I could do anything else. However, I was not ready to capitulate. My son still needed treatment. I was not ready to go home. I did not have the courage to return to Romania.

I went to the hearing room of my God, who always received me without an appointment, and who always honored my petitions according to His will. I knew that *"All things are possible to him who believes" (Mark 9:23)*, and I chose to believe that He would solve my problem in His time.

The next day, I went to work at Dr. Bailey's home and showed Nancy, his wife, the letter. Indignant by the content of the letter, she told me that I had to stay in America and that she would do her best to help me.

She immediately called a lawyer, explained that it was an urgent case, and obtained an appointment immediately.

We dropped everything and went to the lawyer together. After finding out my situation, the lawyer explained to us that, in order to remain in America, I must, within fifteen days, submit another application for political asylum. The chances of success were 50 percent. The cost: at least $6,000.

Nancy paid for the consultation, and we returned home. She was not at all pleased with this lawyer's offer.

She called a lawyer friend who was in charge of a law firm in Los Angeles and scheduled an appointment. After paying my work hours in advance before I completed my job, Nancy took me to Los Angeles to meet that lawyer. After hearing my story and my urgent need for an attorney, this nice woman promised that she would find a volunteer legal attorney who would take care of my case. And so, it was.

A few days later, a lawyer called my sister, asking to talk to Elena. His name was John Mumford. My sister told him I did not speak English. However, he insisted on speaking directly to me. I was very excited and worried, realizing that I could not handle such an important conversation with a lawyer.

The dialogue went unexpectedly well. The most important thing I understood was that he wanted to help me and that his services would be free. Soon after, he sent me a letter to confirm my appointment with him at his office in Beverly Hills.

As my legal attorney, Mr. Mumford had the right to have access to my file at the immigration service. As soon as he obtained a copy of my file, he sent me another copy as well.

I was very shocked to see that the only document in the file was the initial application I filed immediately after my arrival at the Los Angeles airport. All the other documents I had attached to the file with my own hands were no longer there.

How could they disappear after I had carefully put them in my file?

We had to start over.

It was an extremely long process, and my lawyer had to work hard to keep me ashore. I felt safe, knowing that I had a lawyer on my side who would handle my case. Mr. Mumford was a very kind and benevolent man and inspired a lot of confidence. Following the submission of a new application, the deportation order was suspended.

> *I was very shocked to see that the only document in the file was the initial application I filed immediately after my arrival at the Los Angeles airport.*

My lawyer filed an action at the immigration service court for the re-evaluation of my case. The court trial was a long process, more than two years.

On December 22, 1989, I was scheduled for my last hearing with the immigration court judge. After two and a half years of procrastination, the final decision was to be made.

The long-awaited day arrived. I had to appear in court at eight o'clock in the morning. I left home early to avoid the hellish traffic on Interstate 10 to Los Angeles.

I was alone. I met Mr. Mumford on the steps of the courthouse. He was holding a newspaper in his hand.

As usual, I greeted him with a bright and hopeful smile. I froze when I saw his gloomy face with his eyes fixed on the first page of the newspaper. He showed me the headline of the *Los Angeles Times*.

"Bloodshed in Romania!"

Images from the revolution, soldiers climbing on cannons with hands raised in victory, confirmed the triumph against Communist oppression.

When he showed me the newspaper article, I was horrified. My thoughts suddenly flew to my family in Romania. I forgot about myself and the impact of this event on me as an immigrant. Now I realized why my lawyer was so sad.

The news of the fall of Communism, following the revolution in Romania, and implicitly the establishing of democracy, would pave the way for my return home without fear of persecution. The fall of Communism in the Eastern Bloc caused a stir in the capitalist world.

Freedom in Romania! But for me, this freedom carried chains.

Through a string of circumstances, I appeared as a deserted prisoner who must be returned to her homeland after the war was won.

We took our seats in the waiting room of the immigration service court and waited to be summoned to the courtroom.

The hearing was short. But not the last one as we expected. The judge announced the postponement of the final decision until the regulation of the state of emergency in Romania and the installation of a new government. She also told us the immigration court would have to consult the opinion of the Washington D.C. State Department in making the final decision.

I had to submit new evidence to my file that would reflect the current state of Romania after the revolution.

I left the courtroom with a heavy heart. But I did not lose hope. We knew that God was in control and that He loved us. A precious promise from the Bible rung in my ears: *"You whom I have taken from the ends of the earth, And called from its farthest regions ... Fear not, for I am with you; be not dismayed, for I am your God. I will strengthen you, Yes, I will help you"* (Isa. 41:9-10).

***

HAPPY BIRTHDAY, FREE ROMANIA!

The new year, 1990, found us alone at our home in Loma Linda. Just Silviu and me.

I had chosen to be alone after the failure in court the previous week.

I was heartbroken thinking of my country, Romania, wounded by the bullets of the revolution, my loved ones, the victims of the revolution, and what would happen after the collapse of Communism.

The state of uncertainty in Romania right after the revolution also worried me. Would I have to go back? Why not? After all, I had my own home. I had a very good job, a loving brother and sister, and most of all, I had my mother, whose love drew me like a magnet back to my home country.

The reason why I refused to give in to the idea of returning to Romania, however, was the need for treatment for my child. He had already undergone several surgeries and was due to undergo more until adulthood. I was determined to move forward and not give in to discouragement.

The silence in which I had sunk that evening was suddenly interrupted by a totally unexpected phone call. "Hello, Elena! I'm Emil Bujor, and I want to talk to you."

From the tone of Emil's voice, I understood that it was an urgent situation that did not allow postponement. I do not know why my heart started beating fast. I was wondering, what does Emil have to talk to me about? But there was no time to think.

"Hello, Emil! What do you have to say?" I replied in a hasty tone.

"I can't tell you over the phone. I need to meet you in person. Please tell me when and where I can see you."

I hesitated. And because it was my turn to speak, out of common sense and politeness, I let him choose the meeting place, and I decided the day and time. I did not sleep at all that night.

The news of my possible return to Romania caused pain to the whole family and quickly made the rounds of the Loma Linda community.

I later found out that one evening, Eugen, my brother-in-law, met Emil in town and, among other things, told him that I might have to return to Romania.

"Why?" asked Emil, puzzled.

"How come? You don't know?! She has received a deportation order, and now, she is on trial with the immigration court."

"And?"

"And, in the meantime, the revolution broke out in Romania ..."

"I know. And?"

"And the judge suspended the final decision until the establishment of the new government, which seems to be a democratic one."

> **"Well, why doesn't she get married so she can stay in America?"**

"And?"
"And then, Elena will have to leave America."
"Well, why doesn't she get married so she can stay in America?"
"Well, to whom?"
Suddenly, the discussion dropped, and everyone went their way.

CHAPTER 6

THE ROPE BRAIDED IN THREE

"Two are better than one ... And a threefold cord is not quickly broken." (Eccles. 4:9, 12)

At the appointed time and place, Emil was waiting for our meeting. Because he had invited me to a discussion, I let him say what he had to say. I was trying to hide my emotions.

He asked me if what he heard was true. I confirmed to him that my situation was precarious and that I was not sure if I would be able to stay in America. Then Emil suddenly changed the subject and asked me if I was dating anyone.

"No!" I replied unequivocally. "And I'm not even interested in such a relationship!"

To my surprise, Emil did not seem to be intimidated by my abrupt answer. He insisted that it would be good to get to know him after he confessed to me that he loved me—and wanted to marry me.

After hearing such a shocking statement, I was speechless. Emil broke the silence and, without waiting for my approval, encouraged me to pray, as he was also praying that God's will be revealed in this matter.

I only knew about Emil from the words of others from the church we both attended in Bucharest before coming to America. We never spoke to each other. I always avoided eye contact with him, knowing that he was a single man and I was a single woman.

I knew him to be morally and spiritually upright. I also knew that he went through a painful divorce due to returning to the church and renewing his covenant with the Lord. That is it. Nothing else.

But since I was not interested in marriage after suffering a very traumatic divorce six years prior, I did not care to know more about him.

However, Emil convinced me that I needed to pray and trust in divine guidance for such a crucial decision.

He later told me that he had his eyes on me for a long time and gathered a lot of information about me even before coming to America.

Arriving in Loma Linda, his decision to marry me crystallized after keeping me under observation for a while and finding out that America did not change me for the worse; instead, I remained the same Elena he knew from Romania.

He explained to me why he delayed the proposal. Because he had come after me to America, he needed time to make ends meet before getting married. But when he found out that I might return to Romania, he decided to step forward and propose.

I agreed, after much hesitation, to try to get to know each other.

I was very reluctant to advance this friendship because I was a mother, and my child was the apple of my eye.

My reasoning was logical: if his biological father left him, how can I trust a surrogate dad for my son? How would Emil love my son, especially since he had never been a father?

I did not entertain the idea of an intruder in my family to overshadow my love for Silviu. Little did I understand, at that time, my son's need for a father.

Emil had a double mission. He had to win not only my heart but also that of my son. He knew that if he could win Silviu as a friend, it would be much easier for his mother to overcome her prejudice against re-marriage. His strategy was successful.

One day, Silviu returned home from a visit with his Romanian friends. He was very excited to share with me the great news:

"Mom, today I made a new friend. His name is Uncle Emil. He's so smart! He could even fix my bike. And I think ... he loves me. Otherwise, he wouldn't have repaired my bike."

"I'm glad, Silviu, that you have a friend who loves you!" I replied affirmatively.

"And when I play with the boys, and we compete, I can't run, but Uncle Emil carries me on his back and runs with me even faster than my friends."

By virtue of my son's friendship with "Uncle Emil," I became interested in this relationship.

Throughout our friendship, we discovered in each other moral-spiritual values that increased our mutual trust, respect, and appreciation. I understood from Emil that he had a rather difficult life. His mother died at the age of forty-five, leaving behind five children between the ages of two and eighteen.

His father married a widowed mother with two children, and family life became more complicated. Emil, being the eldest, left home first after finishing a technical school for radio and telecommunications. After a few years, two younger brothers finished high school, and both entered the polytechnic university and supported themselves. They were very intelligent and hardworking boys.

Rodica, the baby of the family, was raised by her aunt, while the youngest boy, being the most privileged, remained under his father's care for a long time until he grew up and went on his own.

Although raised in an Adventist Christian home, after the loss of their mother, both Emil and his brothers lost interest in religion. Alienated from their family and church, they made their way in life, ignoring the earlier landmarks they had respected in family life. However, the teachings imprinted by the mother on the minds of the children were not completely obliterated.

They all started families and were highly regarded in society, respected, and appreciated at work due to their special character molded in a Christian home.

At the age of thirty-one, Emil married Ana, a nurse who loved the world and parties, with no interest in the spiritual. This contributed to his spiritual decline and the adoption of an unhealthy lifestyle.

Emil was a self-taught man. His thirst for learning and his passion for electronic science motivated him to accumulate extensive knowledge in this particular field. His professional rise had been remarkable, and he was soon employed at the Institute of Atomic Physics at the Department of Nuclear Medicine.

Here, he asserted himself due to his professional knowledge and moral qualities, and in a short time, he was sent to the Netherlands for special training at Nuclear Chicago Company in Amsterdam.

I must mention that under the Communist regime, leaving the country with legal forms was a utopia. You had to be the "Communist Party man," a party member with a prominent position to have relations with the Securitate and not to be "stained," that is to say, not to have a background considered by the party's policy as dubious.

Emil did not qualify for such a privilege. However, despite these severe restrictions, Emil was chosen to go abroad, not only for his professional virtues but also for his moral integrity and loyalty to his confidant, Dr. Zinca. Dr. Zinca was the head of the Nuclear Medicine Laboratory and guaranteed Emil's return.

Because he solemnly promised to return to the country, Emil resisted the temptation to remain in the Netherlands. The head of the Institute where he was trained insisted on him staying, offering him a very profitable job, but Emil declined.

On his return to the country, after working only four months in the Netherlands, Emil bought a Fiat 1300. This was at a time when only the elite of the Communist regime enjoyed such a car, considered a luxury item.

> **Emil bought a Fiat 1300. This was at a time when only the elite of the Communist regime enjoyed such a car, considered a luxury item.**

In this prosperous period, when Emil was at the peak of his professional success, and the future seemed glorious, something very strange and completely unusual happened in his life. Sadly, he realized that money, success, and fame did not fill the void in his soul.

He visited his brother, Paul, and asked for a Bible.

He began to read it with deep interest. The feeling of guilt overwhelmed him. He identified with the prodigal son in the parable of the Lord Jesus. A deep sadness gripped his soul. He looked like a sick man.

He called Dr. Lucian Turlea, his childhood friend, and told him about the burden that was crushing his soul. Lucian, a gentle and tactful young man, listened to him intently and gave him understanding. Emil decided to go to church. He had not crossed the threshold of the church for nearly twenty years.

The following Sabbath, he was warmly received at church by Lucian and Paul, as well as other fellows, who thought he was a guest. Paul had returned to the Lord two years prior.

Emil was deeply moved by the solemn atmosphere in the church, which reminded him of his innocent childhood. Memories of the children's Sabbath School unfolded like a panoramic film in his memory. The songs learned at that early age came to mind with overwhelming intensity. He read the Bible with passion, and he managed to read it three times in one year. He decided to make radical changes in his lifestyle after carefully studying books such as *Counsels on Diet and Foods* and *The Ministry of Healing*.

Looking back, he realized that a dramatic and genuine conversion had taken place in his heart. He assumed no merit in this mysterious work. It was the work of the Holy Spirit in his heart in direct response to his mother's prayers while she was alive and then to other faithful relatives who were praying for him and his brothers who had gone out into the world.

Emil continued to come to church every Sabbath and, after a few months, asked to be baptized.

When Emil tells of the miracle of his conversion, he will often say, "I regret all those years I lost in the world, far from the Lord!" Ana was not at all pleased with her husband's conversion. Though Emil tried to convince her that he made an intelligent and reasonable choice, his wife refused to accept God in her life. Emil could no longer accompany Ana to parties and all kinds of entertainment, and she was not happy about it. Her freedom of choice was respected. Emil did not impose his beliefs or lifestyle changes on his wife. Even so, after three years, she decided to separate from him and eventually initiated a divorce.

She chose the world and remained in the world until a time when she was struck by a relentless disease and began to seek God. She attended an evangelistic campaign presented by the American evangelist, Mark Finley, and through baptism, she made a covenant with the Lord. A few years later, she went to rest in the hope of the resurrection on the glorious day of Jesus' second coming.

After his conversion, Emil began to have problems with keeping the Sabbath and was warned that he would be fired if he refused to work on Saturday.

He had already worked at IFA for six years. The very day he received this news, returning from work, someone tapped him on the shoulder. It was a doctor from the Ministry of Chemistry who Emil had worked with before moving to IFA.

"What are you doing, Emil? I have been looking for you for a long time! I really need you in the research lab."

"Yes, I can come if you give me time off on Saturday."

"No problem. I'll take care of you."

Thus, Emil left IFA and was employed in the research laboratory within the Ministry of Chemistry.

A year later, a conflict of interest arose at work. And because Emil refused to compromise, he was threatened with being fired.

That same evening, he received a phone call from Mr. Rogers, an engineer from ACIRAM, a company in charge of maintenance of the medical equipment of all the hospitals in the capital city of Bucharest.

Emil was highly recommended by a common friend, Dr. Andreescu, who had known him for a long time. He was hired at this company and had the Sabbath free for ten years until he left for America. Exemplary work ethics and professional competence had been rewarded beyond his expectations. When he left, he was sad to be leaving such a good job.

This is Emil's story in a nutshell.

The Lord led him in an amazing way during the difficult years of Communist oppression when freedom of conscience was flagrantly violated.

Our love for the Lord was the bond that united all three of us. Without much prayer and divine guidance, I would not have been able to decide on marriage.

Emil always supported me in prayer, and he also wanted the Lord to decide and seal our decision. After six months of courtship, on June 9, 1990, our wedding ceremony at Campus Hill Church was honored by God's presence through a glorious display of the rainbow, crossing the cloudy sky over the Loma Linda hills.

Our life together has been marked by the loving presence of our Lord, manifested by innumerable miracles, which could not be contained in this book.

***

IN THE SHADOW OF HIS WINGS

"Because You have been my help, Therefore in the shadow of Your wings I will rejoice." (Ps. 63:7)

The judicial process with the immigration court had been extremely long and difficult. Many court hearings, many other documents, added to the file. Without a lawyer, we would have been unable to overcome the many obstacles that stood in our way. Mr. John Mumford's contributions were remarkable.

After we got married, I added another file to my case: Application for Residence in the USA by Marriage.

Emil already had the status of legal resident, and the lawyer suggested that we start on a new track, having nothing to lose. The initial request for political asylum could fail after the collapse of Communism in the Eastern Bloc. The political changes after the revolution could pave my way back to the now free Romania.

Time passed by, and with it, the less pleasant memories related to the immigration trial faded away.

Silviu's treatment was going well. Usually, he was discharged only a couple of days after the surgery. He was trying to hide the pain, knowing that it hurt me as a mother, maybe worse than for him.

Once, when I asked him if he still had pain, he replied, "I still have pain, but I try to hide it so as not to upset anyone."

If his body's temperature reached over 98.6º F., he would try to hide it, so it would not sadden me.

Once when the reading was higher than normal, seeing my sad face, he immediately found the argument with which to brighten my face: "The thermometer joked, Mama! Don't worry! I'm okay."

This was Silviu, our much-beloved son, who brought so much joy to our lives with the pearls of his innocent childhood.

In the spring of 1991, we decided to enroll Silviu in the fifth grade at the Adventist school in Loma Linda. Adjustment to the new school was difficult. Challenged by the difficulty of walking, he felt frustrated and isolated from the other children. They, in turn, made fun of him, which made him dislike the school. "He's a brilliant boy," his teacher told me, "but he's not paying attention in class and bothers other children."

We could not understand why Silviu, such a good child at home, behaved differently when he was at school. With a lot of prayer, support, and understanding from his parents, Silviu continued to go to this school until finishing the seventh grade.

The following year, at his insistence, we decided to try home school. I had to quit my job and become his teacher. We bought the home-schooling curriculum with the necessary set of books and got to work. During class, he had to ignore the fact that I was his mother, which did not suit him at all. He accused me of being a "Communist teacher" because I was too demanding. While acting as my son's "tormentor," I did some research to find out what qualifications I needed to return to the dental field.

I sent for my dental lab technician diploma from Romania, and it was equated according to the American standards with an associate degree (dental hygienist). Unfortunately, my credentials from Romania did not count in America. Given the experience and love for the profession that I had practiced for almost twenty years in Romania, I chose to qualify as a dental assistant, using this new profession as a springboard to plunge myself into the dental field. I enrolled at the Concorde Career Institute in San Bernardino. It was a difficult year for both of us, but we ended it well.

I graduated as a dental assistant, after which I decided to take the registration exam at Loma Linda Dental School and became an RDA.

***

July 29, 1993

After more than six years of waiting, the day of the final decision at the Los Angeles Immigration Service Court arrived.

At this time, I was no longer alone. I had my family with me, Emil and Silviu. I knew that the Lord would be at my right hand, and I felt safe.

My lawyer seemed a little anxious. After so many years of hard work, he had not given up. His toil had to be rewarded, and our prayers answered.

The atmosphere was quite tense. We were waiting to be called to the courtroom.

During a break, a distinguished gentleman came out of the courtroom and, seeing Mr. Mumford, stopped and stared at him. Soon they recognized each other as former university colleagues. This was the prosecutor who was going to interrogate me in court. His friendly attitude inspired confidence. I remembered the Lord's promise: *"I have put My words in your mouth; I have covered you with the shadow of My hand" (Isa. 51:16).* That gave me courage.

We were soon called inside. I was overwhelmed in the presence of the judge; however, the Lord helped me to formulate honest and intelligent answers to the questions the prosecutor asked me. I had a court-appointed translator with whom I was not allowed to speak beforehand. He could only translate during the trial.

After a thorough examination of the information and the evidence in the file, the judge stood up and uttered the final decision: "Permanent residence in the United States for the applicant Elena Bujor and her child, Silviu Nedea, has been granted!" Then she called me to the front, held out her hand, congratulated me, and said, "Welcome to the United States!"

The whole family was in tears. Our lawyer was at the height of his happiness too. As we were walking out of the court, he stopped and, pointing to the sky, exclaimed, "Up there, there must be Someone who took care of you, Elena." Indeed!

After a brief review of what happened, we realized that God had wonderfully orchestrated all the events related to our coming to America and obtaining residency in this wonderful country.

Amazingly, two weeks after the final trial, my lawyer sent me a document from the Immigration Service: "Legal residence in the USA granted for Elena Bujor through marriage with Emil Bujor, and her son, Silviu Nedea." We were doubly thrilled to see one more evidence of God working in our life. Both Mr. Mumford and I decided to use the first approval through the court, for which he invested so much time and effort.

After another six years of waiting, on March 25, 1999, I was able to submit the applications for citizenship.

Finally, on May 31, 2000, after thirteen years of struggles and earnest prayers, both my son and I became American citizens. Praise the Lord!!!

Many are the wonders and the plans of the Lord for us! We will be forever grateful to Him for the wonderful way in which He protected and guided us step by step and helped us to overcome all the obstacles in our long pilgrimage to freedom.

"Oh, that men would give thanks to the Lord for His goodness, And for His wonderful works to the children of men!" (Ps. 107:8)

Indeed, *"Faith means to believe what you do not see; the reward of this faith is to see what you believe" (Saint Augustine).*

We felt deeply indebted to our lawyer, Mr. John Mumford. We did not have enough words to express our gratitude for everything he had done for us. The long and arduous process required countless hours of work and total dedication, as he himself acknowledged: "It was a difficult journey for you, Elena, to get resident status, but it was worth it!"

We prayed that the Lord would richly reward Mr. Mumford for his amazing contribution.

**

THE FIRST VISIT TO FREE ROMANIA

In the spring of 1994, after seven years of exile, I decided to visit Romania before starting a new job in my new career. I took Silviu with me on his spring break.

Since all of Emil's family immigrated to Australia, we reserved the time and money to visit them in the future.

The meeting with family and friends was very emotional.

On the street, in the subway, wherever I went, I saw sad and gloomy faces. I was wondering, Why?! We got rid of Communism! We are free! Why isn't the world happy now? I learned that the revolution, marked by violence, cruelty, and the sacrifice of many young lives, impacted the whole mourning nation.

> **On the street, in the subway, wherever I went, I saw sad and gloomy faces. I was wondering, Why?!**

Bucharest, riddled by the bullets of the revolution, looked desolate. Buildings of historical significance, monuments of architectural value, hospitals, schools and universities, as well as tall blocks of flats, bore the painful imprint of violence and revenge of an oppressed nation against Communist slavery.

I realized that healing would not come quickly, especially for the generation with which I identified, those who had suffered the rigors of Communism.

A completely unexpected surprise awaited me in my homeland when I visited the small church in Meri, to which I had attached precious childhood memories. I did not expect to meet people I knew when I was a little girl, except my cousin, Stephen, who introduced me to those interested in meeting an "American guest."

A lady a little older than I shyly approached me. I looked at her with bewilderment and some restraint. With teary eyes, she confessed to me the following: "You don't know me, but I know you. I'm in the Seventh-day Adventist Church today because of you."

"How do you know me?" I asked, puzzled.

"Do you remember how, many years ago, you were fired from work because of the Sabbath?"

"Yes, I do!" was my prompt reply.

"At that meeting, where many doctors and medical professionals from town were present, you boldly declared, 'I cannot violate my conscience and come to work on Saturday, even at the risk of losing my job.'"

"Yes, that's exactly what I said! But how do you know these things?"

She then confessed to me how, at a family party, her cousin recounted what happened at a work meeting he had chaired as the hospital director.

"A young woman, an employee at the dental clinic, was threatened with the loss of her job if she refused to work on Saturday. The firmness with which she responded to this challenge stunned the entire medical staff present in that room. Her reply astonished us all: 'According to the fourth commandment of the Decalogue, Saturday is the true day of rest, and I cannot violate my conscience by coming to work on this day, even at the risk of being fired.' After repeated attempts to persuade her to give up these retrograde ideas, offering her compromising solutions, I finally had to terminate her employment contract. Unfortunately, I was the loser; she was the winner in this battle. I violated my conscience, abusing my power; she stepped with dignity into my office and left with her head up, not showing any resentment toward me for firing her."

"I was deeply moved by my cousin's story," the lady continued. "The firmness with which that young woman did not want to violate her conscience made me think. I decided in my heart to find out which religion observed, as a day of worship, Saturday. I got my hands on a Bible and started searching for the commandment that forbids working on Saturday. I found out that the fourth commandment clearly states that the seventh day is the true Sabbath, not Sunday, which I was keeping according to my church's creed. I started looking for the church that kept Saturday as a day of rest and learned about the Seventh-day Adventist Church. Here I discovered the truth and accepted it wholeheartedly. That's why I'm here today, and I'm glad I had the opportunity to meet you in person."

My heart was pounding with joy and gratitude! I thanked the Lord that through my apparent defeat—the loss of my job—a precious soul had been won for Christ.

***

It was a busy summer after returning from Romania. Silviu worked and raised money to buy a new computer. The old one that he bought from a yard sale did not satisfy him. He took it apart out of curiosity to find out what was inside. Surprisingly, he put everything back together, and it was still working!

Emil helped him buy it piece by piece and put it together. Now, Silviu had a new computer, with his own money, built by him, under Emil's supervision, and he was delighted with his achievements.

This was just the beginning of the little explorer's long pilgrimage into the mysteries of computers. We had no idea at the time that his passion for this science would open unforeseen prospects for him to form a beautiful career.

***

In the fall of 1994, we decided to enroll Silviu in ninth grade at the Adventist academy at the Weimar Institute in northern California, where other Romanian friends were attending. He was glad he quit homeschooling. The Adventist school had a good reputation with high moral and spiritual standards.

In the beginning, we were all delighted with the choice we had made.

This was the first flight of our little bird from the family nest. However, it was not long before we realized that he was not ready for such a change. Although we kept in touch by phone and letters, the longing for us, and for the home atmosphere, consumed him.

We hoped that gradually, Silviu would adjust to the new life away from home. But over time, the desire to return home became consuming.

We did everything we could to encourage him, to convince him to stay there until the end of the school year, but our efforts were in vain. We realized that a school so far away from home did not suit our son, and we decided to bring him home. And so, we did.

At the beginning of 1995, we enrolled him at the Mesa Grande Academy in Calimesa, about fifteen miles from home. It was an Adventist school in the same town where Emil worked. Silviu was happy that he rode to school with Daddy in the morning, and they came home together in the afternoon. He had no problems adapting. The fact that he was at home with his parents was the most important thing for him and for us.

***

AT THE CROSSROADS

"Before they call, I will answer; And while they are still speaking, I will hear." (Isa. 65:24)

It was an unusually hot summer in 1995. The air was so polluted that we could barely see the neighbors' houses across the street.

I had a terrible asthma attack without knowing I had asthma. The chemicals I had been exposed to as a housekeeper, to which was added the polluted air in the area, triggered the crisis. I urgently saw a doctor. He relieved me of the respiratory distress and prescribed an inhalant. He also advised me to move out of the polluted area and go somewhere with fresh air close to the ocean. This would be the best treatment for me.

We put the matter before the Lord and asked that if we were to move, He would show us where and open the way for us.

One Sabbath at the church, a doctor gave a health nugget presentation about the importance of clean air. It was exactly what I needed to hear. After the short presentation, someone in the back row stood up and said, "If anyone is interested in moving to a fresh air area, come to Gold Beach on the Oregon coast. I recommend this beautiful area because my family and I moved there a year ago, and we are very happy."

It was Dr. Herman Liem, whom I knew only by sight. I knew he was a dentist. Nothing else. He was visiting his mom in Redlands that weekend.

I wondered if this was the Lord's call for us to move to the ocean for fresh air, or was it just a coincidence?

I contacted Dr. Liem after Sabbath, and he invited us over to his mother's home to discuss the matter. After knowing about me, my credentials, and my background in the dental field, he invited me to come to Gold Beach and see if I liked the area, and if so, we would talk.

And so, I did. We prayed that the Lord would open the way for us and make it possible if indeed it was His will for us to move to Oregon.

I scheduled a short visit to Gold Beach and flew to a nearby airport in North Bend. His mom, Ina, and a couple of friends from church were waiting for me at the airport.

I was taken directly to Dr. Liem's office for a short stop. Ina offered me the local newspaper and suggested I choose a house to rent in Gold Beach.

I was puzzled by such an unforeseeable proposal. I wanted to see if I liked the area in the first place. I was expecting to have an interview with the dentist to see if the offer suited me, then return home and discuss it with my family. It was clear that things had already been arranged and that all depended on my choice.

I understood that there were not many rentals available and that I did not have many options. When I started calling, I discovered that all the houses were rented with one exception. It was a phone number that no one answered. After a while, the gentleman who answered apologized for being at the dentist and not being able to answer the phone. I later found out that at the time I called, he was in the dental chair right in Dr. Liem's office. What a coincidence!!

We were invited to see the house. I really liked not only the house, which was almost new but also the beautiful position outside the city, on the ridge of a wooded hill with plenty of fresh air permeated with the scent of conifers.

Ervin, the owner, understood that I could not decide before going home and consulting with my husband, and he promised to put the rental on hold, waiting for me to call and let him know about our decision.

I was taken for a tour of the small tourist town and, more than anything else, I enjoyed the walk on the beach.

The cool ocean breeze and the double-purified air from the coastal coniferous forest and the ocean were in stark contrast to the polluted air and heat of Southern California.

I was enchanted by the endless expanse of blue water and the roar of the ever-moving waves as they were crashing to the shore. The air laden with aerosols ("medicine" prescribed by my doctor) gave me a new breath of life.

Walking on the sunny beach was the best therapy for my weary soul. I forgot why I was there. I felt as if I had landed in a mini-vacation that I would have extended if I had my loved ones, Silviu and Emil, with me.

The interview with Dr. Liem was short and to the point.

Key question:

"When will you be able to start working?" he asked me. "In two weeks?"

I was scared. I did not know if Emil would agree to move after I brought home the Gold Beach report.

All I had to do was return home and decide with my family, and I would send the final decision to Dr. Liem as soon as possible.

Arriving home, I described to my family the beauty of this corner of heaven surrounded by rolling hills, the cool climate, the perfectly clean air, the impeccable workplace, and the friendly people I met there.

After earnestly praying for divine guidance, analyzing the series of events that occurred in such a short time, we were convinced that nothing happened by chance, that the Lord orchestrated them all wonderfully, and we decided to move to Gold Beach.

We started packing, knowing that we would have to tell our landlord that we would be moving in two weeks. According to the contract, we had to give notice a month in advance in order to get back our $500 deposit or lose the deposit. We asked the Lord to help us.

A few days later, Elvira, a Romanian friend, knocked on our door, looking for an apartment to rent. When I told her that we were going to move and that our apartment would be available in a couple of weeks, she was delighted. So, we received the deposit from the landlord and a refund for all the improvements we had made to the apartment. Silviu prepared a yard sale, and everything went very well. This is how the Lord helped us to raise the money we needed to move to Oregon.

On Labor Day, in early September 1995, we were ready to move. We had a long journey of 940 miles from Loma Linda to Gold Beach. Behind the U-Haul, Emil towed my car to save me from driving on such a long trip.

Emil's car remained at Loma Linda, where he would return at the insistence of his boss and continue working until the end of the year. It was the middle of the night when we finished loading and took off, headed north to the Oregon coast.

Silviu fell asleep quickly, with his head in my lap and his feet in Emil's lap. I fell asleep from time to time, and poor Emil drove slowly the largest size U-Haul. And because it was equipped with a device that limited his speed, our travel time almost doubled. We crossed many mountain ranges with the speed of a snail, and finally, on Sunday, just after midnight, we arrived at our destination.

The owner, knowing that we would arrive late at night, had prepared a sleeping place for us in his house, which was on the same property. He even had a watermelon in the kitchen, which we cut at once and enjoyed with the greatest pleasure. We could not wait to rest after an almost twenty-four-hour long, tiring journey.

Emil fell asleep immediately, as expected. Silviu started crying. He did not like Oregon and wanted to go home. He was tired too. I reassured him quickly, promising that after we get some rest, we would go "home."

And so, it was. The next day, when he saw our new home in the heart of nature, he was delighted.

CHAPTER 7
GOLD BEACH—OREGON'S PARADISE

> *"I love it here. This place is just beyond words to explain. It's almost heaven ... It's so pretty ... Misty in the mornings and foggy in the evenings, perfect days to go strolling along the beach barefooted on sunny afternoons. Words can't explain this place ... It's just wonderful!"*

That's what Gold Beach looked like in the eyes of our teenage dreamer, Silviu.

This tiny, idyllic community nicknamed the "Banana Belt" of Oregon has a picturesque charm quite different from other towns. Strung like pearls on the northwestern coast of America, Gold Beach is a tourist town par excellence, located right on the edge of the ocean, the mountains and the sea harmoniously intertwined.

In addition to the natural beauty of this evergreen place forested with conifers, the emerald waters of the Pacific were in constant motion. The mouth of the Rogue River, famous for its splendor and abundance of salmon, the climate almost constant in all seasons, all of this increased its fame beyond the borders of America.

In early September, on the riverbed which furrows at the mouth of the ocean, the picture is enchanting. Fishermen's boats float like multicolored butterflies on the water mirror.

Dr. Liem's dental office had a strategic position. The large windows overlooking the ocean gave you the impression that you were at a resort. During the lunch break, a bench on the jetty at the mouth of the river was the ideal place to relax and meditate. The seagulls hovered overhead, waiting for you to share your lunch with them. After lunch, a walk on the beach, washed by the waves of the blue, endless ocean in perpetual motion, was available to anyone who wanted to recharge their batteries.

"Agate fever" touched me like most of the newcomers to Gold Beach. I soon became an avid agate seeker. I had the great pleasure of walking on the beach during my lunch break and finding at least one, which I proudly added to my agate collection.

However, life in Gold Beach seemed difficult to me in the first few weeks after moving to Oregon.

Unpacking, adapting to the new climate and a new job, placing Silviu at the nearby Adventist school, all of this I could handle much easier if Emil had been with us. Unfortunately, he had to return to California the very next day and would continue to work for another four months until the end of the year. Emil understood that his employer needed him, and his sacrifice was properly remunerated. A summary of the letter of recommendation Emil received upon leaving revealed his impact on Michael Gross's business.

To potential employers of Emil Bujor:

It was my privilege to have Emil Bujor in my employment for almost 5 years.

Emil was one of the very best technicians that worked for Gross TV in the 46-year history of the business. His knowledge of electronic theory was an enormous help when working on more obscure products. I can't remember any task that Emil was not willing to tackle, and very few that he couldn't effectively repair. When he told me that he would be leaving in December of 1995, I was deeply saddened, knowing I would be hard pressed to replace him. Loyalty, honesty, and a strong work ethic are qualities that are hard to find in today's job market, but always looked for by employers. Emil has them all and would make an excellent employee.

Sincerely, M.G.

I took Emil to the airport, and we parted with difficulty.

The first week, set aside for unpacking, passed very quickly. I enrolled Silviu in the tenth grade at Brookings Adventist Elementary School, about thirty minutes away.

I took him to school every morning, drove to work, and then, after work, brought him home. We commuted for about two months, and then I transferred him to Crescent City Seventh-day Adventist School, where an Adventist family offered to help, hosting Silviu in their beautiful home.

Emil came to see us once a month. It was a long, tiring trip, but it was worth it. The joy of being with us just for Sabbath surpassed all other inconveniences.

Two months later, the Gold Beach Church sponsored an evangelistic campaign. Our joy as parents was boundless when our son made his decision to be baptized on December 9, 1995.

Silviu integrated with ease into the new school, and I quickly took root at work. I was very happy to work in the dental field again, although my new profession as a dental assistant was different from that of a dental laboratory technician that I had practiced for almost twenty years in Romania.

In the laboratory I had worked on stone castings; now, as a dental assistant, I was working on "living matter."

Not long after, Dr. Liem provided me with a small laboratory in his office, which he equipped with the necessary tools and materials for the manufacture of dentures and other dental prosthetic works.

I was delighted to return to my skill as a dental technician outside of chairside assisting during office hours. The wealth of theoretical knowledge, as well as the practical experience, which I brought from Romania, helped me to quickly climb the ladder of professional success.

The working conditions were excellent. Dr. Liem, a perfectionist par excellence, expected the same from his staff. The reputation of the dental office he owned had gone beyond Oregon's borders. He had a well-trained team and continued to invest in each of us to meet the highest professional standards imposed by his practice.

At the beginning of 1996, Emil finally came home. There was a lot of joy, not only in the family but also at church. We made long-lasting friendships with very special people such as Marcia and Adolph Swazak, and many others. Emil enjoyed a cordial reception at my new job, and, not long after, Dr. Liem hired him in a part-time position for maintenance and fixing the dental equipment besides other duties in his practice.

Whenever something was not working, Emil was called, and, through a "magic" touch, he would make it work again. In most cases he would find the solution to any problem. After a while, Dr. Liem sponsored him to be trained in dental radiography. He successfully passed the exam and obtained a state license as a technician in Dental Radiology Proficiency.

Dr. Liem implemented digital radiology in his office when this new technology had just emerged. A device had not yet been invented for the correct and easy placement of the sensor in the patient's mouth. Emil invented an ingenious, durable, and easy-to-handle device that was used successfully in the office for more than eighteen years, as well as after we left Gold Beach.

As I gained seniority at work, I became more and more attached to patients who came regularly to the office for prophylactic or restorative treatment. Those who needed prosthetic treatment (partial or total removable prostheses) were assigned to me for laboratory work.

***

It was a sunny Sabbath day in the middle of summer.

As usual, after the church service, the fellowship meal followed in the annex of the church. Here, during the week, our church provided community service, a soup kitchen, and clothing for needy people. People from different walks of life came for the potluck, eager not only for food but also for fellowship. The door was wide open for everyone.

On this particular Sabbath afternoon, a young, well-dressed lady entered the fellowship hall. Her name was Julie. One of the elders greeted her with a friendly smile and invited her to dinner. "I have an emergency, and I need to talk to Dr. Liem," Julie replied.

Dr. Liem was called and asked her how he could help. Julie told him that she had lost a crown on her front tooth and urged him to help her get her smile back as soon as possible.

Then, he asked me if I was willing to do a good deed on the Sabbath, and without hesitation, I offered to help.

We took Julie to the office, and I made a temporary crown for her, which perfectly resembled her natural teeth. Julie was ecstatic because we offered her such prompt, quality service free of charge.

A few days later, the following article appeared in the local newspaper, which Dr. Liem brought to my attention:

Dear Editor,

On behalf of Summer Recreation and, most importantly myself, this year's director, I would like to thank Dr. Liem and his associate, Elena.

They returned the smile to my face the day of the parade by immediately offering their heartfelt assistance, expertise, and graciousness in the midst of my dental emergency.

I lost a crown from a tooth during the parade, and without any resistance or hesitation, they opened their hearts and their office to aid in my emergency.

For this act of unselfishness, I will be eternally grateful.

Eternally Grateful,

Julie Wilson

My greatest satisfaction was to be able to give back to my patients the smile that they had lost. The anatomical, functional, and emotional restoration of the patients wearing removable prostheses fulfilled me not only professionally but also emotionally.

The smile that blossomed on their faces, the tears of joy, the hugs, and the words of gratitude gave me the satisfaction of a duty fulfilled.

Most of the patients, especially the ones I saw for the first time, asked me where I was from because of my accent. It was obvious from the start that I was not an American. And when they found out where I came from, the question invariably followed: "What brought you to America? Why did you leave Romania? When and how?"

This was always the starting point of the amazing story of my coming to America.

> **The smile that blossomed on their faces, the tears of joy, the hugs, and the words of gratitude gave me the satisfaction of a duty fulfilled.**

Depending on the time I had available, I briefly described the reason for my departure from my native country, as well as the series of miracles by which Providence facilitated my coming to this country. Almost everyone who listened to my story told me, "Elena, you have to write a book!" I promised most of them that at retirement, I would write a book.

***

It was the end of the day at the office. As usual, we were preparing the treatment rooms for the next work day. Suddenly, I heard my name called. Kathryn, the manager at the front desk, was calling:

"Elena, someone is looking for you. Can you come to the lobby?"

I had no idea who would be looking for me after hours when the front door was already locked. I hurried forward, and there I met Diana, one of my patients from the morning.

"Elena, do you have some time for me? I want to talk to you!" asked Diana with a quivering voice.

Something seemed to be wrong. Diana looked troubled and anxious.

I invited her inside, and, with Dr. Liem's permission, we sat down in his office.

With tearful eyes and trembling voice, she asked me: "Elena, I'd like to know—did you pray for me today?"

"Yes, I answered without hesitation. I have a habit of praying for all our patients at the beginning of the day."

I remembered Diana being restless when she was in the dental chair, a reaction typical of patients with emotional trauma. I managed to comfort her with words of encouragement and a warm hug when she left the dental chair.

"Did you pray for me to quit smoking?"

"Not particularly. I saw you agitated, and I asked the Lord to reassure you."

When I took her impressions for dentures, I realized she was a smoker, but I felt uneasy addressing the issue. I believed it was not the right time. I tried not to let the nicotine smell bother me, although I cannot stand it, especially when I'm working in the patient's mouth.

"But why are you asking me, Diana?" I asked in a low, uncertain tone.

After swallowing her tears, Diana told me what had happened to her that morning after she left the office.

"I got in the car, and the first thing I wanted to do was to light a cigarette. The moment I reached out to take the pack of cigarettes out of the glove compartment, I felt a gentle touch on my shoulder, which held me back from reaching for the cigarettes. I was convinced that this must be Elena!

"I quickly turned my head, expecting to see you in the back seat. I was stunned to find out that there was nobody behind me. Perplexed by the strange feeling, I tried to reach for my cigarettes again, but I could not. My hand was simply blocked. The next moment, I felt the urge to quit smoking and noticed that the craving for cigarettes had disappeared. I am convinced that you do not like me smoking, and I am determined to quit!"

Without assuming any merit, I was still deeply moved by Diana's experience.

How did she know that I do not like her to smoke? I never had any discussions about smoking with this particular patient.

I felt that now was the golden opportunity for me to introduce Diana to the Almighty God, who indeed was able to help her quit smoking.

With her permission, I prayed to God to deliver my patient from this addiction and entrusted Diana in His loving care. At the next appointment, Diana no longer smelled of tobacco, nor was she agitated or anxious. Her face reflected the peace that victory brings.

Diana's experience was not the only one of this kind.

On another occasion, a patient from whom Dr. Liem had removed his few remaining teeth, and for whom I had made a set of dentures, returned to the office to confess to me a phenomenal thing that happened to him.

"After you fit the dentures in my mouth, I was so happy, and I decided to quit smoking. And from that moment on, the desire to smoke completely disappeared. In fact, now I hate the smell of tobacco, and I'm so happy I got rid of this disgusting habit!"

"Praise God for giving you victory!" was my prompt response.

Then, I explained to my patient that it was not I, but God who was the author of this miracle, for which I could not take credit.

Upon departure, the patient kissed my hands as a token of gratitude for the beautiful job I had done. And I thanked the Lord that I could make somebody happy with the work of my hands.

**

It was a normal working day like many others. In the morning, I had to assist with a complicated case. In the afternoon, it was Lisa's turn to take the more difficult case, not knowing that Judy was a problem patient.

I noticed from the start that this patient was very agitated. There was no way she could relax and stand still. Even the dentist could not get to work in such conditions. At one point, I heard him shouting, "Elena!"

From the tone of his voice, I understood the state of emergency, and I quickly rushed to the scene.

Lisa had already gotten up from her chair, ready to leave. Without a word, I understood that I had to take her place in the "hot" chair. She breathed a sigh of relief and disappeared from the room. I turned my thoughts to Heaven and prayed. The doctor kept his hands out of the patient's mouth, waiting for her to calm down. The moment I clasped her hands in mine, she turned her head to see who was touching her. Then she closed her eyes and soon fell asleep.

The procedure was long and difficult. Lisa came back and assisted the doctor, and I continued to pray that the Lord would keep Judy asleep.

At the end, when the patient woke up, she asked who the person was who touched her. I was called, and Judy greeted me with a warm, affectionate smile. Then she confessed to me:

> **"The moment your warm hand touched me, I had the feeling that an angel was stroking me with his wing."**

"The moment your warm hand touched me, I had the feeling that an angel was stroking me with his wing."

"Indeed," I told her, "He was the Angel I invited here because you needed a divine touch."

One afternoon, Kathyrn told me that she had a patient in the waiting room who asked to be assisted by me. I accepted without asking who the patient was. To my shame, I didn't recognize Judy until she reminded me of the "angel story."

When the doctor entered the room, Judy shouted loudly: "Dr. Liem, you need more 'Elenas' in this office. Elena must be cloned!" Laughter erupted all around while I was silently praying for Divine presence in the room.

I had the great pleasure of working with my patients, of telling them what God had done for me and what He meant to me. His boundless love for all of us was always the focal point of my conversation with them.

***

Ann was a distinguished lady, a patient who respected and appreciated me in a very special way. Often, when she was scheduled at Dr. Liem's office, if I was not around, she would ask about me and want to see me.

One day, she had an appointment at the office and, among other things, she told us that this would be the last opportunity to see each other, as she was moving from Gold Beach. She wanted me to assist the doctor on her last visit.

Before the doctor came to the room, she offered me an envelope and asked me to open it. Inside I found a greeting card, which, on the left page, had a gold wedding ring glued to it, and on the right page was written the following:

Dear Elena,

This simple ring has been the symbol of a beautiful love. Now, that time is past.

Hopefully, that bit of gold it may produce will contribute to a bundle of love for someone else who needs it.

Thank you for all your extra TLC (Tender Loving Care).

I will miss you so much!

Ann.

Ann had lost her husband recently, and she had shared the pain of her loss with us at the office. She told me that she thought of me and wanted to give me her husband's wedding ring as a gift. Her kindness impressed me a lot. I have fond memories of many of the patients I have bonded with over the years.

***

In the fall of 1996, we enrolled Silviu at Milo Adventist Academy because the school in Crescent City, where he had attended tenth grade, did not have eleventh and twelfth grades.

The new school was located three hours away from Gold Beach, about 145 miles, in a very beautiful area in the mountains. Most of his classmates from the previous school enrolled in this school, which had a good reputation. The day I took him to Milo and installed him in the boys' dorm, I crashed emotionally. I struggled to keep from crying in front of him. Unfortunately, I was alone. Emil was very busy at work to make up for my absence that day.

I returned home with a troubled soul, even though I entrusted my son to God's loving care.

At the new school, Silviu adapted much more easily than in other places. We visited him often and took him home for the holidays and on vacation. We talked on the phone quite often, and, as a mother, I encouraged him not to forget his "seven years" at home.

Toward the end of the year, we had unforeseen financial problems that we could not solve with our rather limited budget. The financial deficit was also felt in the timely payment of school fees. The arrears were $1,000. We realized that we could not pay this amount until the end of the school year, and we asked the Lord to intervene for us in the crisis we were in.

The school year was over, and Silviu came home with the bill that had to be paid in a fairly short time. We continued to pray that the Lord would help us to break this deadlock. I knew from experience that His resources were inexhaustible.

We did not reveal our trouble to anyone. Only to the Lord. And we trusted that He would bring us out, even though humanly speaking, we saw no way out.

A week later, we received a phone call from the school accountant informing us that our debt had been reduced to zero. Someone had donated $1,000 to us. I froze in emotion and bewilderment. We wanted to know who that person was. The accountant told us that the person wanted to remain anonymous. We sent a thanksgiving prayer to our heavenly Father for His miraculous intervention and a "Thank You" card to our benefactor in care of the school address.

***

EMPTY NEST SYNDROME

In the summer of 1998, after finishing high school, Silviu decided to go to college in Sacramento. His plan was to enroll at UC Davis and pursue a career in the computer industry that he enjoyed so much.

The separation was quite traumatic for all of us, especially for me as a mother.

As always, we entrusted him to our Father's care and assured him of our love and support on all levels.

The empty nest syndrome knocked me down. Shortly after he moved to California, we sent him a package in which I included the following thoughts:

My dearest Son,

My heart is longing for you. Your flight from the parental nest has left a huge void not only in the home but also in our hearts.

I know that there is Someone who understands me because His love surpasses even the love of a mother.

I want you to never forget how the love of our heavenly Father manifested itself in a very special way in your life. The history of your life is full of evidence of His divine intervention.

Saving you from certain death when you were only five years old is an indisputable miracle.

Our coming to America is a striking evidence of God's leading in our lives.

The amazing way in which the Lord has opened a way for you to be treated and healed of the infirmity that would have marked you for life cannot be forgotten.

The Lord has endowed you with special talents, and it's your privilege and responsibility to develop and use them to His glory.

Remember everything you learned at home, and apply them in your daily life.

I planted the truth in your soul with love and watered it with tears.

I wholeheartedly trust in the great day of the harvest when "Those who sow in tears shall reap in joy" (Ps. 126:5).

We know that the Lord has a plan for you that will surely come true. We carry you daily in our thoughts and prayers.

We want things to go well for you, and "In all your ways acknowledge Him, And He shall direct thy paths" (Prov. 3:6).

With unspeakable love,

Your Mother.

Being an independent person, Silviu was determined to work and support himself at school.

Not long after, he gladly told us that he was hired by Apple as tech support after a very difficult telephone interview.

After a while, he invited us to his new "home," a nice rental apartment in Sacramento.

The joy of our reunion cannot be described in words. We were received with great warmth and love by our son, whom we missed so much. He shared with great satisfaction the fact that he was doing great, that everything was going well, especially at work, where he was highly appreciated by his superiors.

He did not tell us much about his passion for school education. "It's very boring; it seems like a waste of time to be in the classroom," were his first impressions about school. "I'm learning much more and faster from the books I buy and from the practical experience at work."

We encouraged him to continue his education because this was the golden age when he could cultivate the talents with which the Lord had endowed him.

***

AT THE BORDER OF TIME

The year 2000 was remarkable, as the whole world was on the threshold of a new millennium. Everyone was anxiously waiting to see what would happen in the event of a short circuit of computer programs.

In December 1999, Silviu was already employed through an employment agency at Intel Corporation in Folsom, California, and had been trained in the Y2K crisis.

On New Year's Eve, we received an unexpected phone call from him. We knew he worked that night, and he would not have time to call us.

"Hello, parents! I'm in Portland at the airport. I was rushed on the Intel Corporation jet at the request of my supervisor, who needed me tonight at the Oregon branch. I had problems renting a car. I couldn't rent because of my age; I'm not twenty yet. I asked for help from the corporation, and the problem was solved on the spot. I'm glad I can help my boss in this emergency."

Silviu's contribution was appreciated beyond his expectations.

We were very happy to receive a photo of the Intel Corporation Certificate of Appreciation from him.

The following was engraved on the granite plaque:

Intel

Certificate of Appreciation

Granted to

SILVIU NEDEA

Thank you for your extraordinary contribution in ensuring the successful

Year 2000 rollover.

The year 2000 promised to be a very good one. Silviu's performances at Intel offered him bright prospects, and this filled our souls with joy.

His contract with Intel would expire in May, but he hoped to be permanently employed. We prayed that the Lord would lead everything according to His plan, and we had ample reasons to trust in His divine guidance.

In February, Silviu announced that he would like to buy a new car but did not have bank credit yet and could not obtain a loan. He asked us to cosign for him to get the loan he needed with the promise that he would send us the money on time to pay the installment on the car. We were happy to help him, and he was very grateful for the trust we placed in him.

Before the deadline for the first payment on the car, we received the first check from Silviu, accompanied by a lovely thank-you note.

This was the first and last time we had to cosign for our son. Somehow, he managed to obtain credit from the bank, and after the first month, he took over the loan. We fully trusted his moral and financial responsibility, and he never disappointed us.

> **On May 18, he shared the great news that he was hired permanently by Intel with a great salary.**

On May 18, he shared the great news that he was hired permanently by Intel with a great salary.

We thanked God for His tender care for our son and continued to keep him in our prayers.

Silviu got so busy at work that sometimes he forgot to eat. At the end of the year, Intel discovered that he had spent a large number of hours overtime without reporting them, and as a reward, he received a huge check, as his time was spent on research and innovation.

On the other hand, Dr. Liem's dental practice had been remarkably successful.

I worked full-time chairside, assisting on average nine hours a day, after which I switched to the laboratory. Emil worked part-time in the office, and in the evening, he helped me in the lab. With his inventive mind, he brought many improvements to the workplace. Everything went smoothly because he was always available when a technical problem arose and demanded immediate attention. Life was busy but very satisfying.

CHAPTER 8
THE YEAR OF GREAT PAINS

"This I recall to my mind, Therefore I have hope. ... His compassions fail not. They are new every morning; Great is Your faithfulness."
(Lam. 3:21–23)

The first half of 2001 passed uneventfully. Routine life kept us on track with some exceptions.

I started feeling pain in my wrists, especially at night. It would keep me awake at times, but as long as I could work, I ignored it and kept moving forward.

Thank God Emil was healthy, and I leaned on him whenever I felt weak. His tremendous support made a huge difference in my life, especially in times of crisis. Above all, we both relied on the Lord and His wonderful promises.

It was around the middle of June 2001 when a patient shared with me about the loss of a family member. Cause of death? Hepatitis C. I knew nothing about this disease. I asked for an explanation, and that is how I found out that the virus had been transmitted through blood transfusion. I immediately thought of my son, how two decades ago he had received multiple blood transfusions in Romania. However, I had no evidence that he could have been infected by the virus, and I did not want to succumb to dark thoughts in this regard.

A few days later, another patient at the office told me about her husband, who was going to have a liver transplant the next day at Oregon Health & Science University. The reason? Hepatitis C had damaged his liver. How did he get it? Through blood transfusion.

That evening, Emil and I decided to call Silviu and advise him to have a laboratory test just for peace of mind. And he did.

We entrusted this matter to the Lord and went about our daily routine. After a relatively quiet week, the news came that I did not want to hear. It was June 25, 2001.

After receiving the phone call from Silviu, Emil came to the office during the lunch break and told me, "Hold on, be strong. I have bad news for you! Let's go out for a while."

A terrible fear pierced my heart.

"The boy called. The test result is positive," uttered Emil in a pathetic tone.

This news was devastating to me. I burst into tears and cried desperately, "My son, my son!" The panoramic image of the fierce battle with death fifteen years ago and the miraculous way in which the Lord had saved my son unfolded in an instant before my tearful eyes.

I could not accept this cruel reality. I went back to work without eating my lunch. I was unable to share my pain with anyone and looked forward to the end of the day, so I could go home and talk to my son.

I prayed constantly for him, but also for myself that God would give me words of encouragement for him in this hopeless situation.

To my great astonishment, Silviu was the one who encouraged me, probably feeling from the tone of my voice the pain I was going through.

"We must have faith, Mom. The Lord is in control!" His words first rebuked me and then encouraged me.

"Yes, Silviu! The Lord is in control!" I muttered under my breath. "Then, don't forget that He has the power to heal you. We will pray for you more than ever," I added in a reassuring voice.

I knew that from then on, my life would not be the same. My child was in a precarious situation. Gloomy thoughts darkened my horizon. The battle with discouragement was terrible.

Whenever I thought of Silviu, I would cry. I had shed many, many tears over the years for my beloved son.

Nicolae Iorga was right: "There are tears so heavy and so hot that the eyes cannot cry them ... they lie in the heart, burning it ..."

My only consolation was the Lord. I kept repeating His promises in my mind whenever dark thoughts flooded my mind: ***"You number my wanderings; Put my tears into Your bottle; Are they not in Your book?"*** *(Ps. 56:8).*

Only the Lord can understand a mother's pain for her child. I could not imagine what was going on in Silviu's mind. Being an introvert, he managed to hide his feelings from me out of the desire to protect me, I am certain. I was trying the same thing, fighting with myself, fighting in prayer, asking the Lord to help me convey to my child hope and confidence in God's healing power.

Immediately, Silviu started his research on hepatitis C and shared with us everything he had learned about this disease. So-called "Silent Killer," hepatitis C can stay dormant for many years, in latent form, without symptoms, as was his case. If the Lord had not revealed this to me in His due time, we might have discovered this deadly virus when it would be too late. Indeed, the Lord has been and is always in control.

The most tragic thing we learned is that this disease is incurable in the vast majority of the victims. Generally, the patient can only survive a few decades from the date of contamination. Knowing that Silviu was infected at the age of five, the fear that he would not have a future made me shudder. Prayer and trust in God held me upright, although I often bent over and fell when I struggled to carry my cross alone.

The internal medicine doctor, who registered Silviu, recommended treatment with Interferon without giving him any hope of a cure. Because of the side effects of this drug, Silviu did not rush to try it. Apart from feeling tired, he had no other symptoms.

He went periodically to the doctor for check-ups and sought to be up-to-date with medical science research to find out what else he could do to survive the deadly disease. He also kept us informed with the news and waited with growing interest for the discovery of an antidote for this deadly virus.

Although the liver had been affected by the virus, the result from the biopsy was not alarming. In the opinion of the specialist, considering that the patient contracted the disease in childhood, the body got used to living with this enemy without being attacked by it. The vegan diet, we believed, had made a major contribution to the well-being of our son.

His passion for work, especially doing what he liked, helped him achieve great professional goals, despite the emotional stress he had to deal with all the time.

The desire to learn, the plan of completing his career path that he had made himself as self-taught, everything related to further education, all these were put in the background. His number one priority was his health, then his job, in which he invested so much brain energy.

Although we always encouraged our son to continue his education, after learning that he had hepatitis C, we did not mention anything to him about school. He worked hard and had no time or energy left for school. His health concerned us more than anything, and we knew how important rest was for him.

We continued to encourage him emotionally and spiritually, reminding him that "**With *God all things are possible*"** *(Matt. 19:26).*

We prayed earnestly that the Lord would miraculously heal him, as He had done at the age of five when Silviu was on the verge of death. We prayed also that God would give scientists wisdom in discovering the cure for this relentless disease.

We anchored our weak faith in the many promises from the Bible, our only resort in this terrible crisis. We continued to persevere in prayer for the Lord to have mercy on our son and bring healing at His appointed time and manner.

***

Life went on, in spite of the many challenges, emotional stress, and the constant battle with discouragement.

The long awaited vacation time had arrived. Our trip to Australia to visit Emil's relatives had been scheduled before we knew about Silviu's medical problem.

For me personally, it was good therapy to get away from home for a while.

We had a pleasant time with our dear ones in Melbourne, and, after three weeks of vacation, I expected to return home restored not only emotionally but physically also.

On the contrary, I felt increasingly incapable of fulfilling my duties at work. The pain in my hands became permanent until one day, when I got up with my hands stiff with pain, I realized I could not work anymore. I was in tears when I went to the office that morning. Dr. Liem advised me to go to the doctor. I did not want to get discouraged. I knew the Lord had a way out of this crisis. At lunch break, Dr. Liem called me to the office and gave me a stack of papers to fill out for the SAIF Corporation, the medical insurance for employees who suffer work injuries.

It was certain that my suffering was related to prolonged exertion at work. The symptoms were typical of carpal tunnel syndrome, an inflammation of the median nerve that causes sharp pain in the wrist.

Dr. Liem warned me that this insurance might not approve such a claim, as the syndrome is not specific to dental assistants but to dental hygienists. The process would be very long and complicated. I would have to look for a lawyer because usually, the first claim was rejected. We decided it was still worth a try.

I scheduled a visit to a neurologist in Grants Pass, 125 miles away from Gold Beach, and got my appointment for a month later. We prayed that the Lord would have mercy on us, and my claim would be accepted by SAIF, despite the unfavorable prognosis.

The outlook was bleak if my claim was rejected. The medical expenses would be very high, as it seemed that I would need surgery on both hands. Unable to work, our income would fall substantially. Our faith was to be severely tried.

The days are difficult when you are waiting, especially when it hurts. I had two more weeks until the appointment with the neurologist.

One day, Emil returned from work with his back stiff with pain. "What happened?" I asked him anxiously.

In a calm tone, trying not to amplify my panic, he told me that while he was loading a bulky package into Dr. Liem's truck, a sudden gust of wind turned it upside down. In an attempt to straighten up and not lose the package, he felt a sharp pain in his back. He hoped it would be something of the moment and continued to take care of his business. After a while, the pain worsened, becoming permanent.

> *The days are difficult when you are waiting, especially when it hurts.*

As my visit to the neurologist was approaching, I called the clinic and asked if the doctor could see my husband as well due to his critical condition. We could not wait for another month for his appointment.

We earnestly prayed, and God answered our petition in an amazing way. Emil was accepted to be seen the same day as my scheduled appointment.

It was a cold, gloomy day at the end of November. The appointment was at four o'clock in the afternoon. The doctor gave each of us the diagnosis we had guessed based on the symptoms. It was clear that I had carpal tunnel syndrome, which required surgery, and Emil, by all appearances, had a herniated disc.

I was advised to wear braces, and Emil was recommended a lumbar belt and pain pills.

It was getting dark, and it started to rain by the time we were headed home. Our route took us down Highway 199, passing through the Siskiyou Mountains. At one point, we entered an extremely twisted gorge, with minimal visibility not only due to rain and darkness but also due to very tight curves.

The farther we went into the mountains, the heavier the rain. We remembered a similar situation a few years prior when at dark, we were driving on the same route. Due to rain and strong wind, a huge tree fell on the left side across the road, blocking our access to the right lane. Due to a tight curve, we could not see it in time to stop and avoid the collision. In a split second, Emil turned into the left lane and managed to pass under the trunk of the tree, whose root was propped up on the mountain slope on the left side of the road.

We thanked God that He inspired Emil to make this wise maneuver and that no car came from the opposite direction at that critical moment.

Now, we were again on the same dangerous road with low visibility due to dense darkness and rain. In front of us was a large truck splashing water and blocking the view ahead of us. At one point we heard a loud bang. The car shook and started losing speed.

We were totally bewildered. Not knowing what was going on, Emil pulled off the road before the engine stopped. We quickly got out of the car and looked around, trying to understand what was happening. Behind us was a car that overtook us. In the light of its headlights, we could see a trail of oil, and in the middle of the road and a large stone that had rolled off the mountain. The strong smell of gasoline frightened us. We realized that the stone we ran over had punctured the gas tank and the oil pan.

We were alone, stuck in the middle of the mountains, with no gas, no light source, and, of course, no cell phone, which was not popular at the time. And even if we had it, by no means could we have gotten a signal in that secluded area.

We were totally helpless. Emil with his back bent in pain, and I with my hands stiff with pain. God was our only hope. We cried out to Him: Lord, have mercy on us!

No car passed us except the one that had overtaken us after we pulled off the road. We hoped we could signal someone to ask for help, but there was no other car at that dark hour. We prayed to God to send us the much-needed help.

After about twenty or thirty minutes, we saw a car coming from the opposite direction. They turned and stopped behind us. They were the young couple, husband and wife, who had passed us when we pulled off the road. They confessed that they had noticed the smell of gasoline when they passed us, but it was inconvenient for them to stop. However, the lingering smell of gasoline seemed to haunt them. The man was obsessed with the thought of having to return.

"At one point," his wife testified, "I heard a voice urging me to turn around and see what had happened to the car pulled to the right." She was convinced that God had spoken to her, and, without hesitation, they returned.

We thanked the Lord for sending us the help we so desperately needed. They asked us where we were going and then invited us to their car and took us to Brookings, a neighboring town just south of Gold Beach. From there, we called a friend from church, and he brought us home, whole and unharmed.

Thinking of what happened that night on the road, we could not thank God enough for His wonderful intervention. Only a small spark that could have occurred when that stone struck the gas tank could have engulfed the car in fire and consumed us alive. God's wonderful promise was fulfilled right before our eyes in that critical moment: ***"The angel of the Lord encamps all around those who fear Him, And delivers them"*** *(Ps. 34:7).*

The next day, Dr. Liem called Emil to the office and explained that he also qualified for medical coverage, as he was injured at work. He then handed him the stack of papers to complete and send to SAIF Corporation.

This was further proof that the Lord was in control, and we entrusted our situation to His hand once again, knowing that He would take care of us.

***

IT IS GOOD TO WAIT

"It is good that one should hope and wait quietly For the salvation of the Lord." (Lam. 3:26)

Waiting is not an easy thing to do, especially when the future looks bleak and you do not know what to expect. When it is accompanied by pain, sometimes it becomes almost unbearable. This was the case with Emil. He had to wait for the MRI schedule in order to establish a correct diagnosis and, depending on it, the appropriate treatment.

We were hoping that the pain medication, one of the strongest, would alleviate his pain. Unfortunately, he could not tolerate it due to hallucinations and anxiety and had to discontinue it. For a week, he could not sleep for more than one hour out of twenty-four when his exhausted body would give way under the burden of pain and fatigue.

It was January 6, 2002. My birthday. A sad and gloomy day for both of us.

Suddenly, Emil's condition became extremely alarming. He had such a tachycardia that I could no longer record his pulse.

We were only a few minutes away from the hospital and decided to leave immediately instead of calling 911 and waiting for the ambulance. I could hardly drive the car with my hands stuck in braces.

At the ER, Emil was taken in immediately. His heart rate was so high, over 200 beats per minute, and could only be recorded on the EKG. The incredible pain that had brought him into this situation was removed by intravenous medication. Only then did Emil fall asleep. He did not wake until the next morning. He was prescribed another set of drugs for muscle relaxation and, implicitly, for pain control.

We thanked the Lord that now Emil could sleep and that the pain was bearable. The MRI result was conclusive: disc herniation, requiring surgery.

In the meantime, we were waiting for a response from SAIF Corporation. We heard that it would not come earlier than a month, and usually, the first claim would be denied.

To our surprise, in about two weeks, both Emil and I received the answer we were hoping for. Both claims had been approved. Praise the Lord!!! Our gratitude to the Lord could not be expressed in words. Indeed, **"The Lord is near to all who call upon Him, To all who call upon Him in truth"** (Ps. 145:18).

Almost daily, we received forms that we had to fill out and send back in record time to the insurance. And more than that, we had to present ourselves to all kinds of appointments for medical tests and evaluation to different doctors affiliated with the SAIF Corporation.

We asked the Lord to help us in this tangled situation. We contacted a lawyer who was to be our legal representative, taking a heavy burden off our shoulders.

After a while, we both received an allowance with which we were able to make ends meet every month, and all medical expenses were covered by SAIF.

Given the conditions we were in, neither Emil nor I were able to prepare our daily meals. Without complaining about our condition or asking for help, our colleagues at work prepared us an unexpected surprise. They all decided to provide a food dish for our home by taking turns and cooking delicious meals for us.

We were overwhelmed by the love and kindness of our friends from work who sacrificed time and means to jump to our aid. Each week they brought us a tray with several vegan dishes, accompanied by the corresponding recipe.

We also got heartfelt support from our church family, and we praised the Lord for providing our daily needs.

In February, I was scheduled for surgery on my right hand, and after healing, at the end of March, I had the surgery on my left hand. The healing time took longer than expected. I could not wait to get well and resume a normal life by returning to work.

Emil's surgery was scheduled for May. He was barely walking, propped up by a cane. We thanked the Lord that the pain was bearable. However, from time to time, tachycardia returned, and I had to take him to the hospital immediately in order to stabilize the heart rhythm.

On the appointed date, Emil and I went to a hospital in Eugene for his back surgery.

The operation went well, without complications. The surgeon told Emil that the sharp pain would normally disappear, and the post-surgical pain would subside in about two weeks.

Unfortunately, after recovery, the pain was still lingering in Emil's left leg. We waited more than a month, but to our great perplexity, things did not change for the better. We informed the surgeon about this, and he ordered a new MRI, followed by a visit to his office.

The MRI result indicated scar tissue had formed after the surgery and generated the same symptoms as a herniated disc. The doctor's explanation was clear; Emil's body is prone to such scars, for which there is no cure, and another surgery would be useless. In other words, Emil has to adapt to the new condition, which was a return to the pre-existing one. Thus, he would have to suffer indefinite pain in his left leg.

We returned home with heavy hearts but not discouraged. Knowing from past experiences that God is the Great Healer, we decided to leave Emil's case in His hands and claim His promise: **"Call upon Me in the day of trouble; I will deliver you, and you shall glorify Me"** *(Ps. 50:15).*

In such a condition, Emil would not be able to return to work, and since he had turned sixty-five, the lawyer prepared his retirement file.

He was offered an allowance for college education paid by SAIF Corporation in order to learn a new skill of his choice suitable to his physical limitations.

During this time, while I was still on sick leave, a chronic throat infection that had plagued me for years worsened. No wonder—my immune system was weakened by the stress I was going through.

The ENT specialist recommended a tonsillectomy, the removal of the tonsils. He warned me that due to my age, fifty-two, the risk was high that there could be postoperative bleeding that could not be controlled. I trusted the Lord and gave my consent for surgery. The doctor told me that he must have a pint of blood collected sometime before the operation so that, in case of emergency, my own blood could be used for transfusion.

I was hospitalized for surgery so that in case of emergency, prompt intervention would be available. The surgery was laborious because my tonsils were so rotten and could not be removed as a whole. The doctor was pleased that a blood transfusion was not necessary, and I was discharged on the condition that I would come back immediately if the bleeding started. He prescribed the strongest antibiotics and painkillers. If I did not take the pain meds every four hours, the pain was incredible. The inflammation was so great I could barely breathe. Swallowing was a real torture for me.

I recovered slowly, and we thanked the Lord for complete healing, especially for saving my life from out-of-control bleeding. *"I sought the Lord, and He heard me, And delivered me from all my fears"* (Ps. 34:4).

This is one of God's promises that reverberates in my memory and strengthens my faith in Him each time I'm facing difficult times.

***

BLESSINGS IN DISGUISE

In the summer of 2002, I was able to resume work with great joy and high expectations, thinking the whole ordeal was over.

But after a while, I started having pain in both of my thumbs. Often, they got stuck in a certain position, and it was very painful to straighten them back. After a while, I decided to go to the surgeon who operated on me earlier that year. He knew from the start what it was all about.

This complication, named by him "the cousin of carpal tunnel syndrome," occurs in some people who continue to strain their hands, performing repetitive motions.

This was also my case. The solution: two more surgeries. I had no choice; however, the healing time was shorter and less painful. Little did I know at that time that four other surgeries of this kind would be needed in the future.

A full year of pain and suffering was paid for. SAIF Corporation compensated us in a much unexpected way. Both Emil and I received a substantial settlement for "pain and suffering," and once again, we experienced the truth that, indeed, *"All things work together for good for those who love God"* *(*Rom. 8:28*)*.

***

It had been almost eight years since we moved to Gold Beach. Without complaining, we had withstood the worst weather: storms, floods, and even the devastating "Biscuit Fire." Rain was the order of the day, except in the summertime. Clean air mattered the most to me. I had no problems with asthma at all, and, despite all the troubles we went through, we were convinced that it was worth making the move to the Pacific Coast.

> *Little did I know at that time that four other surgeries of this kind would be needed in the future.*

Emil saw things a little differently, however. He longed for a warmer climate. He got tired of the cool, humid weather, with lots of rain and storms. Sometimes, he could not sleep at night because of the roaring, raging tides of the ocean or because of the gusty wind that made the lamp swing on the nightstand.

Slowly, he began to contemplate the idea of moving to a place with a warmer climate. Every time we went over the mountains to Grants Pass for medical appointments or shopping, we enjoyed the sunshine and clear sky and wondered if it would be a good idea to move to this area. Of course, we began to pray that the Lord would open the way if that were His plan.

First, we had to sell our home. We soon learned that its value had decreased over time on a rental space. On the contrary, it would increase if it was installed on private land permanently.

When we moved to Gold Beach, we ordered a double-wide manufactured home that we had placed in a mobile home park on a rental space within walking distance to work. We thought about the alternative of moving our house to private land. The question was: Where?

Emil took an interest in a nearby company and found out the good news: It would cost us $4,500 to move our manufactured home to the Grants Pass area.

Through a sales agency, we found and purchased one acre of land in Merlin, a rural settlement near Grants Pass. This transaction would not have been possible if we had not received the settlement from SAIF Corporation. The Lord had wonderfully orchestrated all events so that our suffering was not in vain.

For everyone, the troubles that Emil and I went through, both at the same time, were an enigma. Colleagues and friends were amazed that we never complained, despite the suffering and stress we went through. On the contrary, we showed an optimistic spirit, trusting in God's love and His healing power.

It was a beautiful day for April, with no rain or wind. It was moving day. Peter, my brother from Romania, had come to help us with this huge project.

I continued to work in Dr. Liem's office even after we moved to Merlin.

It was very difficult for me to detach myself from that place that I had loved so much and for which I had such fond memories. I stayed at Ina's house (Dr. Liam's mother) from Monday through Thursday, and on the weekends, I returned home to Merlin.

Emil enrolled himself at Rogue Community College, and he chose to study CAD (computer architectural drafting), a one-and-a-half-year course. His tuition, in addition to a monthly allowance, was secured by the SAIF Corporation.

As winter approached, my commuting to Gold Beach became more complicated due to the bad weather.

One Sunday night, I left for Gold Beach in good weather. As I approached the mountain, it began to snow so hard that I could no longer see the road. It was already night, so, for fear of getting stuck in the mountains, I returned to Grants Pass. The next day, Emil took me to Gold Beach, and from then on, we decided that he would take me on Mondays and bring me back on Thursday evenings.

***

2004—A STORMY YEAR

Although we had moved away from the coast, whipped by rain and wind, an unexpected "storm" was about to uproot us from where we had just settled.

As with any storm, it was preceded by a period of calm. We enjoyed the beautiful weather and the gorgeous landscape specific to this area that resembled so much our home country's scenery.

The first winter was especially beautiful. After a heavy snowfall, the landscape was enchanting. The freshly laid snow, bathed in the brightness of the sun, filled the horizon with diamond sparkles. I had not seen such landscapes since I left Romania.

One Thursday evening, Emil had come earlier than usual to take me back. It was my birthday, and according to tradition, my co-workers had celebrated my birthday at work. I now wanted to take the festive atmosphere home with me.

It was dusk, and we were about to enter Highway 199, where a few years prior, we had the adventures that marked me for life. I was horrified by the rain and darkness on this dangerous route.

About twenty minutes after entering Highway 199, the road abruptly narrows and becomes very twisted. Rain and low visibility require maximum caution, especially at sharp curves. Emil was familiar with the road and speed restrictions.

At one point, entering a very tight curve, he lost control of the steering wheel. In the next second, the car spun 180 degrees in the middle of the road. I closed my eyes and cried out in despair, "Lord, save us!" Praise God, no cars were coming from the opposite direction!

The next moment, when I opened my eyes, the car was stuck in a massive rock on the right side of the road, facing the opposite direction. Stiff with fear, we looked at each other in bewilderment. What had happened?! We both were whole and unharmed.

At the moment, we could not reconstruct what had happened. All I could exclaim was, "Thank You, Lord, for saving us!"

Emil could not get out of the car through the left door, which was stuck into the rock. Only after we got out did we realize, in part, the seriousness of the accident. Soon the police arrived, probably called by one of the drivers who stopped to offer first aid.

The policeman helped us to reconstruct the accident. Right next to that very narrow curve, a torrent of muddy water, rushing from the mountain parapet on the left, had covered the road, and the yellow stripe in the middle of the road was out of sight. Emil lost control when the car touched the yellow line, which had become very slippery.

In short, the policeman told us that we had a great chance of rolling over into the precipice on the right side of the road. He told us that every year, exactly in this place, there is at least one accident with tragic consequences. Usually, the car is thrown into the huge abyss, at the bottom of which stretches the bed of the wild mountain river, the Smith River.

Although that dangerous curve was protected by a concrete wall built for this purpose, we were projected to the end of the wall where there was a massive rock that blocked us, thus preventing our car from falling into the deep escarpment.

We looked at each other, terrified by what we heard, and praised God for rescuing us by means of the huge rock, which we named "the Rock of our salvation." One of many Bible promises popped in my mind at that critical moment: *"Unless the Lord had been my help, my soul would soon have settled in silence" (Ps. 94:17).*

After this accident, the third on this mountain trail, I was determined to give up my job in Gold Beach.

March 1, 2004, was my last day of work with Dr. Liem.

The detachment from the people and the place I so much loved was not easy, as he acknowledged: *"I know it's hard for you, and you also know it's much harder for us to let you go. It's hard for us to lose you. We will miss you a lot. But you can come back. The doors are still open for you to come back."*

Having some free time, we decided to visit our son in Sacramento. He had told us that he had decided to try the Interferon treatment, and we wanted to see how he was doing.

We found him in shock. He was shivering even though it was hot inside the house. After a while, he had to interrupt the treatment because it was getting harder and harder for him to tolerate it.

We returned home with a broken heart after seeing our child suffering without being able to help. We continued to pray that the Lord would have mercy on him and strengthen him in the ordeal he was going through.

I started looking for work, submitting résumés to various dental practices. I soon found a new job at Dr. Steven Rogers's office in Grants Pass.

Both the doctor and Donna, his assistant, were very nice. The atmosphere at work was relaxing, and that eased my transition to a new workplace.

Gradually, I noticed that something strange was happening to me. I had insomnia and palpitations; I started losing weight and felt depressed. Despite not getting enough sleep, I was hyperactive. I worked very hard, but I could not rest.

The symptoms worsened from day to day, but I tried to ignore them and move on. It went like this all summer. At work I noticed that my hands were shaking when I was assisting at the dentist's chairside. I had never had such symptoms before.

One Friday, after finishing my chores at home, I felt exhausted. My body was shaking, and I could not relax. I knew that something was wrong with me and asked Emil to take me to the doctor.

When the doctor entered the room, I started to cry. When he asked what bothered me, I could not give any explanation and kept on crying. Nothing was hurting, but I felt very anxious. My heart was pounding in my chest as if I were having a panic attack.

The doctor ordered some blood tests and sent me home. On Monday, I was called at work and asked to return to his office as soon as possible. I was terrified by the thought that the lab results must be alarming, and at the appointed time, I was present at the medical clinic. The doctor warned me: "I have bad news for you. Your thyroid gland is out of control, and you need to see an endocrinologist immediately." He got in touch with Dr. Richard Eddy in Medford, a nearby city, and he agreed to see me at the end of the day.

Usually, an appointment with such a specialist is not obtained earlier than thirty days.

When Dr. Eddy entered the room, he exclaimed in astonishment: "Wow! After looking at the lab results, I was expecting to see a crazy woman in the room."

After a careful examination, Dr. Eddy explained to me in detail the terrible condition I was in. According to laboratory data, the thyroid gland was no longer controlled by the brain through the pituitary gland and was working randomly, bombarding hormones throughout the whole body. The adrenaline was reaching its peak. Because of this, my body was functioning as an engine without brakes, heated to incandescence.

In order to help me understand my condition, he compared my body with a red-hot car engine that I continued to accelerate to the maximum until it blew out. As such, he urged me to quit working immediately. I was on the verge of having a thyroid storm with tragic consequences. Dr. Eddy presented me with two choices: Either to kill my thyroid gland with radioactive isotopes before it would kill me or to try an aggressive treatment that does not always give the desired results.

I opted for the second alternative, based on my past experiences and relying on God's healing power and His loving care for me.

According to the prescription, every four hours, I had to take a handful of pills and check my blood pressure and pulse, which were both much higher than normal. I was going to be checked in two weeks for new lab tests and adjustments of medication.

I was shaking and feeling so tired that I could barely stand. After a week of treatment, I did not feel better at all. Tachycardia stressed me out more than anything else. My heart was pounding so loud that I could not sleep. I called Dr. Eddy's office, and I was scheduled for the next day. He increased the heart medication and asked me to come back in a week.

The lab results were very discouraging. Not the slightest sign of improvement. Of course, I already knew, as my body was telling me as much. Dr. Eddy maximized the dose of medication for my heart and added some new ones. I felt so weak I had to stay in bed.

Although I was exhausted, I could not sleep. I had moments of discouragement, and I wondered if I would ever get well. We prayed earnestly that the Lord would have mercy on me.

After the first visit to the endocrinologist, I informed my employer that I had to quit my job for medical reasons. He was not surprised by this news. He had noticed that something was wrong with me, and he expected to lose me due to illness.

Medical bills were accumulating with each passing day, and in a short time, the financial reserves were exhausted. Medical expenses far exceeded our budget. The only source of income was Emil's rather modest social security and the financial assistance from SAIF.

Our faith was being tested again. In moments of discouragement, I heard the voice of the Lord gently rebuking me:

"Is My hand shortened at all that it cannot redeem? Or have I no power to deliver?" (Isa. 50:2)

Looking back on the wonderful way Providence intervened in our lives, we decided to pray and silently wait for God's help.

Both Emil and I clung to God's promise: *"Behold, the Lord's hand is not shortened, That it cannot save; Nor His ear heavy, That it cannot hear"* (Isa. 59:1).

We endeavored to keep fresh in mind the past experiences, and we asked Him for faith, patience, and wisdom so that we would know what to do.

> *Our faith was being tested again.*

After three months of treatment, no improvement was noticed. Was it worth continuing the treatment? Dr. Eddy decided to try something else. Despite the fact that my plate was already full, he prescribed hormonal treatment on top of the medication I was on. I accepted it.

In the winter, as the weather was getting cold, I felt a little better, but Emil was shivering around the wood stove because I did not allow him to kindle the fire. I could not understand poor Emil until one day when some friends came to visit us, and they were squatting around the stove, with their coats on, wondering why Emil did not light the fire.

I was sweating so hard that my clothes were sticking to my body. The red-hot engine needed cooling.

Something amazing happened after a month of intensive treatment.

At the next medical check-up, laboratory data indicated that the thyroid gland had reconnected to the brain, and thus its function was to be gradually regulated.

Although I did not feel any improvement, the hope of healing was rekindled in my exhausted soul. The family provided us with emotional and financial support.

Medical expenses were rising constantly, and I needed to pay them out of pocket since my health insurance was terminated after I quit my job.

When there was a due date for paying the medical bills, the money always arrived in the mail just in time. Once, we received from a relative exactly the amount we needed to fill the prescription. That check was accompanied by an explanatory note: "The Lord has inspired us to send you this money."

Another time, a family member sent us a substantial amount of money with which we were able to pay all the pending medical bills. And so, the blessings flowed abundantly, and our weak faith increased as well. We praised the Lord and felt so unworthy of His boundless love.

One particular day, we could not figure out how to pay a large medical bill. We asked the Lord to intervene. Later on, Emil went to the post office to pick up the mail. He brought home a large envelope via FedEx from the mailbox. We had no idea who the sender was or the contents. When we opened it, we were moved to tears. Inside, we found a lovely card signed by our friends from out of state and a very substantial check.

A few years ago, this family had suffered a severe trauma, and, inspired by the Lord, we sent them financial help. Exactly the same amount of money came back to us, just when we needed it most. How these friends knew about our trouble, we have not known to this day. We have always sought not to complain or ask for help from people, but only from the Lord. God's promise, *"Cast your bread upon the waters, For you will find it after many days" (Eccles. 11:1),* has been fulfilled literally in our lives, and we praise Him for His wonderful care for us.

Out of the desire to protect our son, who also had his own struggles related to hepatitis C, we decided not to burden him with our troubles. On the contrary, we sought to encourage him and turn his attention to the Great Physician.

In the summer of 2004, we contacted our friend in Romania, Dr. Doru Laza, regarding Silviu's situation. He suggested natural treatment and was very kind to help us. At that time, he ran a health clinic in Romania and encouraged us to send Silviu there.

Silviu agreed to try, although he was quite skeptical about it. There was no concrete evidence that hepatitis C could be cured naturally.

He took a leave of absence from Intel and went to Romania for treatment. He was well received at our friend's clinic, and he complied with the natural treatment protocol. Upon returning home, he shared with us, among other things, the fact that he met Alina, a young girl about his age, and sent us her picture. We learned that Alina was the only child in her family, she was a dentist like her parents, and Silviu seemed interested in this friendship. We entrusted this matter in God's hands and continued to take care of our own problems.

***

THE YEAR OF DIFFICULT DECISIONS

Right from the beginning, the year 2005 brought us to the threshold of a series of problems with which resolve was imperative. My health condition, which had not improved much, required a difficult decision. If I could not get well soon, we would be on the verge of bankruptcy.

Emil would finish school early in the summer, SAIF medical insurance would be suspended, and the financial aid would cease.

We were deeply grateful to the Lord and to our family and friends who helped us stay afloat. But, there is a measure in everything! We put our rather precarious situation before the Lord and earnestly asked Him to show us what to do. We were praying and waiting for an answer.

Time passed, and nothing promising was on the horizon. With the end of school, Emil's allowance ended. The only source of income was his social security, of which very little remained after paying the mortgage for the house.

Well-meaning friends suggested the idea of selling the house and moving to a more affordable region or state. Thus, we could get rid of our mortgage and ease our financial burden.

We prayed to God if it really was His will for us to move, that He would open the way.

One day we received a call from my brother Cornel. He was in California, staying with our older sister. Knowing the situation, he suggested we try Arkansas, where he lived. He told us that he was returning home in a few days and proposed that we go with him. He told us that the market was much cheaper there, and we decided to give it a try, even though we did not like the idea of leaving Oregon.

> *We prayed to God if it really was His will for us to move, that He would open the way.*

It was the beginning of February. We went to Loma Linda, and from there, we went with Cornel to Hot Springs, Arkansas. We left our car at my sister's place and prepared for a two-day journey, about 1,700 miles.

After eleven hours of driving, it started getting dark. We had just entered Texas on Interstate 10 in El Paso. We looked for a place to rest overnight. There was no traffic at that hour in the evening. I was already asleep in the back seat when suddenly, I woke up screaming, terrified by a powerful commotion and a sudden, squealing brake.

The car stopped abruptly. The explosion of the airbags scattered a dust that was drowning me. We were all scared and puzzled. When we exited the vehicle, we saw that the front of the car had been severely damaged.

The oil stain beneath it suggested that the oil pan had been broken. A massive metal bar was stuck under the car.

As Cornel tried to unravel the mystery, Emil noticed several police cars with flashing lights stopped on the other side of the road. A car had fallen into a precipice separating the two lanes of the freeway.

Nearby was a bridge over that ravine, and Emil decided to go to the place and find out what had happened. There, the policemen were talking to the man who had managed to get out of his car propped on its hood. Emil reported our bizarre accident and was told we had to wait.

Meanwhile, Emil was still looking around, trying to understand what had happened. He noticed that a large piece of the guardrail missing from the other side of the freeway resembled the piece of metal under our car.

After a long wait, the police came to our side and found that the two accidents occurred at about the same time. The massive piece of rail from the other side of the freeway was projected onto our side. Cornel could not see it and drove over it. Our totaled car was towed, and we were taken to a place where we could rent a car. We thanked God for protecting us from an accident that could have been fatal. Again, He had intervened to rescue us, according to His promise: ***"God is our refuge and strength, A very present help in trouble" (Ps. 46:1).***

After this long, difficult journey, we arrived at our destination. After a much-needed rest, Cornel took us to see the town of Hot Springs and its surroundings.

It was a beautiful spring day in February. There were flowers everywhere. The freshly flowering magnolia trees looked gorgeous. On the roadside, wildflowers strewn on the green grass carpet were decorating the landscape along the freeways.

We went to a sales agency and took various leaflets with advertisements for houses and land available in this area. Prices were incredibly low compared to Oregon. An advertisement caught our attention in a special way. It was a vacant lot in a new neighborhood with beautiful houses located at the foot of a wooded hill. It enticed us. The owner was a contractor who was going to build a house on it. We contacted him, and he showed us a model house nearby, which we really liked.

We contacted the owner's agent for details. He told us that the house would be ready in about four months. In the meantime, we had to sell our house in Merlin. The contract would stipulate that the purchase of this home would be contingent on the sale of our home in Oregon. We asked for some time to think and pray about it. The next day, we returned to the agency, discussed in detail the terms of the contract, adding some options to the house plan as well as some necessary work around the property. We realized that a retaining wall was needed behind the house to prevent the erosion of the nearby hill. Due to the fact that the land was below the level of the street, we requested an underground drainage system to be installed around the house to prevent flooding. These additional works were stipulated in the contract.

The owner agreed to everything we asked for, and we signed the contract. The final price, after adding the options and landscaping works, was $80,000. It sounded like a very good deal for a brand new home with 1,300 square feet, three bedrooms and two bathrooms, a garage, and plenty of space for gardening.

The agent assured us that he would keep us posted with the construction work. We were not asked for a down payment, and we were not given a deadline to buy the house. We would not be stressed out about selling our house in Merlin.

We rented a car, said goodbye to Hot Springs, thanked my brother for helping us, and set off. By God's grace, we made it home safely.

We started making plans for selling the house and decided not to put it on the market but to let the Lord sell it for us if it was His will indeed.

We had consulted with a realtor friend about the price and settled on $180,000. Emil stuck the sale sign on a conspicuous spot, and we prayed earnestly that the Lord would send us the right client at the right time.

Shortly after the sale sign was displayed, we had a customer who told us that he would be able to buy the house in four months. We accepted the proposal. The new house in Arkansas was going to be ready in the summer, so we were not in a hurry.

As the deadline for selling the house approached, the potential buyer informed us that he had changed his mind and was no longer interested in the deal. We did not panic, knowing that God was in control.

A few days after the apparent failure, a young woman saw the sign and told us that she was interested in our home. We invited her in to take a look, but she refused. She asked us if we had an agent, and we told her we were trying to sell it ourselves in order to keep the sale price low.

The young woman said that she wanted to be helped by an agent, and she left.

Soon a young man came to our door. He introduced himself as an agent from Century 21 and offered to help us in selling the house. His name was Tim.

Surprised by such an unexpected visit, I asked him: "How did you find out about us?"

"A young woman came to the agency, told me you had a house for sale, and gave me your address," he replied.

"Where is the young woman? Didn't she want to see the house?"

"She didn't want to come," said the stranger.

"And yet, why did you come to see us without having a client for our house?"

"I want to help you sell your house," the uninvited agent answered in a convincing tone.

"No, thank you! We are trying to sell it ourselves to reduce selling expenses," I replied.

"Yes, I understand. That's why I want to help you. It doesn't cost you anything. I just wanted to offer you my services for free."

We looked at each other in bewilderment and then looked long at Tim, the unsolicited agent who came to our door.

Very politely, he asked for permission to take a look at our house. After a long hesitation, we invited him in.

He was impressed by the excellent condition of the house and suggested the price of $215,000. What a surprise! His estimation was a lot higher than the initial one set by our friend a few months prior. Tim then asked permission to take some pictures inside and outside the house, after which we filled in the necessary forms for the sale.

It was Friday afternoon. Tim told us that he would post the pictures on the agency's sales list and let us know when he had a client for us. We asked him not to bother us on Saturday, as this is a special day for us, the Sabbath. We told him we did not do business on Sabbath. Tim understood us and promised to respect our beliefs.

After he left, we tried to recount what happened. The young woman who came to us, seemingly interested in our house, but not having the desire to see it; her visit to the agency, looking for an agent to whom she gave our address without wanting to be shown the house; Tim's appearance and his proposal to sell our house without a sales commission—everything seemed so bizarre.

We asked the Lord to explain to us the dilemma. Without trying to unravel the mysteries of Providence, we had abandoned ourselves, with all confidence, into the arms of our heavenly Father for protection and guidance. On Sunday, at eight o'clock in the morning, the phone rang.

"Hi, it's Tim! I have a client who wants to see your house. When may I come and show it to them?"

I could not believe what I heard.

"Anytime!" I replied in a friendly tone.

"Right now?" asked Tim in a rushed tone.

"Sure!"

Not long after, Tim showed up with his clients. They were a couple about our age, who came from California six months earlier, looking for a home. They had rented an apartment and started searching without finding what they wanted.

We realized we were dealing with picky people and did not have high hopes for them. However, we withdrew and let Tim do his job.

> **We told him we did not do business on Sabbath. Tim understood us and promised to respect our beliefs.**

After touring the house inside and outside, the clients told us frankly: "We really like this property, and we want to buy it at the asking price. That's $215,000."

Both Emil and I became speechless. Too good to be true! We did not expect those people to be so straightforward and immediately communicate their decision to us. That was the agent's job after consulting with his clients.

And, to make sure that we would not change our minds, they asked us to vacate the house as soon as possible because they were paying cash and wanted to move in as soon as possible.

The client was a retired agronomist and was in a hurry to plant trees on the property. He was delighted that we had plenty of space around the house, a large garden, and a well that yields a high debit of water.

Before deciding on the move, we called the Hot Spring agent and asked him what stage the house was in and when we could move in. We were told that in three weeks, the house would be ready, that he would leave us the key for the house inside the electrical panel, and that we could move in whenever we wanted. He went on to say that the house would go into escrow the next day in preparation for closing.

We were pleasantly surprised by the news and announced to our buyers that we would vacate the house in three weeks, more precisely on July 4th.

Said and done.

After signing all the papers, we started packing and scheduled the U-Haul. The three weeks of packing were very stressful for me.

The long journey we had to take, moving to an unknown place to a house we had not seen yet, all these things exacerbated my anxiety.

We said goodbye to our dear friends who had been with us through all the troubles we went through. Loretta and Phil, who had always been around us and on whom we had relied for their support. Jim and Carolyn Sutton, who gave us invaluable moral and spiritual support, and many others.

CHAPTER 9
THE MYSTERIES OF PROVIDENCE

"He does great things which we cannot comprehend." (Job 37:5)

On the morning of July 4, 2005, we were ready to take off. Chuck, a very kind neighbor, had helped Emil load the truck. The small car was towed behind the U-Haul.

Poor Emil had to drive a long and tiring trip of 2,200 miles. From the start, I was already tired. I could not wait to get to our new home and breathe a sigh of relief. Four and a half days later, with God's help, we reached our destination.

We were not going to unload anything until the next day. We informed my brother of our arrival, and while waiting for him to come, we went around the house. It looked gorgeous on the outside. But something caught our eye.

The retaining wall behind the house did not exist. Nor did the drainage system around the house. These two works stipulated in the contract were non-existent. We kept calm and decided to wait until the next day.

Cornel took us to his home and gave us the comfort we needed after the long journey. The next day, we returned to "our house" to take a closer look at the land around the house.

We were shocked to see the change of scenery overnight. It had been raining hard all night. Behind the house, a waterfall had formed, flowing from the top of the hill, crashing furiously toward the house. Water was pooling around the house.

I took pictures and videos of the waterfall. We decided to rent a storage unit for our belongings until the work around the house could be completed. Cornel offered us unlimited accommodation.

We contacted the agent and asked him to come with the contractor to the scene. They were not happy with what they saw, but they had nowhere to go. They had to acknowledge their responsibility to comply with the contract and promised to remedy the situation. We then did the house inspection, and we really liked it. We had nothing to object to, and we decided to complete the transaction after the work was finished.

The contractor solemnly promised to keep his word. In the following days, he set to work. He cut from the hill next to the house and built the retaining wall that would protect us from flooding. During the excavations, he accidentally bumped into the high voltage line. The power company was called in to fix the problem. The contractor had to pay $2,500 for the installation of the electrical cables to the depth required by law. He asked us to contribute half of this amount, but we refused, considering that it was not our responsibility.

The work continued, and, in a short time, we were to finalize the transaction and move into our new home.

One evening, as we usually came to see the progress of the work, we noticed an Oklahoma car parked in front of the house and a pile of cardboard boxes scattered around. We got scared. We stood at a distance to see what was going on. The gentleman carrying the boxes in the house motioned for us to come closer. A friendly elderly couple invited us into the house.

"You must be our neighbors, and we want to meet you!" said the stranger.

"Kind of. We are living a little higher on the hill," I answered, swallowing the knot in my throat and trying to put on a friendly smile.

"Come on in!" Our neighbor said in a lovely tone. "We want to tell you how we got this house. But first, we want to offer you this flyer and, if you want, some other religious literature. We are Christians, and we want to tell others about our faith."

I politely accepted the offer and hurried to get to the subject.

"Okay! Tell us how you found this beautiful house?" I asked in a self-induced enthusiastic tone.

Emil and I tacitly agreed to keep our mouths shut.

They were so excited that we did not want to interfere in their joy. We listened with deep interest and curiosity to their amazing story.

"We came from Oklahoma," the gentleman began, "looking for a house. On Sunday, we went to church and told the folks why we came to Hot Springs. One of them, a professional builder, told us that he has a house for sale. He brought us here and, here we are! We really like both the place and the house."

I congratulated the new owners, thanked them for their hospitality, and we left. The poor people were not to blame.

How about us?! What had we done wrong? Why were we treated like this?! I believed that the dispute between the contractor and us had been resolved peacefully. We considered that we had the right to know why we were treated this way.

We called our agent, who was, in fact, also the contractor's agent, and asked to talk. He invited us to the agency, and we told him what had happened.

Of course, he was aware of it, and without giving us any explanation, he threw his hands in the air and, in a malicious tone, said, "I don't want to get involved in this. If that doesn't suit you, look for a lawyer and sue the contractor."

We tried to reason with the guy, but he refused to talk to us. "We will see you in court!" were his last words, then he walked away.

The contractor would not answer the phone when we called him.

We started looking for a lawyer, and we chose the best one from Hot Springs. After presenting our problem, we asked him if it was worth taking our case to court and if we would have any chance of success.

The lawyer agreed to take our case, being a very simple one. The defendant would be required to pay all the court fees to compensate us for moving expenses, accommodation, and storage rent. In addition, he had to return the value of the household items already installed in the house at our expense.

We had kept receipts for these items, storage rental fees, plus traveling and lodging expenses. The trial was scheduled in less than thirty days.

On the appointed day, at eight o'clock in the morning, we appeared in court, accompanied by our lawyer. In the waiting room, we met the two defendants, the builder and his agent, plus the new owners of the house in question.

They were all happy, relaxed as if they were the innocent party in the process. We greeted each other respectfully.

We were soon summoned to the courtroom. Here appeared the lawyer of our opponents, an old man who did not look like a lawyer. The judge was also elderly.

Our lawyer took the floor. His plea was full of indisputable arguments. Even our opponent, the builder, when questioned, acknowledged the truth.

His lawyer, in a brief presentation, without persuasive power, tried to defend his client who was accused of non-compliance with the contract. His pleading did not have any legal support. At noon, we were given a one-hour lunch break, after which we resumed our seats in the courtroom. Our lawyer made strong arguments that could not be overlooked. The transparency of the evidence presented by him was indisputable. We did not understand, however, why the judge delayed the trial until the end of the day. At five o'clock in the afternoon, he stood up and, instead of uttering the sentence, informed us that, due to lack of time, he could not make the final decision. He would mail the court order to all persons involved in the process.

A trial as simple and clear as black and white, debated for a whole day, without any result! Unbelievable!

Why? The judge had only our case on his agenda for the entire day. This was an enigma not only for Emil and me but also for our lawyer.

> **A trial as simple and clear as black and white, debated for a whole day, without any result! Unbelievable!**

He told us that this judge was in a temporary position, replacing another one, who had retired, and this was not his field of expertise. We gave him the benefit of doubt and decided to wait. Of course, we were firmly committed to success.

About a week later, the court letter arrived in the mailbox.

With anticipated joy we opened it, expecting the good news we justly deserved. At the first reading, we did not quite understand what it meant. We were not familiar with the legal terms. We read it over and over again and got really confused.

We could not believe it. The roles had been reversed. Justice was grossly violated. The defendant was acquitted. We lost the case and were required to pay the court fees. The only refund was for household items we paid for. That was it.

The day after receiving the letter from the court, the lawyer called, confirming that he had received the court decision. He was stupefied. "Incredible! I cannot believe my eyes!" He exclaimed in an indignant tone.

We understood that the judge was "bought." We later learned that in this state, judicial corruption is the order of the day.

This was our rationale: It seemed the bargain with the house was done at the church. Most likely, this judge went to the same church with the contractor or at least was a friend of his. And by virtue of the "law of love," he justified the guilty, declaring him innocent because he confessed his sin at the trial.

Now I understood why everyone in court had a serene and happy face. They were in control of the situation. The trial had been nothing more than a masquerade.

At our last meeting with the lawyer, he expressed his outrage at this deplorable failure. "Is there anything else that can be done?" I asked distrustfully.

"Unfortunately not!" said the lawyer. "It's not worth it. If we appeal, the court fees will be much higher, and the chances of success will be zero." Thus, we decided to give up.

With the money recovered from the trial for the items we bought for the house, we paid the lawyer's fee.

We trusted in God, even though our thoughts did not match His, according to one of the Bible verses: ***"For My thoughts are not your thoughts, Nor are your ways My ways,' says the Lord. For as the heavens are higher than the earth, So are My ways higher than your ways, And My thoughts than your thoughts"*** (Isa. 55:8–9).

The most important thing for which we thanked the Lord was that my health was improving, despite the stress I had gone through. I continued the treatment and kept in touch with Dr. Eddy, who was monitoring me from a distance. I kept him up to date with lab tests, and he was very pleased with the results. After a while, he gave me permission to resume work.

Now on the prayer list, in addition to finding another home, we added the request of finding a job. We struggled to forget the troubles we went through and continued on.

It was a Sabbath day. We were at the Seventh-day Adventist Church in Hot Springs.

Being quite new to this church, we did not know any of the American brethren. We knew only a few Romanians, but it was difficult to recognize them among the Americans. At the end of the service, someone came to us asking in the Romanian language, "You are Romanian, aren't you?"

"Yes," I answered with a smile on my face.

"I'm Angela, and this is my husband, Costel. We would like to invite you to our home for lunch."

We thanked them for the invitation and followed them closely as they headed home.

As soon as we arrived at their home, the first thing that caught our eye was the sale sign posted in front of the property. We did not want to ask questions to avoid discussions about it on the Sabbath.

We had a pleasant time together and, on leaving, we thanked them for their hospitality. I asked for their phone number and promised to keep in touch.

***

A NEW PERSPECTIVE

After the Sabbath, we decided to talk to our new friends about the sale of their house. The fact that we were invited to their home was not a coincidence, we thought. Of course, they had no idea of our intention to buy a house in Hot Springs.

We asked them bluntly: "How much are you asking for your home? We saw you had it for sale."

"Are you interested?" asked Angela, taken by surprise.

"Maybe. We would like to know the price first," was Emil's answer.

"$105,000. Negotiable. It's a pretty new house. It was built five years ago."

We decided to see it, and on Sunday, we were on the spot. The house looked beautiful! Inside and out. Just the perfect size for two of us: three bedrooms, two bathrooms, double garage, etc. A fenced property with a large backyard for gardening and nice porch and flowerbeds in the front.

When we told the owners how much we could afford to pay for the house, without hesitation, they lowered the price to $97,000. Done deal!

They were happy to move to their new home, and we were even happier that the Lord had given us a more beautiful house than the one we had lost.

Cornel, my brother, helped us a lot with moving, installing in the new place, and other work around the house.

The news of our arrival in Hot Springs spread quickly, not only among the Romanian community but also among the Americans. That is how Dr. C.C. in Amity found out about us.

THE MYSTERIES OF PROVIDENCE

Learning that I was a dental assistant, he became interested in meeting me and called for an interview at his clinic. I was hired on the spot. A few days later, I started commuting to Amity, a little town about thirty-three miles from Hot Springs.

I was so happy to resume my normal life after almost a year of sick leave. Very nice people and a pleasant atmosphere made me feel welcome in my new workplace. The only inconvenience was the daily commute. It took me an hour and a half back and forth. We had sold one of our cars before moving to Arkansas to simplify the moving, so, with just one car, Emil drove me every day to work.

I must admit that after moving to Arkansas, the weather disappointed me deeply. In July, when we arrived there, the climate was so different from the one in February when we had gone to check out the area.

Although I did not like excessive heat, weighing the other benefits offered by this state, especially the affordable house, I had decided to not complain about the weather. But humidity became a major problem for me, especially in the summer. My asthma had started bothering me again.

In December 2005, I established care with a family doctor and had my annual check-up. My new physician ordered a mammogram. The result was dubious. A lump appeared on the film that needed to be investigated. The doctor sent me to a surgeon who recommended an excisional biopsy. Black clouds began to overshadow my future. If the result was positive, what could be done? I did not have medical insurance.

I accepted the procedure in order to elucidate the nature of that nodule. Prior to the biopsy, the surgeon did not mark the area to be incised. I did not say anything, thinking he knew what he was doing. After the biopsy, I had to take time off from work for healing. Dark clouds hovered over my head, turning the waiting time for the biopsy result into an ordeal.

Our faith was once again being tested. We prayed for divine intervention. There was nothing else we could do.

During this difficult time, we received a phone call from Silviu, informing us that he had decided to marry Alina and inviting us to their wedding in Romania on January 13, 2006. Unfortunately, our going to Romania was not feasible due to the precarious situation I was in. I was still in pain after surgery. I was looking forward to the biopsy result. I could hardly think of anything else.

When the pain subsided, I tried to palpate the incised area and felt that the lump was still there. I immediately remembered that the surgeon had not marked the area in question before the biopsy. I was very upset about the whole situation, and I was anxious to see him again and to show him that the nodule was still in place.

Three weeks later, I was back at the surgeon's office. Although confronted with the fact, he flatly refused to admit his mistake. The biopsy result was negative. But it was not conclusive for me, knowing that the tissue examined was not the nodule itself but an adjacent tissue. Convinced that the tissue examined in the laboratory was not harvested from the area suspected as a nodule, I sought the opinion of an oncologist. After the examination, the oncologist ruled in my favor. The area suspected as a nodule was actually an inflamed mammary gland, which posed no danger. The chunk removed for biopsy was an innocent tissue, not the so-called "nodule." Both Emil and I breathed a sigh of relief after a month full of tension and uncertainty. We praised the Lord for getting us out of this difficult trial.

In addition to the physical and emotional pain, we were left with $4,000 in medical debt for an unnecessary surgery. This is Arkansas! It was our choice to be here, so we refused to complain about any inconveniences. If I had gone to that oncologist before the biopsy, I would have been spared this unfortunate experience.

Meanwhile, Silviu and Alina got married without us being able to take part in this great family event. Although far from each other, our soul has been and will always remain with our children, whom we love so much.

***

WHERE DOES YOUR HEART DRAW YOU?

The winter holidays, with their noisy procession, passed in the darkness of the past.

The old year, hunched over by the burden of troubles and hardships, seemed prematurely aged. It was time to gather under his ragged cloak all his memories, good and bad, and disappear into nothingness.

The New Year, 2006, was promising to be an auspicious year, and we looked to the future with confidence, wanting to keep only fond memories of the past year.

We had submitted to the Lord our plans for the future, asking for His will to be done in all things. I resumed my work at Amity, and Emil took care of his chores around the house. The weather had cooled down, and I was glad to get rid of the hot, sticky days.

One morning, when Emil was taking me to work, before entering the freeway, we had to return home because the road was slippery and covered with ice. The trees were bent under the weight of the icicles. It was very cold, and very few people were on the road.

Commuting was getting more and more tiring for us. Emil was spending three hours back and forth on the road every day. Dr. C.C. had suggested we move to Amity. He showed us a brand-new house for sale, close to his office. It was a modern one, provided inside with a special place of refuge for tornados. That area was exposed to such weather, and people built very thick concrete bunkers outside, partially buried into the ground as shelters from the storm.

He had even offered Emil a job to encourage us to settle permanently at Amity. We had barely recovered from moving the year before. We did not want to move again! The best option was to look for work in Hot Springs and get rid of commuting.

A friend of ours recommended Dr. E.S., a well-known dentist in town with a good reputation.

He happened to be present at the front desk when I submitted my resume. I was very surprised when I was called for an interview at the end of the day. The office was already closed. Only the girl at the reception counter was present and attended the interview.

But the biggest surprise was that I was hired on the spot. The question was, "When can you start working?"

One of his assistants had resigned, wanting to go to school to continue her education, and Dr. E.S. was in great need of hiring another assistant.

I asked for two weeks' notice for Dr. C.C., after which I would report for the new job. He was not happy about my decision, but he understood the situation. Emil was glad he was able to repair the dental x-ray machine at the office as well as other appliances, reliving fond memories. Dr. C.C. expressed his appreciation for our contribution.

The long-awaited day had arrived. No more commuting.

On the appointed date, I showed up for my new job, my face radiating with joy. I walked through the back door, as any employee. The first person I met was Karla. Unpleasantly surprised by my unexpected appearance, she asked me in a repulsive tone, "Who are you? Whom are you looking for"?

At first glance, I felt like I was in the wrong place, even though the smell specific to the dental clinic indicated that I was in the right place. I cautiously took a step back.

"My name is Elena, and I was hired by Dr. E.S. as a dental assistant at this clinic," I mumbled timidly.

"What?! You were hired without my knowledge? Did you have an interview with Dr. E.S.? When?"

"Yes," I answered. "Two weeks ago."

Then I decided to shut my mouth so as not to get into more trouble. Just then, Dr. E.S. entered the door. The dialogue stopped abruptly. I was officially introduced to Karla and the rest of the staff as the new assistant.

Later on, the doctor took me to the lab and asked me how I could help him in this area. He knew from the interview that I was also a dental lab technician. He was very happy when I told him everything I could do in the laboratory, thus relieving him of certain technical operations he had to perform himself.

The office was well equipped with modern equipment, very clean and tidy. I felt privileged to work for this dentist in such a nice environment. In addition to professional excellence, he was a very kind man both with patients and staff.

If I had forgotten the first impression, everything seemed to be in perfect order at my new job. But, as first impressions matter, I decided to be prudent in my relationship with Karla. I had no idea what she was hiding behind the facade.

I tried to be myself, ignoring the apparent small inconveniences. Always kind and benevolent to carry out orders without hesitation, even if they were often irrational.

I was the happiest when I worked in the laboratory, far from the scrutinizing eye of my colleague, who, due to lack of competence in this area, could not find anything to complain about.

However, I must mention that at first, it was not so. When Karla saw me working in the lab, she said bluntly, "You're not allowed to work in the lab. This is the doctor's business, not for the assistants."

When I told her I was doing this with the doctor's permission, after investigating the matter, she left me alone.

I was appreciated by the doctor and the rest of the staff, and this helped me to overlook the unpleasant moments. However, the relationship between Karla and me was still strained, although I made a desperate effort to improve it.

When everything seemed shrouded in mystery, without being able to understand my colleague's unjustified attitude toward me, an unexpected surprise radically changed things for the worse.

One morning, a new colleague appeared at work. Her name was Lori. It did not take me long to understand that Lori was "new" only to me. I soon found out that she was the girl who had resigned prior to my arrival. I did not know why she had returned to work. It was not my business to know.

> *I had no idea what she was hiding behind the facade.*

From the beginning, this young colleague looked at me as an intruder and openly expressed her displeasure toward me. There was no way I could please her. I had learned to strictly follow the rules imposed by Karla. But Lori's rules were diametrically opposed to Karla's, and I constantly got in trouble. I did not know whom to obey. I did not understand what the hierarchy was in this office.

Until that moment, I believed Karla was "the head." Now, I was dealing with two highly polarized heads. What surprised me was that the two got along well and made a common front in their hostility toward me.

I knew I could not serve two masters, and although I hated to complain to my boss, I decided to vocalize my concerns. Dr. E.S. listened to my plea and solemnly promised that things would change in time, encouraging me to be patient. I took his word for it and continued to defeat evil with good, becoming inoffensive to my opponent's attacks.

However, things did not change for the better, and soon, the cup of my forbearance was almost full. Only one more drop before I had to quit.

Although I did not want to bring home the problems from work, I had to share my trouble with Emil and unite in prayer, asking the Lord for patience and wisdom in making the right decision.

Despite my efforts to hide the pain, I often shed tears. Things were going from bad to worse, and I could not see a way out. A wise saying came to my mind: *"You can't change the people around you, but you can change the people you choose to surround you"* (Ileana Vulpescu).

We prayed that the Lord would intervene either to change things or to get me out of there. The question was: If I leave, where will I go?

Where does your heart draw you, Elena? My heart was drawing me back to Gold Beach.

The idea of another move did not fit in our minds. Enough is enough! At times, I was confused and disappointed about our move to Arkansas, wondering if indeed it was God's will for us to move there.

However, all of the events related to our moving to Arkansas, succeeding one after another, could not be a coincidence.

Although the path had been extremely thorny, we always had the feeling that God was in control and that everything was allowed by Him with a great purpose, which, most of the time, we did not understand.

***

July 2006

It was a hot summer like I had never seen before. It was our first summer in Arkansas. Maximum humidity.

The earth was exuding hot steam that turned into water on contact with the body. The sauna effect of the hot and humid climate incited my asthma symptoms again.

Nostalgically, I was thinking of the coolness of the Pacific Coast, the fresh air packed with natural aerosols, and the lovely atmosphere at my old workplace. My heart kept pulling me in that direction. Yet, I did not have the courage to share my feelings with Emil. Another move?! No way!!

Even though I could not foresee any alternative on the horizon, I chose to pray and trust in divine guidance.

One day, Dr. E.S. informed us that he would be gone for ten days and that we would be free to go on vacation. I breathed a sigh of relief at the thought of getting rid of the nightmare for a while.

Neither Emil nor I had the desire to leave on vacation in such a distressing situation. I was so tired, especially emotionally, and I wanted nothing else but to stay home in my comfort zone and relax for a while.

Shortly after, we received a phone call from Lucian, our friend from California, and his family. They told us they were on vacation in Gold Beach, and they missed us so much. For years our friends: Lucian, Constantza, and their three girls, Cristina, Irina, and Daniela, had spent their vacation with us, delighted with the natural beauties of the coast and the joy of being with us.

"Gold Beach has lost its charm and its attraction since you are no longer here," they said.

Stirred by the fond memories that connected us to our friends and implicitly to Gold Beach, I thought out loud and told them how much I would like to be together again.

Among other things, we mentioned that in a week, we would be on a short vacation but that we had decided to stay home.

The next day, Lucian called again and informed us that he had booked for us four nights at the motel where they were staying and that they were looking forward to spending a few days together in Gold Beach.

We were stunned at such an unexpected surprise and asked for time to think and pray about it.

We made up our minds, thinking that even though we would waste six days on the road back and forth, we could spend four days at Gold Beach with our friends and, at the same time, visit our loved ones there. And so, we did. At the appointed time, we set out, asking God for traveling mercies.

After three days of driving, thirteen hours a day, we finally arrived at Gold Beach. And where do you think we stopped first? Dr. Liem Family Dentistry.

The meeting with colleagues was an occasion of great joy. We were received with much warmth and love. We did not stay long because it was during working hours. It was enough for them to know we were in Gold Beach. Dr. Liem asked us to come back after work because he wanted to talk to us.

In the meantime, we met our friends, the Turlea family, who welcomed us and directed us to our motel room. We had a great time together, and we thanked them for inviting us and offering free accommodation.

The meeting with Dr. Liem was very emotional for me. One thought tormented me terribly: What if Dr. Liem would propose we come back?!

Although I longed to return to Gold Beach, the thought of another move made me shudder. Emil agreed with me. We prayed that the Lord would lead the discussion with Dr. Liem in harmony with His will.

I set out to be very reticent in this discussion and to let the Lord's will come true and not mine. After a brief presentation of the current situation in his office, highlighting the fact that after our departure, the team, being incomplete, did not work at optimal parameters, Dr. Liem urged us to come back. Both he and his team wholeheartedly wished for our return.

In those moments, a wise thought came to my mind: *The best place in the world is where you are desired.*

Finally, he presented to us the package of benefits waiting for us upon our returning to work. This was the most tangible way to express not only his desire to be together again but also the need to revitalize the workforce in his business.

I was in a big dilemma. Emil, out of love for me, granted me free will, and thus, I would seal my own fate. A Romanian saying flashed through my mind: *"Life is the most difficult school because you never know what grade you're in, what test you're taking, and you can't even cheat because your test is different from all of the others"* (J. Dryden).

My desire to get rid of the nightmare of Hot Springs and return to the place where I worked for nine years and had been loved and appreciated overcame all the disadvantages of a new move.

Dr. Liem offered us free and unlimited housing on his property, as well as a place to store our belongings. His mother, Ina, had a big and beautiful house, where we could settle and where we would be received with much love. The thought that I was escaping the unbearable climate of Arkansas, that I would go to work with the feeling that I belonged to that place, gave me wings.

I took the courage and said YES! with all my heart.

The critical moment was over. The next day, the good news was received with great enthusiasm both at the office and at church.

After a four-day mini-vacation, with our batteries recharged and our souls refreshed, we returned home to Hot Springs and put the house up for sale. Friends at church did not know what to think. They did not understand why we were moving, because we never complained about our problems.

A few days later, Dr. Liem informed me that he had booked my trip and that he expected me to return to work in two weeks. My schedule was already filled with patients awaiting my return to the office. There was no time to waste.

On the first day of work after vacation, before resuming work, I went to Dr. E.S. and officially announced my resignation, giving him two weeks' notice. This news was like a hammer blow for him. He refused to believe what he heard and told me we had to talk after hours.

THE MYSTERIES OF PROVIDENCE

At the end of the day, he called me to his office and asked why I had made this hasty decision. Without going into details, I told him why I decided to quit. Between the lines, he could read my frustration at the fact that I was not welcome in his office. Deeply saddened, he was trying to buy some time to remedy the situation.

He promised that in time things would change, but I made it clear that I made up my mind, and I was adamant in my decision. Another heavy burden was lifted from my heart, and I thanked the Lord for giving me the boldness to stand firm on my position.

The last days of work seemed shorter than ever. The countdown had begun. For me, the work atmosphere was no longer tense, despite the oppressive silence floating in the air. The thought of my soon liberation was very comforting to my troubled soul.

No one asked me anything except the girl at the front desk, who had attended the interview and wanted to know why I was leaving. Karla was stressed because she had to find another assistant in my place. Once, when I went to the reception desk, she was sorting job applications. I could not help but notice that she was bent over the trash can, tearing a piece of paper and muttering: "Overqualified!" When I looked closer, it was a résumé.

Now I understood why I could not fit in this place: I was overqualified, and she did not want competition. Hence, her aversion toward me from the first day I showed up at work without her consent.

I reconstructed the scene of my first visit at the office and remembered that on that day, Dr. E.S. was present when I submitted my résumé, and I was called for an interview at the end of the day. My misfortune was that my résumé did not get in her hands; otherwise, I would have qualified for the trash.

I thanked the Lord for solving the dilemma and helping me understand the real cause of my colleagues' hostility toward me. There was only one fault of mine. Very simple. I was overqualified.

From now on, I was not frustrated about anything. I felt free as a bird, soaring to the sky, and could not wait to take my flight to the West Coast.

My last day of work at Dr. E.S.'s was the shortest and the easiest. All the staff was gathered in a working meeting, which I did not have to attend. A business evaluation committee had come, and no patients had been scheduled for this particular day.

I worked alone in the back room, and I was at ease. As always, I put my heart and soul into everything I did, and at the end, I went to say goodbye to everyone.

> **There was only one fault of mine. Very simple. I was overqualified.**

It was known to be my last day of work. I shyly opened the door to the conference room, and without entering, I waved goodbye to everybody. Immediately, Dr. E.S. got up and came out after me. He accompanied me to the door and, with a sad face, addressed me a short but pointed statement:

"Elena, I'm really sorry to let you go! You are leaving a sweet aroma behind you. Thank you for your impact on my practice!"

I left that place with teary eyes but with a grateful heart that God pulled me out of this painful experience.

From now on, I started counting the days until my flight to Oregon. Emil and I had to pack almost everything before leaving. After that, all the burdens would be on his shoulders—selling the house, loading things, and the long journey alone with a heavy load behind him.

I also packed my luggage, not knowing how long we would be separated from each other. On the last Sabbath, I said goodbye to my friends at church. I was especially attached to Alex and Sigilda, a very nice couple whom we felt very close to. We got a lovely card from them as an encouragement that our coming to Hot Springs was not in vain. Here is a brief statement that gave us the assurance that God had a purpose in sending us to Arkansas:

"We hope you don't forget your investments in Hot Springs. Eternal investments ... time, energy, generosity, smiles, hands outstretched for better or worse in meeting the needs of others...."

***

The day of my departure had come. Emil took me to the airport in Little Rock, and from there, I was to fly to Oregon.

The parting was dramatic. Especially because we had an unknown future ahead of us. We had no idea when we would see each other again. Emil would be left alone with unresolved problems.

I knew where I was going, and from this point of view, I was the happiest. But much of my soul would remain in Hot Springs attached to Emil's soul. The most painful moment was at the airport when I disappeared beyond the checkpoint, and Emil was left alone. He later confessed to me that, after I had disappeared from his sight, he withdrew to a corner and, with tears of pain, prayed for me and for our soon reunion.

When he returned home, he felt lonely in an empty house, with the moving boxes piled up in the middle of the living room.

Emil and I were now so far from each other. We entrusted ourselves to God's care, waiting for His divine intervention in our lives. For better or worse.

I arrived safely at my destination. I was met at the airport by Marcia, Adolph, and Ina, all three trustworthy friends from church. I had the best conditions in Ina's house. Having no means of transportation, I was going to work with Dr. Liem and Ina, who was helping her son with office work.

At work, I was warmly received by my colleagues. My "coming home" was a day of celebration for Dr. Liem and his team. A long list of patients had been waiting for my return. I was glad to see these precious people to whom I was emotionally attached and who were longing for my return.

Although I was very busy at work, my thoughts were with Emil in his loneliness. He called me every night and kept me posted with the news regarding the sale of the house. We had been warned that in Arkansas, houses do not sell easily, and our faith would be heartily tested. From the past experiences, we knew that with God, all things were possible and continued to trust in His loving care.

At the beginning of October, two months after my departure, Emil called up and gave me the most exciting news: "The house has been sold!" Praise the Lord!

Our joy was boundless. Soon, very soon, we would be together again.

Then, Emil rented the moving truck and, with Alex's help, loaded it and hitched his car behind it.

We prayed fervently for God's protection on the road. He had a long way to go, and being by himself made him feel insecure. His only hope was in God Almighty, our strength and our shield in times of trouble.

Soon after he hit the road, something very strange was happening. Each time when he was passing over little bumps, the truck was shaking, and over larger bumps, was losing direction. Emil was terrified and could hardly recover. He realized that this vehicle had a technical problem that could not be solved on the road. If he would ask for help from the rental company, another truck would be sent to him, and he would not be able to transfer the heavy load to the new one.

He pulled off the road and prayed that the Lord would show him what to do. He took courage and set off again, being very careful and praying all the time.

The moments of shaking and unbalance were as numerous as all bumps on the road. It was a permanent terror that demanded maximum precaution. And, of course, a lot of prayer and faith in divine protection.

At one point, the imbalance was so great that Emil lost control and crossed several lanes without any turn signal or hazard warning. All the cars around him stopped until he managed to regain control of the truck and pull it alongside the road.

I knew nothing about these troubles until he arrived at Gold Beach, totally exhausted.

We thanked God for helping Emil cope with the incredible stress and preventing a horrible accident that could happen on the road during the five days of driving under a lot of pressure.

He confessed to me how much he missed me and how much it would have mattered if I had been with him in this long nightmare on the road.

We unloaded all our belongings into Ina's garage and settled temporarily in her beautiful house on the top of the hill, twenty minutes from town.

After our return to Gold Beach, we were geographically closer to our children, Alina and Silviu, and decided to visit them in Sacramento. The meeting with our children was wonderful. We had the great pleasure to meet Alina, Silviu's wife, whom we learned to love as our own daughter as soon as she became a member of our family.

Since her diploma from Romania had to be validated, Alina understood that she had to work hard to become a dentist in America. First, she had to learn English and pass a difficult exam (TOFEL) before enrolling in the international program at the university. She knew some French, Spanish, and Italian, but not English. Speaking English had become mandatory in the family.

Alina learned English so well that she passed the exam in a rather short time. There was still a long way to go and a lot of hard work in order to pass the two exams for the National Board. The first part was general medicine and the second part was the dental exam.

Silviu was well-rooted at Intel. His priority was to help Alina, to provide her with the necessary material and optimal study conditions. Meanwhile, Alina had to adjust to family life as well as to American culture.

In order to get acquainted with the dental field specific to America, she decided to volunteer in a dental office. She was accepted as a volunteer at a dental office in Sacramento, where she worked for a while, after which she was offered a part-time paid job. In addition to individual study, she worked for a full year at this clinic.

Alina successfully passed the preliminary exams, thus qualifying for the university admission exams.

***

Once we moved back to Gold Beach, we started looking for property. In early January 2007, Karl, our agent, told us that he had found a piece of land for us, which we liked very much. It was out of town, in the woods, up the hill, not very close to the ocean, in a secluded and quiet place.

What we did not like was the price; it was a lot more than we could afford. We continued to pray while Karl continued to look for a reasonable piece of land for us. We were not in a hurry, as Dr. Liem wanted us to stay as long as possible with his mom, who enjoyed our company very much.

One day, in the middle of summer, Karl came to the office and asked to talk to me.

I suspected he had found something for us. And I was right. To my great surprise, he told me that the piece of land that we liked very much, but which was too expensive for us, was still for sale at a very low price—$48,000 less than the previous listing price. Exactly the price we offered in January when we first saw the land.

A little later, at the end of the day, I was called again to the lobby, where I was greeted by a stranger.

He introduced himself as the owner of the land. He confirmed what Karl had said to me and asked if we were still interested in buying it at our initial offer of $90,000.

The owner knew we had cash and wanted to finalize the transaction as soon as possible.

Thus, in a short time, we became owners in Gold Beach. We had no words to thank God for His divine intervention. Once again, we saw His hand at work on our behalf.

First, we needed to harvest the trees from the property. With the money obtained from the sale of the trees, we covered most of the costs of excavating and clearing the land.

In the meantime, we looked for a manufactured home, which Emil had already designed for our taste. The miracle was that we did not have to order one at the factory. When we visited the Homes Company, we found exactly the model we were looking for; moreover, we were given a $10,000 discount because the house had been on display as a model home for some time. The house was bigger and much nicer than all the others we had so far.

The Lord had wonderfully arranged all things for us in His time.

I need to mention another miracle we had been blessed with. In time, God healed Emil completely from the scar tissue growth that was pinching his spinal nerve, and thus, he became pain-free and capable of doing all kinds of physical work on our property.

He worked very hard to build a permanent foundation for our new home and a deck on the back of the house with a breathtaking mountain view. Also, he was able to do a lot of landscaping in order to beautify our new settlement.

On August 1, 2007, we moved into our home, just in time for our three weeks' vacation to move and settle at our new residence. A month later, our children, Silviu and Alina, visited us and we had a great time together.

Shortly after finishing our projects, including landscaping, we ordered the necessary equipment, and Emil set up a laboratory next to the house, where I could work after hours and on my free days from the office.

At Christmas, as our children announced that they would not come home, we thought of making someone happy by inviting him to our home. Bryan, one of Jesus' "most insignificant brothers," came to mind. He was a middle-aged man, homeless, with nothing but ragged, filthy clothes covering his tall, slender body. We knew him from the fellowship hall at the church. Almost every Sabbath, he came only for food, then went to his place under the Hunter Creek Bridge. I asked him what he needed, planning to give him some presents when he came to our home on Christmas Day.

Humbly, he told us that he needed a pillow and a clock. After we found out what size of shoes and clothes he wore, we bought a pair of leather boots, a thick wool sweater, a waterproof outfit and, of course, a pillow and a watch.

On Christmas Day, we went under the bridge and found him crouched under a large bush.

We invited him into the car and brought him home. Assuming that he needed to take a bath, I prepared the necessary things, and then I invited him to the bathroom. After a while, since he was not getting out, I sent Emil to see what was going on. The poor man had come out of the bathtub and tried to get dressed on his wet body without wiping off first. Emil helped him to come out of the bathroom dressed but not clean. He smelled even worse than before taking the bath. After he left, I found the white towel blackened with dirt, the brand-new bar of soap untouched, and the smell in the bathroom unbearable. I realized that Bryan had not actually washed himself, just softened the dirt on him.

He enjoyed the Christmas dinner with us, and although incoherent in his speech, he told us something about his mother, whom he barely remembered because he had not seen her in a long time.

We tried to tell him about God and His love toward each of us, and then we offered him our gifts. Everything suited him perfectly. With tears in his eyes and words of gratitude, Bryan confessed to us that the love with which we treated him he had received only from his mother. We were glad we made him happy. At least for a while.

The following Sabbath, Bryan came to the fellowship hall as usual, but still in his rags, holding in his arms the new boots, clothes, and everything else we had given him for Christmas.

He came to us and, with a sad face, he returned the gifts to us, saying that he did not like them, that he did not feel good in them, and that actually, he did not need them.

Deeply saddened by Bryan's refusal to accept our gifts, we took the things back, and he quickly disappeared from our sight. We realized that he was not used to these "luxury items," and he felt more comfortable in his shabby clothes.

Shortly afterward, we read in the newspaper that a homeless man was found dead, frozen under the Hunter Creek Bridge. It was our Bryan, who never showed up at the Sabbath fellowship meal after he returned the presents.

Don't we do the same with God's grace?

How often we reject His gift of salvation and refuse to allow Him to cleanse us and exchange our filthy rags with His robe of love and compassion!

> **We realized that he was not used to these "luxury items," and he felt more comfortable in his shabby clothes.**

At the end of the year, after a retrospective look at the events of 2007, we had only words of praise and thanksgiving for the wonderful way in which God guided us and overwhelmed us with His blessings.

Along with a gift received from Dr. Liem and his family, we also found the following words written on the Christmas card:

Dearest Elena & Emil,

What a blessing to have both of you helping in my office. Always smiling and portraying God's character at the workplace. We love you both. Special thanks from my mother, who appreciates your care, love, and patience toward her.

May God bless you both in the coming year!

Love,

The Liems.

***

GREAT PERFORMANCES—DRAMATIC CHANGES

Alina found 2008 was a most challenging year. She was ready to register for the admission exam at the university. Competition was very high at the international dental program, with 500 candidates per ten seats. To make sure she did not miss a year, Alina decided to enroll for the exam at three universities: Loma Linda University, UCLA (University of California Los Angeles), and San Francisco University.

It was not easy to take three difficult exams at these prestigious universities in a short period of time. The news that Alina passed the exam at Loma Linda University overwhelmed us. Our joy as a family was

THE MYSTERIES OF PROVIDENCE

boundless. Her hard work had been fully rewarded. Our prayers had been answered. Praise the Lord!

We soon received two more amazing pieces of news from Alina. She had passed the exams at Los Angeles University as well as San Francisco University. We were all very proud of our daughter and her amazing performances. We were expecting radical changes in our family over the next two years when Alina would complete her education and get her license to practice dentistry in America.

We were already settled at our new home in Gold Beach, and we were very happy that everything was going well. I was also happy to work in my new laboratory. We had a wonderful summer until the day we got a call from Silviu, informing us that he was hired by Hewlett Packard Corporation. He would start his new job in Texas in one month. Dark clouds, with gloomy premonitions, darkened our horizon.

It was a done deal, and we could do nothing about it. They decided that Alina would enroll at UCLA, having a direct flight from Houston-Los Angeles, even though she had already reserved her seat at Loma Linda University. Silviu would begin his new job, thus easing the financial burden of the family. Especially since Alina had to borrow over $200,000 for her tuition.

Both Alina and Silviu would face radical changes. Alina as a student, far from home, and Silviu adjusting to a new job, a new climate much different from the one in California, and mostly being so far away from his wife.

For two years, until Alina's graduation, Silviu was split between Houston and Los Angeles. The new job allowed him to leave for a period of time, running his business from a distance. On her birthday, in her first year of school, Silviu surprised Alina by buying her a new car, a Volkswagen Jetta.

Silviu's success was remarkable at his new job. At a meeting with the leaders of the HP Corporation, Silviu stood out in a special way, astonishing his superiors, not only for his vast knowledge but for his personality marked by his upbringing, in stark contrast to those of his generation.

At the end of each year, our son sent us a review from HP that thrilled our hearts. Below is just a summary of a few of them:

Employee Performance Review.

Silviu joined HP and HRIT in 2008 as a Business Analyst in Roseville, CA—after 7 years in key roles supporting customer facing programs for Intel Corporation.

During his 5-year tenure in HRIT, Silviu has played key roles in several large-scale worldwide programs.

2011 was another great year for Silviu. He demonstrated leadership in managing different projects.

He executed against FY 11 goals and was recognized with two pinnacle awards for innovation in several key projects.

Silviu wore multiple hats and demonstrated leadership in areas of project planning by contributing to the foundation of what would become the standard project planning template to use in FY 12.

As a reward, Silviu was chosen to continue and lead the LDSM project into FY12 which has an overall targeted cost savings to HP of $250m.

Here is what his manager had to say about his performance in 2013:

2013 was another successful and productive year for Silviu, offering many opportunities to excel, learn, develop and deliver.

Silviu was awarded Q2 CIO Excellence for exemplifying leadership qualities on the LDSM project.

Silviu is an Excellent PM (Project manager) and a strong Solution Manager. He has great organizational and planning skills, is very customer oriented, and is well regarded by his team and business partners (we received feedback from RT Systems that said they rated Silviu the highest of anyone in IT).

His other key strengths are: analytic skills, process methodologies, teaching / consulting, communication skills and meeting management.

He is a leader and a motivator and always displays a positive attitude that is contagious. I would like to thank Silviu again for all his help and support this year, and wish him a great 2014!

***

A PLEASANT SURPRISE IN ROMANIA

In the summer of 2009, Emil and I decided to visit Romania to see our relatives and friends again.

One Friday night, Emil and I had the opportunity to visit one of the new churches built after the collapse of Communism in Romania.

We did not expect to know anyone there. We were told that the members were mostly new converts after the revolution when the gates of religious freedom in our country were widely opened.

We arrived a little late, after the opening of the program. The church was full. We thought we would sneak in unnoticed and occupy our seat on the last row.

However, we noticed a familiar face on the platform. The guest speaker that evening was one of our friends, Othniel, a pastor from Loma Linda. His presence surprised us because we did not expect to meet him in Romania.

As soon as we stepped into the sanctuary, the speaker was also surprised by our presence there and made a loud announcement: "We have some visitors from America, and we want to welcome them in our midst."

At the end, our American friend wanted to talk to us. While waiting for him, a young woman approached me with open arms, saying:

"Ms. Elena, Ms. Elena!"

Then, as she hugged me, she burst into tears.

"The Sabbath, Ms. Elena, the Sabbath!"

I froze. I did not understand what was going on. I did not know who the young woman was or what she meant about "the Sabbath …"

"But who are you?" I asked her, puzzled. "I'm sorry, but I don't know you."

"I'm Mia, your colleague from Vidra!"

This time I burst into tears, hugged her, and I could not let go.

Mia's presence in the Adventist church astonished me. "You're Mia!!! What brought you here, my dear?" I asked in bewilderment.

"The Sabbath, Ms. Elena! You did not come to work even once in more than eighteen years of working together at Vidra. You kept the Sabbath faithfully all those years, and I was wondering why you were so adamant about not working on Saturday. Remember how I asked you why you were keeping Saturday instead of Sunday and how you explained to me the fourth commandment of the Decalogue? And each time I was asking questions, you always gave me clear, plausible answers straight from the Bible. After you left the country, I decided to search the Bible on my own, and thus, I was convinced that you were right. Then, I started looking for the Seventh-day Adventist Church you told me about. After an in-depth study of the whole doctrine of this church, based on the Bible alone, I was baptized, and here I am. I prayed to the Lord, if it was His will, to see Ms. Elena again before seeing her in heaven. And behold, the Lord heard my prayer and sent you tonight to this church."

Indeed, our coming to this church was not a coincidence. Overwhelmed by the mysterious ways of God's workings in our lives, I became deeply interested in renewing my friendship with Mia after twenty-two years of separation through my living in America. Spending time with her during our stay in Romania, I learned that Mia was a devoted Seventh-day Adventist, and she had a great impact on her family, raising her three daughters in the church.

Mia's conversion, following my departure to America, was another stark evidence of the amazing way God had turned an apparent failure in my life into a great victory. The bitter experience of losing my first job in Rosiori was allowed by Him not only for my own benefit but for His own glory. Two precious souls had been won for the kingdom: the lady from my home church, then another one in my new workplace, Vidra. Indeed, our God is an awesome God.

***

TALKING WITH DR. LEONARD BAILEY

"Mom, I talked to Dr. Bailey a while ago and told him about my hepatitis C problem. He promised to speak to his colleague, who is a specialist in liver diseases, and ask for his opinion on my case. Today, I found out that I was scheduled for a consultation with this doctor, who wants to see me. I'll fly to Loma Linda in two weeks."

I was amazed how Silviu managed to speak directly with such an outstanding personality in the medical world, Dr. Leonard Bailey.

I think Silviu dared to call him by virtue of our friendship with this honored family from the time when I was their housekeeper.

His wife Nancy, a wonderful woman, helped us tremendously, especially in obtaining our residence in America. Their children, Connor and Bruce, loved to play with Silviu when, with Nancy's permission, I took my son with me to work. We still remained friends, even after our move to Oregon.

I was eagerly awaiting a favorable response from the expert.

After his appointment with the liver specialist at Loma Linda Hospital, unfortunately, Silviu gave us the worst news. The sub-type of hepatitis C, specific to patients from Europe, is the most difficult to address. It does not respond to Interferon nor to a liver transplant.

He did not express his feelings regarding the verdict. And I hardly managed to hide my pain, trying to encourage my son to trust in divine intervention.

We continued to pray fervently for the Lord to have mercy on our son in his prime and help the scientists discover the cure for this relentless disease.

**

2011 was a remarkable year in our family: Alina's graduation. With boundless joy, we had anticipated this great festivity.

Alina's efforts to learn English in record time, training, and admission to three of the most prestigious universities in one year, graduating from the University of Los Angeles, all these incredible performances had placed her far above the common standards.

How difficult it must have been for her to adapt to the American education system, totally different from the one in Europe, only she can tell us.

It was not easy at all for Alina to be alone among foreigners, far from Silviu and the rest of the family, her parents, who were still in Romania at that time. And yet, she never complained about anything.

After graduation, Alina returned home to Houston and got a job as a dentist at a corporation. After a while, our kids were able to buy a beautiful home in a satellite town near Houston. A very nice place, resembling a park with lakes, water fountains, and lots of greenery.

**

Although I still had almost three years until retirement, I was thinking about the time when I would have to say goodbye to my profession and to those with whom I had collaborated throughout my career and with whom I was emotionally attached.

Just as I was planning to reduce the workload, I got a phone call from Dr. Westfall, a local dentist, who asked me if I would be willing to provide lab services for him.

The offer was appealing at the thought that in a few years, I would retire, and major changes would occur in our lives. We still had to pay the mortgage for our home, and we wanted to pay it off prior to my retirement.

The cooperation with Dr. Westfall was fruitful. He had complete confidence in me, and both he and his patients were delighted with the results.

My work was fully rewarded. I was sometimes happier than the patients after restoring them not only aesthetically and functionally but also emotionally. The new smile on their faces after replacing their missing teeth was my greatest joy.

> **The new smile on their faces after replacing their missing teeth was my greatest joy.**

Although I retired in 2013, I continued to work in the lab for both Dr. Liem and Dr. Westfall. It was much better for me after I reduced the workload. I had worked very hard my whole life, and it was time to slow down.

Both Emil and I had been involved in different voluntary activities at the local Adventist church in addition to other responsibilities we assumed after our transfer to this church.

As the church treasurer, Emil was highly appreciated each year by the auditor for 100 percent accuracy in his work. In addition, he was in charge of the operation and maintenance of the local Adventist church radio station, founded by Dr. Liem.

***

A NEW HOPE

The most important event of 2014 was Silviu deciding to enroll in a clinical trial. This was an experimental treatment of hepatitis C with stem cells, which would give hope for healing to those infected by the deadly virus. Although it did not guarantee healing, it was worth a try. Among other types of blood tests, a DNA test was performed after Silviu consented to be enrolled in the experimental trial. The treatment was easy to tolerate with no side effects. Silviu was able to continue working without any discomfort.

Periodically, he went for laboratory tests, and the results were promising. We prayed earnestly that the Lord would work another miracle in Silviu's life, according to His great mercy.

Silviu kept us updated with the lab results, and we continued to keep him in our prayers.

At the end of October 2014, he informed us that everything was going well and that he would finish the treatment in two weeks. A month later, he had another test. Anxiously, we looked forward to great news from our son.

***

November 13, 2014

A text message from Silviu brightened our day and renewed our hope. "Just got my results 5 minutes ago. The virus remains undetectable."

Oh, how glad we were for this amazing news! However, the final result after a year would be decisive.

We thanked the Lord from the bottom of our hearts and continued to pray for complete healing.

***

In the fall of 2014, Dr. Westfall informed me that he had sold his practice and would move out of Gold Beach. He assured me that the new dentist received the best references about me, and he was positive that I would continue to provide lab service for this dental clinic.

However, the new owner was a large corporation owned by the government, and I soon learned that the new dentist was affiliated with a specific dental lab network.

After finishing the pending cases, I said goodbye to Dr. Westfall and staff, knowing that God had a plan for us, and He would reveal it to us in His time.

Since Dr. Liem's lab workload had dropped gradually, we realized that our stay in Gold Beach was no longer profitable for us. Reserves were beginning to dwindle, and work in the laboratory had become thinner.

As in Elijah's case, the spring had dried up. Could this be the sign that we needed to move?

We began to pray earnestly for the Lord to help us understand what His plan was for us and to make wise choices to accomplish it.

Our goal was to become debt-free and move to an area with a warmer climate, where we could grow a garden and live a less stressful life.

The area that attracted us was Grants Pass. We were familiar with this region because we often went there for shopping and doctors' appointments. Land and houses were also much cheaper.

We put our wish before the Lord and waited for His intervention.

As we entered the winter, we knew the season was not good for selling the house. Waiting for the spring would be a better option.

One day, Emil heard the sound of heavy machinery on the property behind our house.

Curiosity pushed Emil to find out what was going on there. To his surprise, he saw that construction of a house had already begun.

He talked to the supervisor and gleaned some information about HiLine Homes, the company that was building the house.

When he returned home, we looked online and learned more about this company.

We focused on one of the smallest houses that would fit our budget. The price was much lower than we would have expected.

This was the first step in starting a huge project in which we relied on divine guidance.

We went to HiLine Homes to gather information, nothing else. Knowing that we were not ready to build a house since our home had to be sold first, we hesitated to get into details about our intention to engage in business with this company.

"No problem! We are here to help you," replied Scott, the man in charge of the contract work.

He explained to us in great detail the terms of the contract and the advantage of starting the project early enough to provide the necessary time for the architect to draw the blueprint of the house and submit it to City Hall for approval. The contract would be valid for one year. During this time, we would be able to sell the house and buy the land.

We stepped out in faith and decided to sign the contract after paying the $7,000 down payment.

We wanted to put the Lord to the test, and so we ventured to try selling the house on our own if indeed it was His will to sell it.

Emil took some pictures of our home and posted them on Craigslist along with the appropriate information.

It was January 2015. The worst time to sell houses.

One day, we received an advertisement from a company that would put our house for sale on MLS (Multiple Listing Sale) across America for only $99.

We could not believe it. It was too good to be true.

Shortly after sending the money, with our permission, this company transferred our home pictures from Craigslist to their list.

After a few days, we checked online and recognized our home posted on MLS. Unbelievable!

The biggest surprise, though, came a few days later when we got a call from someone in Portland.

"Hello, my name is Angela. I saw your house for sale, and I really liked it. I also have my house on the market, and after I sell it, I will contact you."

We did not have high expectations from this client. We were glad, however, that the advertising was working.

We left this matter in God's hands and decided to pray for His will to be done on our behalf.

In mid-March, Emil and I went to visit my sister, Viorica, in Southern California. After a week, we got an unknown phone call.

"Hello! My name is Cathy; I'm from the Gold Beach Real Estate Agency. I have a client who wants to see your house."

We were very surprised by this good news and prepared to return home. A few days later, at the appointed time, the agent and her client appeared at our doorstep.

After taking the tour of the house, the client pulled me aside while Cathy was talking to Emil and whispered to me, "I really like your house, and I want to buy it."

I thanked her, and out of curiosity, I asked her, "Are you Angela?"

"Yes, I'm Angela!"

Cathy was stunned. I tried to hide my emotions even though I was overwhelmed by such an unexpected surprise.

"How do you know each other?" asked Cathy in bewilderment.

The agent did not know about my encounter over the phone with her client three months prior.

And she kept her word; only she did not call us directly. Since she was determined to buy our house, she wanted to have an agent to facilitate the transaction.

A few hours later, we received an email from Angela that confirmed once again her decision to buy the house.

While Cathy would take care of her business, Emil and I started to pack things up, and in the meantime, looked online for a property around Grants Pass.

We would have liked to find a place in the country, but we could not afford it. What we needed was a smaller piece of land with access to all utilities.

Emil picked up some addresses from the Internet. Among other things, we saw a vacant lot almost on the outskirts of Grants Pass with street utilities. What attracted us most was a nearby large green area that looked like a park. We like to walk in nature every day, so this would be the ideal place for us.

We went to Grants Pass to check out all the properties from the Google map. We did not like any of them except the one we had already set our eyes on. It was only a few minutes away from a beautiful park along the Rogue River, Reinhart Park.

Although we liked this lot, we let the Lord decide for us.

Our buyer had problems with the lender, a bank that required all sorts of inspections and imposed very strict conditions.

One of these conditions was to have an earthquake protection system installed under the house. We were not asked to do so when we installed the house on the property. Earthquake installation is not mandatory in the state of Oregon.

We flatly refused such a claim and decided to hire Karl to handle this transaction on our behalf. Things were delayed, and we were willing to resign the deal. Our potential buyers, however, did not want to give up. They had accepted the asking price from the start without trying to negotiate it. So, they decided to change lenders.

Everything seemed to be going well.

The documents were submitted to escrow, and we were told that in three weeks, on June 1, 2015, we would close.

We panicked because we did not expect things to go so fast. We were facing two major problems: finding a place to store our belongings and finding a rental for us to live in until the construction project was completed.

For both, we needed to submit two months ahead and have our name on a waiting list.

We started making phone calls every day, just in case something came up.

Time passed, and nothing could be seen on the horizon.

We decided to go to Grants Pass in person and take an interest in all the storage facilities where we had signed up on the waiting list.

Invariably, we were getting the same answer: "You have to wait. We'll call you when it's your turn."

Eventually, we went to Merlin, just a few miles from Grants Pass, and there was one unit available and just the size we needed. It had been vacated just minutes prior. We rented the unit and returned home praising God for this blessing.

The problem with a house rental remained unresolved. We called friends and acquaintances in the area, and everyone told us this was a very thorny issue, and the chances of finding something in such a short time were slim. We were not discouraged, knowing that the Lord would take care of us.

CHAPTER 10
GOODBYE TO THE OCEAN!

"He has made everything beautiful in its time." (Eccles. 3:11)

The nostalgia of parting from the ocean again grieved my soul. The ocean witnessed my pains, swallowing in silence the tears I wanted hidden from human eyes.

Before leaving Gold Beach, I wanted to go once more to the beach and write there my unfulfilled dreams so that after my departure, they would be washed away by the waves and thrown into the sea. We only had three days until leaving Gold Beach. We were exhausted both physically and emotionally. We still did not know where we would stay after arriving in Grants Pass and where we would live until our new home was built.

We had scheduled the loading of our household belongings for Friday, May 29, to set off on Sunday, May 31. On June 1, we were to close, then hand over the keys to the new owner.

On Thursday, Emil rented a U-Haul of the largest size and started loading it on Friday morning. We hired a young man to help us, and our neighbors, Ron and Jean, offered to help arrange the furniture and boxes inside the truck. I focused on gathering the last things that we would use during our temporary stay until we moved to a new house. It was difficult for me to sort things out. I had to be careful to remember what I put in the boxes, and label them accordingly.

We set aside a futon instead of a bed to sleep on in our rental. It was to be loaded and towed on a trailer attached to the small car, which I had to drive.

While we were in the fever of packing, we received a call from Karl, our real estate agent, informing us that some problems had arisen, and the lender would not provide the money until June 11th. He suggested that we could continue with the move and return on the date set for closing. We had already rented the truck and decided to go ahead with the moving.

On Friday night, before sunset, the loading was done. Both Emil and I were wiped out. For the past two weeks, we had not slept more than four hours a night.

The only unresolved issue was where we would stay. We waited for the Lord to tell us what He had prepared for us. Would we have to stay in a hotel? If so, for how long?

Shortly before the beginning of the Sabbath, the telephone rang.

"Hello, Elena! This is Sharon Hyatt. When are you moving? Did you find a place to stay?"

"Yes, Sharon, we're moving on Sunday morning! But we still don't know where we will stay. We couldn't find anything to rent."

"We have thought of you," Sharon continued, "and decided to offer you accommodation in our son Bob's house until you find a place elsewhere. He no longer lives in that house. If it suits you, you can stay there as long as you need."

Upon hearing this unexpected news, I burst into tears. I was not able to control my emotions, not even to tell Sharon how happy I was with the news I received. I was exhausted from stress, lack of sleep, and overwork.

"Elena, if it doesn't suit you, no problem. It's just a proposal," Sharon added modestly.

"Oh, Sharon! You can't imagine how happy you made us," I replied immediately. "This is the answer to our prayers. The Lord has inspired you to come to our aid. Praise be His name!"

We already knew the place where we would be hosted because we had visited Bob Jr. years ago. He had a large, beautiful house that was almost empty after he moved to Brookings. The Hyatt family was very special to us. They had always been willing to help us each time we were facing complicated situations. However, at this time, we did not ask for their help. Their kindness overwhelmed us. We breathed a sigh of relief, and the Sabbath was like an oasis for our weary souls. We saw God's hand at work and were very grateful for His intervention on our behalf.

Our last Sabbath at church was emotionally charged not only for us but also for our friends. Before parting, we took pictures together and said goodbye to everyone. In a farewell card, our friends laid out special thoughts for us.

Dr. Herman Liem, my former employer and my mentor from whom I learned a lot in the dental art, also had something to say.

These were the last words he wrote to Emil and me at our last meeting at church.

Indeed, the last ones!

Dear Emil and Elena,

We will miss you for sure! Certainly, there will be two gaps left in the church that cannot be filled. We know that you will also be a blessing wherever you go.

Come and visit us as often as possible. You will have a place to stay.

You will always be in our hearts!

Herman Liem

Just three days after we moved from Gold Beach, we received the shocking news that Dr. Liem had suffered a stroke and was being airlifted to a hospital in Eugene. We prayed fervently for the Lord to save him from death, and, by His mercy, Herman survived the multiple strokes he suffered on the way to the hospital. He partially recovered after a long period of intensive therapy.

***

In the evening, after the Sabbath, I began to gather the last things so that we could get up the next morning and set off for Grants Pass.

> **The Sabbath was like an oasis for our weary souls.**

My biggest fear was that I would not be able to drive on Highway 199 with its winding road. I was horrified because of the accidents we had suffered in the previous years. I also had to tow a trailer in which we had loaded the futon and everything we needed at our temporary residence. Being so tired, I was afraid I would fall asleep behind the wheel. Emil was going to drive the U-Haul filled to the top. The experience of moving from Arkansas made him shiver. What if this vehicle also had mechanical problems?!

On Sabbath evening, when it was already dark, Emil wanted to check once again if everything was in order with the U-Haul.

When he opened the cab door, he noticed a pool of black fluid on the floor on the driver's side.

He immediately realized that something was wrong. On Thursday, when he rented the vehicle, everything looked good. He had not noticed anything that caught his attention in particular.

We needed to contact the company and report the problem. I was on the phone all night. It was the weekend, and we had great difficulty connecting with someone. After we reported the problem, we were clearly told that we were not allowed to move the vehicle from its place. As we were in a rural area, it would be very difficult to find a specialist who would come to assess the problem and give us the necessary help.

The best solution would be to transfer the load to another U-Haul. When they found out that we had rented the largest size, we were told they did not have such a large one in our area, and they would send two smaller ones instead.

This proposal scared us. Transferring such a huge load would have been a nightmare. We no longer had the help to start all over. And, more than that, who was going to drive the second moving vehicle? In an adamant tone, I refused the offer.

"Such a thing is unacceptable. Is there any other solution?"

"No!" The gentleman firmly replied. "Anyway, you'll have to wait until tomorrow."

Our night of rest turned into a nightmare. The thought that after a night of sleeplessness and stress, I would not be able to drive obsessed me.

Sunday, late in the afternoon, the specialist arrived. After a brief assessment, he told us the vehicle must be emptied and taken to repair. We flatly refused the proposal.

Then, by God's grace, he came with another possibility. He found a towing company from Grants Pass that offered to tow the loaded truck and take it to its destination.

I jumped for joy! The double blessing was, I did not have to drive the small car with the trailer behind, and Emil did not have to drive the U-Haul either.

The promise of Romans 8:28 came to my mind again: *"All things work together for good to those who love God."*

Now, we could sleep one more night in our house. The last one. We slept very well, although we lay on the floor on an air mattress because the futon was already loaded.

The next day, June 1, 2015, Caveman Towing towed our truck and took it directly to the storage unit we had rented a few days prior in Merlin.

Praise God! Our move to Grants Pass was the easiest possible. Our friends, Bob Hyatt and his nephew, helped us unload the U-Haul. Then we settled into our temporary residence, and we really liked the place. The house was located on top of a hill, in the heart of nature from where we could see in a panoramic image the picturesque Grants Pass surrounded by mountains and watered by the famous Rogue River. Bob, the owner, offered us unlimited housing in exchange for a decent rent.

The next day we went to see the land we spotted on Google some time ago. The sale sign was still there. Through a real estate agency, we made an offer that was accepted. Since the closing of the sale in Gold Beach was postponed to June 11, we called our friends and asked them if they could lend us, for a short term, the money we needed to buy the land. Without hesitation, they deposited the necessary amount in our account, and, in a few days, we became land owners in Grants Pass.

When we went back to Gold Beach to close with escrow, a thought came to our mind: to stop by the U-Haul Rental Company and let them know about our trouble with the defective moving truck. Without expecting compensation, we got a full refund of the rental fee.

What else could we say? The Lord turned an apparent misfortune into the greatest blessing. Praised be His name!

***

GRANTS PASS—A NEW BEGINNING

2015 was a very eventful year that culminated with our move to Grants Pass and the building of the house where we set out to spend the twilight of our pilgrim life.

Even though the moving was quite adventurous, we thanked God for His wonderful interventions in our lives.

On the first Sabbath after the move, we visited the Seventh-day Adventist Church in Grants Pass, where we were well received as visitors.

Although we had visited this church in the past, we did not expect to recognize anyone here. We sat in the back row, and not long after, a lady who seemed familiar to me sat down next to us. I remembered meeting her as a health educator at a seminar many years prior. We were invited to her home, and that is how we made our first friends at this new church, Marcella Lynch and her husband, Jack.

First impressions mattered. As such, it did not take us long to choose the Grants Pass Seventh-day Adventist church as our church family.

In October, Marcella, as the leader of a cooking class organized by the church, invited me to participate in this event, and I gladly accepted the invitation.

One day, while I was helping her in the kitchen, I got a phone call from Silviu.

"Mom, I received the final result from the lab one year after finishing the treatment. The virus has completely disappeared. I'm cured of hepatitis C!"

I cannot articulate how I felt when my son gave me this most wonderful news! I had been waiting fifteen years to hear those words. This was the second miracle by which the Lord saved our son from certain death. We would be eternally grateful to Him, and we will never forget the many miracles He has done in our lives.

I wanted to shout for joy, for everyone to know what a wonderful God we serve. My heart burst into a song of thanksgiving: *"Sing aloud to God our strength; Make a joyful shout to the God of Jacob" (Ps. 81:1). "Oh, that men would give thanks to the Lord for His goodness, And for His wonderful works to the children of men! Let them sacrifice the sacrifices of thanksgiving, And declare His works with rejoicing" (Ps. 107:21–22).*

I could not wait to talk to Emil and share with him this wonderful news. We rejoiced together and thanked our Heavenly Father for the miraculous healing of our son. From now on, our fears were forever dispelled, and we could see the future from a new perspective. There was a future for our son!

***

The time had come for us to prepare the land for the building project. We were responsible for preparing the house pad, as well as digging the necessary ditches for the sewage system, water, and electricity.

We contacted two companies for an estimate, and the quotes were between $5,000 and $7,000.

Emil remembered the Copeland Company, which ten years previous, had helped us with a similar project in Merlin. We went to their office, and there we met Steve, a very nice gentleman who came to the site for evaluation.

On this occasion, we found out that Steve was the owner of this company. We were impressed by his kindness and desire to help us. He inspired a lot of confidence, and we agreed to start the job as soon as possible.

The next day he called us to the office and presented us with the list of the proposed works and the estimated cost. When we saw this list, we were amazed. Especially after reading the comments at the bottom of the price list:

Dear Emil & Elena,

Since you are such very nice people, we will do the work items on a time & material basis, and hopefully save some $.

Please keep in mind that I have tried to be certain that we can complete each of these for the amount listed.

Total ... $3,175

Incredible! This estimate exceeded our expectations. We had no words to thank Steve for his kindness toward us. Once again, we saw the Lord's hand in this transaction.

Later on, we learned that Steve Copeland's company was one of the most prestigious in this area, and we felt blessed to do business with him.

The work started much sooner than we expected and was completed before the set time.

One evening, after we returned from the construction site, we received a phone call from our friends, who wanted to know how the work was progressing. Among other things, they asked us if we needed some money. We thanked them for the offer and told them we did not want to borrow money because we did not want to owe anyone anything.

Little did we know at the time that many other unforeseen expenses would arise along the way, and we would not have the necessary funds.

However, they insisted. "We want to help you. It's good to have some spare money. What do you think? How about $15,000?"

Their proposal simply baffled us.

"Definitely, NO! We cannot afford such a loan that will burden us in the long run."

"No problem! We will not give you a deadline for returning the money. You will return it when you can."

With much hesitation, we accepted the offer and thanked our friends for their kindness toward us.

The next day, the promised amount was deposited into our bank account. Such a thought had never crossed our minds. We thanked the Lord for such an unexpected blessing.

The construction project was completed shortly before the end of the year. Thus, on December 31, 2015, after the final inspection, we were able to move into our new home.

Our joy and gratitude to God could not be humanly described.

***

GREAT IS THE LORD!

"Remember to magnify His work, Of which men have sung." (Job 36:24)

The New Year, 2016, found us at our new home, happy and satisfied with this great accomplishment. We have fondly remembered the wonderful way the Lord has guided us over the years and especially in the year 2015.

We wondered what surprises the Lord had prepared for us this year!

> **We wondered what surprises the Lord had prepared for us this year!**

One month later, in February, we received an envelope in the mail from Volkswagen. Inside we found two cards worth $500 each. They were "loyalty cards." From the attached explanatory note, we understood that we were honored with this amount of money for our loyalty to Volkswagen.

It sounded strange to us. We were in possession of a VW we bought a few years ago, and we owned another VW ten years ago. Were we considered loyal to this company because we bought this car model twice?

We were not going to refuse the cards because we did not understand the reason behind the gift. The money was welcome, and we thanked the Lord for this pleasant surprise.

The mild and calm winter of 2016 was followed by a beautiful spring. We managed to make many improvements to our property, turning it from a vacant lot full of weeds into a small botanical garden.

***

May 24, 2016

A sunny day, greeted by the spring breeze, invited us outside. It was the month of flowers. The air vibrated with the chirping of birds and the humming of bees. The trees displayed their multi-colored crowns, bathed in the silver rays of the sun at its zenith.

After a leisurely walk in the park, we were returning home, animated by thoughts of gratitude for our Creator, the author of the beautiful nature surrounding us.

When we got home, Emil went straight to the computer, and I resumed my household chores. Suddenly, he grabbed my attention, wanting to show me something exciting. When I looked at the screen, I saw a car.

Nothing new. This is one of my husband's passions, and he often enjoys looking at all kinds of cars online.

"Look at this car, Elena! It was put up for sale twenty minutes ago. It's a silver Prius, our favorite color, with only 68,000 miles on it. It looks new, and it is only $6,800. And it's right here in Medford."

"So what? We have a pretty good car; we don't need another one," I replied indifferently.

Emil was contemplating selling the Volkswagen and buying a hybrid car, maybe even a Prius like the one we had lost in the accident ten years ago.

"It's an economical car, and it benefits us!" added Emil, trying to stir up my interest in the matter.

This was the strong argument with which Emil justified his interest in such a car. But I did not see how such a thing would be feasible since we had no money for the second car.

Emil was convinced that this time he would see his dream come true. And trying to allure me, he added, "Let's call to see if the car is still available! At this price, with such low mileage, it won't stay long on the market".

"And if it hasn't been sold, how does it help? We don't have the money to buy it," I replied, trying to bring Emil to his senses.

"That's my problem. You don't have to worry, Elena!"

I called the owner, hoping that the car was already sold and Emil would take his mind off this bargain.

However, to my surprise, the car had not been sold. Emil, in the background, insisted on asking if we could go see it tomorrow.

"Certainly!" The owner's daughter, who handled the transaction, replied.

Said and done!

The next day we were going to Medford to see the car. I could not recognize Emil in this state! He was always cautious and did not plunge into any business until he had the money available. I was burning with curiosity to see what was going to happen.

"And if you like the car?" I asked him sarcastically.

"Wait, and you'll see!" he replied.

The next moment Emil made a phone call to our friends. I walked away, not wanting to hear such a conversation. I totally disagreed with Emil's audacity to ask these friends for money. It was enough that they had remitted us such a big debt. After a brief conversation with our friends, Emil gave me the most exciting news:

"We got the money. If we like the car, we will have $7,000 in our bank account the next day."

I was outraged that, for the first time, Emil was deciding on his own, against my will. We had always agreed in our plans and decisions in everything we had undertaken in family life. However, I hoped that the Lord would not let us make a mistake and then regret our hasty decision.

The next day, we were at the scene. The car and the ninety-eight-year-old owner, along with his daughter, were waiting for us at the appointed place and time.

As Emil examined the car, I prayed that the Lord would open his eyes so that he may see any flaws that would make him change his mind and return home at peace. But the car looked impeccable. It passed all the tests, Emil was satisfied, and the deal was made with only a $200 down payment. A few days later, we became the owner of the Prius and thanked God for fulfilling Emil's dream in an amazing way.

We were going to return the borrowed amount to our friends as soon as our VW was sold.

Blue Book estimated our car at $7,000, exactly the amount of money we needed to pay off our debt.

The next day, we started preparing our VW for sale.

Meanwhile, on their walk to the park, our neighbors, Pastor John Witcombe and his wife Sharon, while passing by our house, noticed the new car in our garage. They stopped, and Pastor John asked Emil, "Emil, did you get a new car? I see a new one in your garage."

"Yes, we did!" Emil replied happily and invited our friends to see our new car.

Seeing that we were detailing the old car, he asked Emil, "What's your plan with the VW?"

"We want to sell it," Emil answered enthusiastically.

"No!! Don't sell it!" Pastor John prompted him.

Both Emil and I looked at him puzzled, not understanding what he meant. Of course, Pastor John did not know that we had bought the car with borrowed money and that we were in a hurry to sell it to pay our debt.

Then, because he also had the same car model, he briefly explained to us that our car was part of the VW TDI 2009–2015 series of cars, in which the computer program was modified to falsify the pollution rate. That violated US standards imposed by the Environmental Protection Agency, and thus, the US government, through the EPA, had sued the VW Corporation.

Later, Pastor John sent Emil a site where he could register the car, and VW would keep him informed of what to do in the future. A few days later, we received the confirmation online that our car fell into the category of those involved in the dispute, and eventually, it would be bought back by the VW Company.

We waited for the trial to end and find out what the court's decision would be in this litigation of international proportions.

We also remembered the $1,000 gift from VW that we had received some time ago and tried to connect it with what we found out now. We decided to wait and not sell the car.

We told our friends about our new situation and asked them if we could delay the refund.

"No problem!" They answered kindly. "No need to hurry!"

The Prius we bought met Emil's requirements. It was in excellent condition, with all service records from the Toyota dealer. Although I did not understand why Emil was so determined to buy this car because the Lord fulfilled his desire against my will, I resignedly accepted His will, knowing that it was the best for us.

***

2017—A YEAR OF MYSTERIES

"How precious also are Your thoughts to me, O God! How great is the sum of them!" (Ps. 139:17)

As at the beginning of every year, Emil and I wondered what God would have in store for us. What would this year bring to us?

In February, we received an email from VW asking us to schedule an appointment with the nearest dealership to return our car to the VW Corporation.

At the appointed time, we returned the car, signed some papers, and left. We were told that in two days, the money would be deposited in our bank account. To our astonishment, two days later, we found in our account the amount of $14,650. Via email, we got an explanatory note pertaining to the money we received from VW.

The company paid us $9,550 for our car; we expected to sell it for $7,000, according to the Blue Book estimate. On top of that, we received an additional compensation of $5,100 and a little later, another $350 from the Bosch Company involved in the litigation. By adding the $1,000 in loyalty cards received six months prior, we ended up with the amount of $16,000 in our bank account.

Undoubtedly, God's hand orchestrated in an amazing way all the events in our favor and blessed us abundantly.

We remembered how Pastor John, passing by, saw the new car in our garage and advised us not to sell the VW. Little did we understand at that time God's plans on our behalf.

Even when Emil wanted to buy the Prius, I could not discern why God helped him to carry out his desire against my will.

After paying back the $7,000 debt to our friends, we had $9,000 left. Thus, we consider our Prius car as a gift from God, and, with grateful hearts, we praised Him for the many miracles He had performed in our lives.

One more time, we experienced the truth from the book of Isaiah: *"'For My thoughts are not your thoughts, Nor are your ways My ways,' says the Lord. 'For as the heavens are higher than the earth, So are My ways higher than your ways, And My thoughts than your thoughts'"* (Isa. 55: 8–9).

***

In the spring of 2017, Emil and I decided to take another trip to Romania. Emil searched for tickets online and found an incredible deal for March with only one drawback: departure from San Francisco.

Although we had to rent a car to San Francisco, we concluded that it was worth it, as the tickets were half price, and Emil made the reservation.

On the morning of March 27, 2017, before daybreak, we left for San Francisco, and after eight hours of driving, we arrived safely at the airport. Late afternoon, we boarded a huge, Paris-bound Boeing aircraft with 500 seats. From there, we boarded a smaller plane and landed in Bucharest.

Although very tired, after more than thirty hours of traveling since we left home, Emil and I could not fall asleep.

As always, jet lag was a major problem, especially for me.

We struggled to adjust to the new time zone. Romania was ten hours ahead of the West Coast.

Even though my brother, Peter, provided us with a comfortable, quiet apartment just for the two of us, we could not rest for the first week. We were fully awake most of the night and drowsy during the day.

One week later, Emil developed flu symptoms with fever and vomiting. After a few days, I got sick, too.

It was a very unusual incident for both of us, and we suspected that exhaustion and lack of sleep overtaxed our bodies, compromising the immune system, and triggered the sickness.

In about a week, Emil was feeling better. I partially recovered. I needed rest, but I could not sleep more than two or three hours a night.

My sister Mari invited us to her home in Constantza, and over there, I was able to sleep a little better.

A week later, we returned to Bucharest. As time went by, I was feeling more exhausted and started having fever, sore throat, chest congestion, and difficulty breathing.

My brother, Peter called the ambulance. When I saw the doctor and his assistant wearing a mask, I was scared, wondering if I had a dangerous, contagious disease.

The doctor prescribed antibiotics and adjuvant medication to alleviate the symptoms. Instead of feeling better, I developed severe nausea, no taste, no smell, and no appetite.

My friend, Carmen recommended a friend from church, a pulmonologist, who came to see me immediately. I could not speak at all. I was communicating in writing with the doctor and those around me. The specialist doctor prescribed the appropriate medication for airway decongestion and another dose of antibiotics. She told me that asthma was the cause of my suffering, although I had initially acquired a viral infection. After a few days of treatment, even though I had no voice and could not talk, my breathing improved slightly. However, I still could not sleep. In four days, we were going to leave the country, and I was afraid that I might not be able to return home in such a pitiful condition. My brother called the pulmonologist friend again, and she administered aerosol medications and gave me an inhaler as an adjuvant to ease my breathing. As the day of departure approached, my anxiety increased, and I felt worse than ever.

The night before our departure, the doctor came to see me again and decided to administer an intravenous steroid, which opened the airways and provided instant relief.

My breathing started to improve, but unfortunately, I did not sleep at all the entire night. The side effects of the steroid medication hit me harder than I thought. But under the effect of adrenaline, I was eager to go home, no matter what. An aerosol spray was supposed to help me in case of emergency.

Parting at the airport was painful for all of us. We sadly had to say goodbye to our loved ones and were very grateful for their love and care. It was a gloomy day, darkened by unpleasant memories of our visit to Romania.

> **Parting at the airport was painful for all of us. We sadly had to say goodbye to our loved ones and were very grateful for their love and care.**

Again, we flew in a smaller plane to Paris, and from there, in a hurry, boarded the trans-Atlantic aircraft to San Francisco.

When we got on the plane, I breathed a sigh of relief. Knowing that we had a long way to go, we earnestly prayed for divine protection. I wore a mask all the time due to the cold air in the aircraft, which bothered me. I felt very awkward for not seeing anybody around wearing a mask.

Neither Emil nor I could even slumber in the fourteen hours of flight. For me, it was the fifth sleepless night. I was exhausted. We could not wait to reach the ground again, go to the nearest motel, and, free of stress, sleep peacefully after such a long journey.

When we finally touched the soil of America, I felt at home again. We could not get out of the hustle and bustle of San Francisco Airport soon enough.

It took us a long time to get our luggage, arrange for the rental car, and get out of that commotion. The traffic was horrible. Only those who have passed through there can understand the stress you are exposed to in that extremely crowded area. At one point, the traffic was blocked.

We were horrified, not knowing how long we would be stuck on the road. It was a big crash at a large intersection. We prayed for patience and endurance, and, eventually, the road was cleared, and we were able to continue our trip.

When we finally reached the outskirts of San Francisco, out of the jammed traffic, we breathed a sigh of relief and thanked the Lord for His loving care and protection.

We pulled to the side of the road, and Emil searched on GPS for the nearest motel in the area. The route took us on an adjacent road along an endless orchard. After a long drive through a secluded area, feeling that we were heading in the wrong direction, I lost patience and asked Emil to turn around.

He was quite tired, and I was afraid he would get frustrated, also. I was constantly praying, "Lord, please help; don't leave us in the middle of nowhere!"

We finally got back on Interstate 5, and Emil checked the map again and found a Motel 6 about fifteen minutes away.

I gathered my strength, gritted my teeth, and prayed continually that I would not lose hope. I had indescribable anxiety, but I hid my feelings not to distract Emil from driving. He was also quite stressed and tired and needed assurance and understanding.

We were in the middle of nowhere, in a totally unknown place. It was getting dark. I shuddered. If we could not find this motel, where would we go?

When we finally saw the motel sign on the side of the road, we felt safe. We were both longing for a resting place.

The motel was one of the cleanest I have ever seen. The location was beautiful, in a very quiet place, away from the traffic.

We rented a room, quickly took a shower and went straight to bed. Emil fell asleep instantly, as soon as his head hit the pillow.

We had the best conditions for sleep. And yet, I could not relax. I felt like a boiling pot. I had a state of anxiety that I had never experienced before. I could feel and hear my heart pounding in my chest. My breathing was getting worse. The inhaler did not help me at all. The feeling of suffocation exacerbated my anxiety. I was propped upright on pillows, looking for a more comfortable position. My every breath was a prayer: "Lord, do not forsake me!"

After more than two hours of turmoil, I got out of bed and dressed, ready for the hospital. I had the feeling that I would die soon if I did not get help.

I did not dare to wake Emil, knowing that he needed rest in order to be able to drive back home the following day.

I wrote him a short note, and I posted it in a conspicuous place on the nightstand next to his head:

"Emil, I can't sleep. I'm very, very sick. I am calling the ambulance. Elena. Seven o'clock p.m."

Although my mind was tormented by stress and clouded by lack of sleep, I thought of doing Emil a favor and let him sleep as much as possible.

I tiptoed out of the room and went to the reception of the motel. Because I could not speak, I wrote the following message on a piece of paper and gave it to the receptionist:

"I need help. Extremely tired. I haven't slept for five days and nights. I am very sick. Please call 911. I need help."

> **"I need help. Extremely tired. I haven't slept for five days and nights. I am very sick. Please call 911. I need help."**

Instantly, I heard the siren. In the next minutes, the ambulance arrived. "It just so happened that we were around the corner," one of the EMTs said.

When asked what was wrong with me, I wrote on a piece of paper what the problem was and gave them my personal information.

Since my blood pressure was rising quickly, reaching 180/50 in just a few minutes, I was informed that I had to be taken to the hospital immediately. I had never had such high blood pressure in my life. I was hooked up to an IV, and, little by little, I started feeling better.

By the time the ambulance arrived at the hospital, I was able to speak in a whispered voice. I must have been dehydrated besides the physical and emotional exhaustion.

The doctor in charge at the ER ordered chest x-rays to check on my lungs. After a long wait, he gave me good news: No pneumonia.

He prescribed sleeping pills and an antibiotic. The same one I had taken in two doses in Romania.

He asked me if I had anyone to take me back to the motel; otherwise, they were going to call a taxi. Now, I was worried about Emil. I had no way of knowing if he had awakened and read my note. Had he found out about me being taken by the ambulance?

Just when I was prepared to ask for time to call my husband, Emil appeared at the door. What a relief! I felt safe, having him with me again.

The doctor gave me a sleeping pill and warned Emil that I would fall asleep soon and would not wake up for the next eight hours. I longed for sleep as for air.

Emil prepared my "bed" on the back seat, and we set off. I was awake the entire way back to the motel. It was already midnight.

I went to bed immediately, waiting to fall asleep quickly and not wake up until daybreak, according to the doctor's assumption.

I had no idea what Emil had been through since my disappearance from the room and how he got to the hospital. There was no time for sharing stories. We both needed to sleep and get in shape for the next day's trip to our final destination.

Unfortunately, I could not fall asleep as the doctor predicted. And I could not understand why the sleeping pill did not work for me. Time passed by, and anxiety increased. My condition was getting worse with every passing moment. The suffocation sensation terrified me.

I cannot adequately describe how I felt in those moments of struggle between life and death. For the first time in my life, I felt like I was dying. Every breath seemed to be the last. Anxiety and fear of death terrified me. In exasperation, I was ready to capitulate. Life had become unbearable for me in such a hopeless condition, and I cried to the Lord to put an end to my suffering.

I entrusted my children, Emil, and the rest of the family to God's care and then abandoned myself in His arms.

Only someone who has gone through a similar crisis can understand how terrible it is to be exasperatedly tired and unable to sleep. After three weeks of prolonged fatigue and illness, ending with five sleepless days and nights, I was at the end of the rope.

The fear of not being ready for death exacerbated my anxiety. Every breath of mine was a prayer. Satan tortured me with foreboding thoughts. I felt abandoned by the One I loved so much and had served all my life.

If He cares about me, why doesn't He hear my cry?! I agonized in prayer as never before, wondering if this could be "Jacob's night of trouble" experience I had to go through.

Emil had no idea of my ordeal. He, too, was exhausted and needed rest. I had to drink this cup alone, and in despair, I cried to the Lord, "Thy will be done!"

As no one can realize the moment of falling asleep, neither had I any recollection of when it happened to me.

At this time, Emil was the one who could not sleep until daybreak. And, so as not to bother me, after noticing that I was asleep, he decided to leave the room. And he walked around the motel for the rest of the night to keep himself from freezing.

Around five o'clock in the morning, he quietly entered the room. I was still sleeping. He wished he would not wake me up, but at an almost imperceptible noise, I suddenly woke up.

From then on, he was eager to go home. He had not slept all night, except for the three hours when I was taken to the hospital.

I later realized that God inspired me to not wake him up when I went out to call for help. He was also exhausted from the long trip overseas and two sleepless nights. My first thought after I woke up was, "Let's go!"

Poor Emil was afraid I would not want to go, being so tired. He was eager to go, and after we prayed for traveling mercies, we set off.

The fact that I survived the ordeal of the night gave me courage, and we thanked the Lord for this miracle.

Now I was more worried about Emil because he had to be awake for eight hours of driving, in spite of lack of sleep and all the stress he went through the previous night. I could barely wait to find out what happened to him last night after my disappearance from the motel room.

His story overwhelmed me. About three hours after I left the room, he woke up and noticed that I was not there. Without seeing the note I had left on the nightstand, he looked for me in the bathroom and, not finding me there, started calling my name. Silence. He hurriedly got dressed and went outside, looking for me everywhere. Panic-stricken, he went to the motel office to report his wife's disappearance.

I had left a brief note for him with the receptionist and asked her to provide the necessary information to Emil that I had been taken to the hospital. After finding out what happened to me, Emil took the two notes and left. When he tried to call the hospital to ask for information, he found out that the phone number was wrong. He panicked at first, but after finding the address in the GPS, he managed to arrive at the hospital, just as the doctor was telling me that he had to send me to the motel by taxi. Both Emil and I breathed a sigh of relief because we found each other after a nightmarish evening.

By God's grace, we arrived home safely and thanked Him for watching over us in our long and tiring journey.

Emil's biological clock had been adjusted without any problems. I still struggled with insomnia, but I was able to sleep a few hours at night, being extremely tired and weak. I scheduled a visit to Dr. W. Heidinger, my family doctor.

When I told him that I had already taken two doses of antibiotics and was on the third dose, he advised me to discontinue the antibiotic immediately since I was dealing with a viral infection. When he asked me, "How is your motivation?" I started crying. Realizing that I was depressed, Dr. Heidinger, instead of prescribing antidepressant medication and sleeping pills, encouraged me to trust in God, the Great Physician.

Both Emil and I prayed earnestly for healing, and our prayers were answered. After discontinuing the antibiotic, I started to feel much better and gradually regained strength.

It took me almost three months to get back to normal. The best remedy for depression was God's promises from the Bible, which I claimed whenever I felt crushed emotionally. This one was one of my favorites: ***"In the multitude of my anxieties within me, Your comforts delight my soul"*** *(Ps. 94:19).*

***

Toward the end of summer, in August 2017, Texas and the neighboring states were devastated by Hurricane Harley. Knowing our children were in the risk zone in Houston, we went through great emotions.

The water level was rising outrageously, and many residential areas were evacuated. Silviu and Alina moved valuables to the attic of their house and waited anxiously to see if they would get an evacuation order.

We were greatly distraught. The images posted on the news channels were frightening. We prayed earnestly for God's protection not only over our children but for the whole area devastated by the hurricane.

By the mercy of the Lord, our children were not physically affected by this calamity, only emotionally.

Shortly afterward, another overwhelming piece of news took us by surprise. Wildfires, breaking out in California, Oregon, and many other states on the West Coast were threatening us also.

Although a big fire erupted in the nearby forest, we did not get an evacuation order. We were tormented all fall with thick smoke and ashes, which forced us to wear a mask. The Lord took pity on us and sent the necessary rain, which cleared the air and finally extinguished the fires.

***

December 30, 2017

We were at the end of the year, trying to forget the bitter experiences we had gone through that year by counting the blessings we had received by God's grace.

A phone call from our son, Silviu, was going to impact our lives forever.

He was in New York, at the airport, on his return from a short visit to Romania. He had just gotten the most exciting news from Alina and was eager to share it with us.

"Mom, Alina is pregnant! The baby is seven weeks old!"

At first, I was speechless, and then, in amazement, I burst into joyful shouting: "Praise the Lord!"

For several years, our children had been waiting to become parents.

After Silviu received confirmation that he was cured of hepatitis C, he wanted to become a father and Alina to become a mother. The time had come!

Our emotions as future grandparents could not be expressed in words. We now included the little baby in our prayers, and we were all looking forward to finding out if it would be a boy or a girl.

About a month later, when I was returning from a visit to my sister in California, I received a message from Silviu on my cell phone. It was an ultrasound, the first "picture" of the sixteen-week-old baby with the words: "It's a girl!"

We were all delighted with the great news and congratulated the parents for the baby girl, the most precious gift from God.

The following summer, 2018, we were surrounded by smoke coming from fires in California.

Paradise, the pride of northern California, was almost completely wiped off the map. Emil's cousin and his family were among the many people that lost everything and needed to relocate. Soon after that, many fires broke out in Oregon, including our county.

Again, we were choked in smoke and ashes. The masks had become a necessary evil for us in recent years due to the smoke that persisted for months during what officials were now calling "fire season." We made the necessary preparations, ready to leave in case of emergency.

The time was coming for the baby to be born. Emotions for parents and grandparents alike were running high!

On the evening of July 28, 2018, Silviu informed us that the family was at the hospital. Alina was ready to give birth.

Soon after, we received a picture of the baby on our smartphone. "Emma has arrived!" I exclaimed with unspeakable joy.

Now, Silviu and Alina had taken on the role of parents, and Veronica, Alina's mother, had taken on the role of grandmother. We could not wait to fly to Texas to see our precious baby Emma.

> **"Emma has arrived!" I exclaimed with unspeakable joy.**

The brand-new parents suggested that it would be good to wait for a while in order to protect the baby from the viral exposure during the trip, and we respected their wishes.

At the beginning of September, Silviu gave us the sad news that his grandmother from Romania had passed away. A few days later, we received the tragic news that Grandpa Octavian had also passed away.

Silviu was much loved by his grandparents, and it was hard on him to lose them both in such a short time. Both of us treasured precious memories about them, their love and care for us, especially after I became a single mother and Silviu became a fatherless little boy.

At the end of the month, I flew to California, called by my sister, Viorica. I left Emil alone, knowing that he could manage loneliness for ten days while I was gone. Only one thing I asked him—not to ride his bike while I was gone. I had an unreasonable fear of a possible accident. And Emil promised my wish would be respected.

I had two more days before coming home. It was Friday afternoon. The phone rang. It was Emil. "Elena, it's so beautiful outside! But I don't like walking alone in the park. I would rather ride my bike. May I, please?"

Without hesitation, I replied, "You may go, but be careful!!!"

"Don't worry!" he replied. "I'll call you when I get back home."

After a short time, Emil called me again. I wondered why he came home so quickly. I had a hunch that something was wrong.

"You know, Elena, please don't get upset ... and don't be worried ..."

"Come on," I interrupted abruptly, "tell me what happened!"

"I want to let you know that I fell off the bike, and I'm at the ER with a fractured hip. Please don't panic! The surgeon told me I need surgery, and I am scheduled for it tomorrow morning."

I froze in fear. Emil in the hospital with a fractured hip! I could not believe it. I immediately cried out, "Lord, have mercy on Emil!" Then, I reassured him that the Lord was in control and all would be well with him. I did not ask him for details about the accident. It was not the appropriate time for such investigations.

I would have liked to talk to someone on the medical staff, even with the doctor, if possible. Emil was sedated, and I did not expect much from him. I left him alone, telling him we would talk later. I asked the Lord to put me in touch with a medical professional from whom I could find out details about Emil's situation. Shortly after, I got a call from the hospital.

I was very surprised when I heard someone speaking Romanian. It was the doctor on duty, a very kind young Romanian woman, who was in charge when Emil was brought in by ambulance to the ER. She assured me that Emil was in good spirits and everything was under control. What a relief hearing straight from the doctor, speaking Romanian, what was going on with Emil. All my questions had been answered, and I was at peace, entrusting Emil in God's hands.

He called later and informed me that he was scheduled for surgery the next day and promised to keep me posted. And he kept his word. The next day was the Sabbath. I was constantly praying and waiting for the result of the surgery. Emil was the first one to call me, but I could not understand his slurred speech under the effect of the anesthesia. In broken English and an exuberant tone, his first words astonished me: "I love you, my darling! You are the best wife in the world, and I love you very much! I love you ... I love you ...!"

I had to interrupt him and advised him to go to sleep, promising that we would talk later. The most important thing I needed to know was that he came out of the surgery, and the details would be taken care of later.

The next day, on Sunday, I flew back from California. By late in the afternoon, I was in Emil's hospital room.

He was very excited to see me again, and his cheerful countenance lifted my spirits.

Later on, the surgeon came into the room and explained to me what the surgery consisted of: replacing the broken femoral head with a metal one. He assured me that everything went well and praised the patient for his determination to walk shortly after the operation.

Emil tolerated the surgery very well, not complaining about anything. He was cheerful and optimistic, telling everybody what a wonderful God we have and how grateful he was for the divine intervention in saving him from a tragic accident.

Being very motivated to regain his independence, he worked hard and, through physical therapy and exercise, resumed normal life sooner than was expected. We gave God all the credit for the miraculous healing.

Although we had planned to fly to Texas to see our granddaughter Emma, plans failed because of Emil's accident.

When he was fully recovered, our kids booked our tickets to Texas for February 2019. But we were asked for something "sine qua non" in order to meet little Emma: the flu vaccine.

For the sake of our children and to protect the baby, we agreed for the first time in our lives to get the flu vaccine. Emil received a higher dose, being considered more vulnerable, due to his advanced age.

After a week, I started having flu symptoms, which lasted only a day.

Unfortunately, Emil's reaction to the vaccine was much more severe, and the flu symptoms were worsening from day to day. We were going to fly to Texas in a month, and we were afraid we would miss this golden opportunity. I have never seen Emil in such a pitiful state. At times, I was afraid he might not recover from the critical condition he was in.

I took care of him as best I could, and with a lot of prayer, after ten days, he started feeling better.

By the end of the month, he was fully recovered, and we praised God for His healing touch.

***

NEW YEAR 2019

On January 17, we received a message from Silviu that blew our minds.

After eleven years at HP, he had decided to move on and had accepted an offer at another company, which would offer him a 40 percent pay raise and better benefits.

This unexpected news brought us to our knees. We assured Silviu that we would pray for him and encouraged him to trust in the Lord, our source of wisdom and strength.

The long-awaited day, the flight to Texas had arrived. It was February 5, 2019.

Silviu picked us up from the airport. It was late in the evening. When we arrived home, the baby was sleeping.

We were asked not to touch Emma for a week because of being contaminated from the plane. We had learned that Grandpa Victor, who had come from Romania before us, had been subjected to the same protocol, and we resigned ourselves to the thought that we would only pass through this once in our lives.

After a week, the restriction was lifted, and we were able to hold the "golden nugget" in our arms as brand-new grandparents. Emma was an adorable baby. We would rarely hear her crying. The nights of terror were over. Now she was peacefully sleeping most of the time. The short moments when she was awake were the most precious for us. Body language was the only one she knew at that time. Her smile was charming, especially when she was sleeping.

The visit to our children passed quickly. During our stay in Houston, Silviu was in orientation for his new job, and, working from home, he spent most of the day in his office.

He worked hard during this period, having to learn new things to retain a huge volume of information necessary for passing all the exams prior to starting the new job.

On February 18, the day before we returned home, Silviu left for Chicago to take his exams.

On March 8, we received a photocopy of the final exam result:

"Silviu Nedea: PASSED 100%"

We had no words to thank our heavenly Father for answering our prayers. Looking back, we marveled at all that He had done for our family and us, and with grateful hearts, united in a thanksgiving song: **"Oh, give** *thanks to the Lord! Call upon His name; Make known His deeds among the peoples! Sing to Him, sing psalms to Him; Talk of all His wondrous works!"* (Ps. 105:1–2).

Despite the fact that Silviu is very busy with his new job, he continues to study online. His goal is to earn his master's degree in economics. His avidity for learning motivates him in his endeavors of climbing the ladder of professional success.

CHAPTER 11

IN THE TWILIGHT

"Bless the Lord, O my soul, and forget not all His benefits: Who forgives all your iniquities, who heals all your diseases, Who satisfies your mouth with good things, So that your youth is renewed like the eagle's." (Ps. 103:2–3, 5)

May 2020 was marked in red on our calendar hanging on the kitchen wall. It was the month when we were going to visit our children. It remained to be seen when they would schedule our flight to Texas.

Who would have thought that in the near future, the entire planet would be devastated by the Covid-19 pandemic? Who could have imagined that it would hold us captive in our own homes for an unlimited time?

The whole world is living in confusion and insecurity. The entire human fabric is infested by this enemy who ruthlessly reaped thousands of humans around the entire planet.

Voltaire's words find their fulfillment in the pandemic crisis that had terrorized the whole world: "One day everything will be well, that is our hope. Everything's fine today; that is our illusion."

Unfortunately, our visit to Texas was postponed indefinitely. In this time of maximum uncertainty, we had resigned ourselves to the thought that our health and, above all, the health of our children must prevail.

This year we also celebrated thirty-four years of our coming to America and the thirty-first anniversary of our marriage. Our hearts were full of gratitude toward God for filling our home with His blessings. The many trials that Providence had allowed us to go through had bound us closer to each other and anchored us even stronger to God, our Fortress. Looking back over the years, our souls light up with joy when we see the flowers of faith rising among the wrecks of many shattered dreams.

Nicolae Iorga was right in one of his thoughts: "After the storms of the soul, as well as after the storms of nature, it raises flowers that we thought were dried."

We humans often become discouraged when we do not receive an immediate answer to prayer and do not understand God's reason for the delay.

God offers wonderful promises to those who are patiently and confidently awaiting their fulfillment.

We thanked the Lord even for unanswered prayers, later realizing that "What seem to us to be bitter trials are often blessings in disguise" (Oscar Wilde).

Most of the trials we went through ended with a "happy ending." Some, however, left us with a bitter taste in our mouths without understanding their purpose. One thing we have learned from such experiences is hard to understand and practice: The greatest test of faith is when you do not get what you want, and yet, you are able to say, "Thank You, Lord!"

Sometimes we tend to lament and get discouraged because of the painful experiences and disappointments that make our lives bitter instead of being grateful to the Lord for the blessings we receive. I found somewhere this idea realistically expressed by an anonymous author: "You can cry that rose bushes have thorns or you can be glad that thorn bushes have roses."

Both the ability to overcome trials and their impact on character formation largely depends on how we relate to them. To a very small extent, the statement of a great woman of faith, Helen Keller, fits me: "Character cannot be developed in ease and quiet. Only through experience of trial and suffering can the soul be strengthened, inspired, and success achieved." Before reaching the age of two, she became blind and deaf due to an illness but became famous for her performance despite her disabilities.

In retrospect, we recognize that we have not always made the wisest choices. We all are liable to make mistakes. Emil and I have made mistakes, and the consequences were inevitable and sometimes very bitter, but the most important thing we strive to learn from the past mistakes is not to repeat them.

I remember a wise Latin proverb I learned in school: "Erare humanum est. Perseverare diabolicum," which in English means "To err is human, but to persist in error is diabolic."

Despite the white hairs, both Emil and I look to the future with confidence, trying not to worry about tomorrow because it doesn't belong to us. The Savior said: ***"Therefore do not worry about tomorrow, for tomorrow*** *will worry about its own things. Sufficient for the day is its own trouble" (Matt. 6:34).*

The same truth is expressed by Ovidiu in other words: "You are afraid of old age that you are not sure you will reach."

Emil and I seek to make each other's lives beautiful, to take care of our health, following the laws of health as much as we can. Healthy eating is the only "medicine" we take twice a day. I learned this from the father of medicine: "Let thy food be thy medicine" (Hippocrates).

We have been on a plant-based diet since we came to America, and we are absolutely satisfied. The results are amazing. Despite our advanced age, we enjoy full health and thank God for the light of the health reform.

Knowing that a sedentary lifestyle brings disease into the body and shortens life, we choose to live an active life. Walking in the park for at least half an hour a day, as much as possible, is a pleasure for us.

The promises of God's Word, which I have sprinkled abundantly on the pages of this book, are and will remain, our anchor for the rest of our lives. In everything we have accomplished in life, we recognize God as our source of wisdom and strength. He is an inexhaustible source of blessings, and to Him, we owe all praise, honor, and love.

With the world events unfolding rapidly around us, it should be our number one priority to prepare for the imminent and glorious Second coming of Jesus Christ in the clouds of heaven.

My desire for you, dear reader, is to get to know Jesus personally. Thus, He will fill your life with love, joy, and hope in a better world.

TEACH Services, Inc.
P U B L I S H I N G

We invite you to view the complete
selection of titles we publish at:
www.TEACHServices.com

We encourage you to write us
with your thoughts about this,
or any other book we publish at:
info@TEACHServices.com

TEACH Services' titles may be purchased in
bulk quantities for educational, fund-raising,
business, or promotional use.
bulksales@TEACHServices.com

Finally, if you are interested in seeing
your own book in print, please contact us at:
publishing@TEACHServices.com

We are happy to review your manuscript at no charge.

www.ingramcontent.com/pod-product-compliance
Lightning Source LLC
Chambersburg PA
CBHW071156160426
43196CB00011B/2100